Design After Decline

THE CITY IN THE TWENTY-FIRST CENTURY

Eugenie L. Birch and Susan M. Wachter, Series Editors

A complete list of books in the series
is available from the publisher.

DESIGN AFTER DECLINE

How America Rebuilds Shrinking Cities

Brent D. Ryan

PENN

UNIVERSITY OF PENNSYLVANIA PRESS

PHILADELPHIA

Published by
University of Pennsylvania Press
Philadelphia, Pennsylvania 19104-4112
www.upenn.edu/pennpress

Printed in the United States of America on acid-free paper

10 9 8 7 6 5 4 3 2 1

A Cataloging-in-Publication record is available from
the Library of Congress

ISBN 978-0-8122-4407-6

To Lorena, who sustains me every day

Contents

Preface   ix

Chapter 1. "The Burden Has Passed": Urban Design After
Urban Renewal   1

Chapter 2. Shrinkage or Renewal? The Fate of Older Cities, 1950–90   37

Chapter 3. "People Want These Houses": The Suburbanization
of Detroit   84

Chapter 4. "Another Tradition in Planning": The Suburbanization
of North Philadelphia   128

Chapter 5. Toward Social Urbanism for Shrinking Cities   174

Notes   225

Works Cited   227

Index   245

Acknowledgments   263

Preface

In the summer of 1993, on break from architecture school, I paid a visit to friends in the city of Detroit. I knew of Detroit's fearsome reputation, and the city's vacant lots, burned-out homes, and bleak, empty skyscrapers confirmed Detroit as the paradigm of urban blight. The sense of emptiness was overpowering; I was shocked to see that even the city's train station, designed by Warren and Wetmore at the same time as their Grand Central Terminal, had been left open to the winds of fate. Entering the station's burned-out, rubble-strewn great hall early one morning, I felt as if I was walking into the ruin of America. To me, Detroit was a half-dead declaration that the decades-long attempt to rebuild what were then known as "declining" American cities had utterly failed. What place was there for optimism in such a landscape?

As I researched cities further, I discovered that optimism did exist in Detroit and other Rust Belt cities such as Philadelphia and Cleveland: new housing was being constructed in small quantities, some commercial areas were thriving, and downtowns still attracted visitors for sports, conventions, and tourism. But my overall sense of disappointment was scarcely allayed by the scattered new neighborhood developments that I saw in declining cities. Many of them seemed to imitate suburban developments, complete with iconic culs-de-sac. In the late 1990s public housing towers began to disappear, replaced by townhouse communities allegedly modeled on the historic city but to me more reminiscent of suburban condominiums. The overall effect of these "revitalization" efforts struck me as not only formally unadventurous but sadly underscaled against the evident abandonment of declining cities. Was no one else noticing North Philadelphia and Detroit, I wondered? Why weren't we doing anything about these places?

I was well aware that older American cities had gone through a substantial rebuilding process only a few decades earlier, during the heyday of Modern architecture. My hometown of New Haven, Connecticut, was littered with the concrete and steel remnants of such efforts—an unfinished highway, a gargantuan arena, and lots and lots of empty land marked the results of the last time urban planners had tried to "save" the city. New Haven showed that the death of these so-called "urban renewal" policies had not been such a bad thing for the city—the brutal clearance of city neighborhoods ended, as did the construction of alienating buildings such as Roche and Dinkeloo's Knights of Columbus tower. At least the federal government was no longer subsidizing the dislocation of urban residents, and cities were no longer celebrating their own "sacking," as Jane Jacobs (1961, 4) had trenchantly put it. Architects were mostly building their large-scale work in the suburbs or on other continents, and many urban-renewal-era Modernists like Paul Rudolph had finished out their careers overseas in tremendous style. As I learned more about urban planning I saw that planners too had abandoned the notion of utopia; rather than projecting new visions, they sought to patch, support, and assist the modest but sincere visions espoused by city dwellers. In places like Boston, with a robust economy and substantial historical urban fabric, this postrenewal approach seemed to be working well.

But what about shrinking cities like Detroit? As far as I could see, not much at all was happening to help the Motor City, or the depressed areas of a half-dozen other large declining cities that I came to know well: Cleveland, Buffalo, Philadelphia, Baltimore, St. Louis, and Chicago's south and west sides. The overwhelming modesty of these cities' 1990s rebuilding lacked Modernism's arrogance, but these projects also seemed to say that the future of shrinking cities was now the single-family detached home, perhaps constructed by a small nonprofit organization and housing a fortunate low-income family. Social planners celebrated this "community-based" rebuilding, but the tools and scope of this rebuilding, as far as I could see, were limited to the generic models provided by the suburban building industry and to the feeble funding still being provided by the federal government. If this constituted a victory over urban renewal, it seemed a pretty hollow one, for most shrinking-city neighborhoods were being abandoned, not reconstructed.

Unlike Jane Jacobs's "attack on current city planning and rebuilding" (1961, 3) in the *Death and Life of Great American Cities*, I found it hard to blame an obvious actor for the parlous condition of America's shrinking cities. The "master planners" of the 1960s were retired, large-scale neighborhood clearance was no longer occurring, architects were not building anything substantial outside of downtown facilities, planners claimed to represent the people, and city politicians all claimed to want to help their cities. It was clear that the failure I was witnessing, if one even perceived this urban shrinkage as failure, was a collective one, attributable to the entirety of actors responsible for rebuilding deteriorated, low-income, depressed areas of cities. There was no single actor to blame. The federal government mostly left cities to their own devices through decentralized funding mechanisms such as block grants; public-private coalitions worked hard to activate cities, but they focused on places like downtowns where developers could make money; nonprofit corporations struggled to generate and sustain modest amounts of housing; urban designers, where they even existed, were regulators more than they were builders.

But where cities like Boston and San Francisco were evidently on the way back from decline as early as the 1980s, it was equally clear that the departure of urban renewal had left shrinking cities like Detroit and Philadelphia adrift. The professional, political, aesthetic, and theoretical unity that had motivated Modernism had withered away, and in its place was a growing desolation, filled haphazardly and modestly by rebuilding strategies that were mostly not formal strategies, by planning departments that had lost the ability to plan; by real estate developers who quite sensibly wished to maximize profits; and by communities, most of them racial minorities, that sensed the scale of their problems but that had a collective memory of urban renewal and feared insensitive outside interference. Amid a narrative of urban revitalization success stories, I suspected that I was also witnessing the concealment of failure, for no one could convince me that a place like Camden, New Jersey, represented a policy or design success.

This book is my effort to better understand and explain what I saw happening in America's shrinking cities in the 1990s and the first decade of the 2000s. My central argument is that the end of urban renewal in the mid-1970s brought both a sense of relief and a sense of disillusionment: relief, because urban renewal projects like the federally sponsored Cedar-Riverside New Town In-Town in Minneapolis treated existing neighborhoods with great brutality; and disillusionment because these developments also projected a vision of the future that was nothing if not optimistic. The late-1970s projects that followed them, such as Charlotte Gardens in the South Bronx, possessed neither this brutality nor any of this optimism. Instead, these projects set a tone of small-scale, incremental rebuilding that would continue, at least in city neighborhoods in the United States, for the next thirty years. From this sequence of events emerged a narrative of brutal Modernist urban renewal, and of restorative contextual design, that remains in force today. But I suggest that this argument elides an alternative narrative in which Modernist urban renewal, recovering from the insensitivity of the 1960s, reformed almost exactly at the same time as the federal policies driving urban redevelopment collapsed. To make this argument, I review the experience of the Greater London Council Architecture Department, which designed a reformed Modernist version of social housing that corrected for many of the errors of the 1960s, at least until this organization too was shut down.

In the United States, a review of the population and housing trajectories of the largest cities during a fifty-year trajectory from 1950 to 2000 demonstrates that the end of modernist urban renewal in no way interrupted the downward economic trajectory of many of these large cities. In places like Philadelphia and Detroit, losses continued uninterrupted after 1975, suggesting that no single policy regime was destroying (or saving) these places. In the middle chapters of this book, I offer detailed histories of these cities' neighborhood redevelopment efforts, which distinguishes my study from more traditional studies of downtown development, such as that found in Frieden and Sagalyn (1989). Detroit and Philadelphia were both heavily industrial cities, but otherwise they were quite different in terms of geography, design, housing stock, social trajectories, and experience during the urban renewal decades of the 1950s and 1960s. In particular, Philadelphia carried out its rebuilding with greater sensitivity, utilizing urban design and planning judiciously and generating some substantial successes, such as the Society Hill and Yorktown developments, even as it made some of the same mistakes as other cities. Detroit, conversely, was in some ways a much newer city with a recent and relatively disposable housing stock, and its midcentury redevelopment set a precedent of substantial displacement and destruction that arguably contributed to the city's precipitous decline in the 1970s and 1980s. Certainly by the time market interest began to return to these cities around 1990, Detroit had not only fewer intact neighborhoods but also a weaker capacity to redevelop itself intelligently.

Without any centralized housing, planning, or urban design policy, Detroit focused on attracting developers to build market-rate housing with the aid of city subsidies. In the Jefferson-Chalmers neighborhood, for example, this strategy achieved notable success, but developers imposed the proviso that the only marketable housing model was the suburban single-family home. After some initial success with the heavily subsidized Victoria Park development, the Detroit process went awry when the city ran out of the easily developable large parcels that urban renewal had generated in the 1970s. The next large Jefferson-Chalmers project was an unmitigated disaster, as the city had to condemn inhabited homes in order to provide a site large enough to meet the demand of a politically connected developer selling market-rate houses. In a struggle reminiscent of the 1960s, bitter community protests delayed the development for years. Detroit headed into the market crash of 2007 having achieved little redevelopment success outside of those few areas where developers were willing to build.

In Philadelphia, a city that actually had less market-rate demand for housing in the 1990s than Detroit, the city pursued an interventionist social housing strategy in its hardest-hit neighborhood of Lower North Philadelphia using momentum from the election of an ambitious new mayor in 1993. Over the next seven years the city carried out a series of social housing developments whose mostly uninspired designs were guided by a larger-scale spatial planning strategy of some sophistication. As the market recovered and then boomed after the turn of the millennium, the city's policy of building low-density social housing persisted. At the time of this writing (2010), suburban-style social housing was still being constructed even as developers were building high-density, mixed-use housing only a few blocks away. Nevertheless Philadelphia's rebuilding strategy made sense from the policy level, if not the design level, and multiple reformed Modernist design precedents existed from the 1960s and 1970s to provide a guide for better building in the future. No such precedent existed in Detroit except for tabula rasa urban renewal projects like Lafayette Park that denied the validity of the existing city.

As the cases of Philadelphia and Detroit suggest, the development precedents from the past thirty years are not exactly promising, and shrinking cities today are focused more on demolition than construction strategies. Moreover, the currently dominant theories of everyday, landscape, and new urbanism all have limitations in the context of shrinking cities and their neighborhoods. That said, I do think there is cause for optimism. In particular, the design trajectory of "reformed" Modernism (Rowe 1993, 264) that was mostly cut off around 1980 may still reconcile projective design with the social expectations of shrinking-city residents. To establish a new trajectory for shrinking-city rebuilding, I lay out a set of five design and planning principles: palliative planning, which argues that action is important even if full recovery is unlikely; interventionist policy, which argues that serious problems demand equally serious responses and that the decentralized action of the past thirty years has been ineffective in responding to the scale of shrinking-city problems; democratic decision making, which argues that planners must consider the needs of shrinking cities' least able and empowered residents as a central concern; projective design, which argues for rekindling the future-oriented spirit of Modernism while retaining the humanism required for any social design intervention; and patchwork urbanism, a theory that portrays the landscape of the future city as a patchwork of settled, partially empty, reconstructed, and empty areas. Shrinking cities, and cities in general, will always be incomplete, always in flux, yet always moving toward a better future under the aegis of the previous five principles. I conclude with a portrait and illustrations of a "semi-topian" future for a typical shrinking city.

Many of the economic changes, social shifts, and physical deterioration that have afflicted cities like Detroit and Philadelphia are irreversible. But I believe that the recent history of inconsistently managed change is one that can motivate urban designers, planners, and politicians faced with the prospect of future change to reconcile disciplines, reorient policy directions, and reformulate design strategies to face problems head on. In many ways, shrinking cities represent the richest opportunities that currently exist for urban designers in the United States.

Chapter 1

"The Burden Has Passed": Urban Design
After Urban Renewal

The End of an Era in Minneapolis

In 1970 (Montgomery 1971, 35) the United States Department of Housing and Urban Development, or HUD, announced a new program to rebuild urban neighborhoods across the United States. Coming at the end of two decades in which American cities had been reconstructed, reshaped, and rethought as never before in their history, many people must have found it difficult to imagine that bolder moves were possible. What could surpass a decade in which hundreds of low-income housing projects totaling hundreds of thousands of units had been built (Thompson 2006, 6), tens of thousands of miles of interstate highways had been constructed ("National Transportation Statistics 2002"), and acres of slums had been cleared from city centers? Was it possible to imagine an urban future more dramatic than that which was already under construction around the country?

Any doubters were silenced when Congress passed the Urban Growth and New Community Development Act, later named the Housing and Urban Development Act, on December 31, 1970. This act envisioned the construction of ten "HUD-guaranteed new communities" (Jackson 1972, 6), also known as "New Towns In-Town" (10), across the country. Such a concept may have been novel for a nation inclined more to suburbia than to density, but the British had provided ample precedent across the Atlantic. Ten years earlier the Barbican development, a concrete, elephantine, "complete neighbourhood, with housing, open spaces, schools, and amenity buildings" that contained more than 2,100 units (Carter 1962, plate 7) had opened on the site of a blitzed neighborhood at the edge of the City of London.

HUD's aim was ambitious. The agency envisioned each New Town containing up to several thousand new housing units, as well as associated retail, commercial, institutional, and even manufacturing facilities. HUD's description of the new communities aptly communicated their almost utopian quality: "Our nation certainly is not lacking for innovative urban ideas. What it has lacked is the opportunity to put a series of ideas together in a systematic matter, then actually implement them in an integrated, experimental setting designed to prove our best thinking on urban needs. New communities provide such a setting; they offer opportunities for major advances in every facet of urban design, social and physical, and a chance to test and prove new concepts in living. They are setting new standards of excellence for future urban growth" (Jackson 1972, 7). True to HUD's word, the 1971–72 fiscal year provided $2.9 billion for housing and "urban renewal," or neighborhood clearance and rebuilding, programs (Herbers 1970, 32), including funding for the planning, design, and construction of two HUD-guaranteed New Towns In-Town in New York City and in Minneapolis, Minnesota. The scale and complexity of these projects surpassed any federally subsidized development that had ever been proposed for these cities. In New York, a linear New Town, a miniature Manhattan, would rise on Roosevelt Island (then Welfare Island), a long-marginal East River island directly facing the Upper East Side. Minneapolis was a much smaller city than New York—430,000 to New York's nearly eight million (*CensusCD NCDB*, 2001)—but its Cedar-Riverside New Town would equal New York's in scale, with a cluster of tall buildings, almost a second downtown, replacing an older neighborhood 1.5 miles southeast of the city's central business district. Designed by noted architect Ralph Rapson, Minneapolis's New Town, with 12,500 units anticipated (Special to the *New York Times* 1971, 29), would have been one of the largest urban renewal projects ever constructed in the United States. It would also, though few could have known it at the time, be one of the last.

Many felt that Ralph Rapson was the perfect designer for this ambitious new effort. By the 1960s Rapson was one of the most successful architects in the United States. Trained, like many of his generation, at the leading schools of Cranbrook Academy and the Massachusetts Institute of Technology (MIT), Rapson rose to fame in the 1940s through his graceful designs for furniture and small homes in partnership with other noted Modernists such as Eero Saarinen (University of Minnesota News 2008). In 1954 Rapson assumed the directorship of the School of Architecture at the University of Minnesota. He would live in Minneapolis for the rest of his life. By the early 1970s, with highly regarded designs for embassies, cultural facilities, and housing under Rapson's belt, the Cedar-Riverside commission, which Rapson rhapsodically described as a "dream of an all-new way of life for the rejuvenation of the city" (Goldberger 1976, 1), must have seemed the perfect culmination to an already highly accomplished career.

Like many urban redevelopment projects of the time, Cedar-Riverside's design required near-complete clearance of its site, which like much of Minneapolis was a mix of small one- and two-story commercial structures mixed together with housing. Cedar-Riverside dated from the early decades of the twentieth century (Cedar-Riverside Associates 1971, 2), and it might not have seemed particularly decayed or threatening to one accustomed to older, denser eastern cities. A 1966 City Planning Commission report testified, however, that it was one of Minneapolis's most "blighting" neighborhoods: "The Riverside area . . . consists of a chaotic mixture of land uses. These mixed uses are mutually destructive. West Cedar [the principal street], in particular, shows clearly the blighting effects of the intermixing of uses . . . in addition, the mixture of uses makes it difficult to attract new uses that will add needed stability" (Minneapolis City Planning Commission 1965–66, 11). The Commission concluded that nothing less than a complete reconstruction of Cedar-Riverside was needed: "Up to 98 percent of the structures require renovation and rehabilitation to meet contemporary needs and standards (23) . . . major reconstruction or rebuilding (is required) for over two-thirds (of the neighborhood)(37) . . . it will be necessary to alter both street and land use patterns if the many hazards are to be ameliorated (45)." Rapson's New Town In-Town design rectified these existing "hazards" in spectacular fashion. Cedar-Riverside would consist of five high-density residential developments surrounding a mixed-use commercial district, and it was projected to house 30,000 people in 12,500 units by 1992 (Miller 2006, 40; Christensen 1973; Bryan 1972). Most of the land was already in the possession of a single owner, a philanthropist named Gloria Segal who had begun to purchase land in the early 1960s and who saw in Rapson and the New Communities program the perfect means to realize her dream of rebuilding a "blighted" city neighborhood into an ideal community.

Cedar-Riverside initially proceeded on schedule. On June 29, 1971, HUD guaranteed the project a $24 million loan for its first ten years, a sum that required a local match of up to $40 million (Special to the *New York*

Times 1971, 29; Bryan 1972, 127; Martin 1978, 95; Christensen 1973, 137; Segal 1972, 162). Completion of the first phase was scheduled for 1976 (Cedar-Riverside Associates 1971, 1). Because Segal had purchased most of the land in the 1960s, construction began almost immediately (Martin 1978, 111). By 1973, phase I of Cedar-Riverside, about 10 percent of the proposed project, was complete, and its new residents began moving in, a mix of low-income tenants displaced from other urban renewal projects and middle-class tenants paying market-rate and even "deluxe" rental prices (Goldberger 1976, 1; Martin 1978, 115).

Cedar-Riverside's design was monumental and spectacular, showing a clear affinity with what the architectural press had labeled "megastructures" (Wilcoxon 1968, 2, in Banham 1976, 8) (Figure 1.1). Rapson's Minneapolis megastructure was a connected series of tall residential towers, each between thirty and forty stories high, interspersed with lower blocks of four to eight stories high. Each lower block defined partially enclosed parkland with play areas and recreational space (Bailey 1974, 33). Rapson eliminated through streets; roadways into the superblocks ended in culs-de-sac that left most of the ground open for pedestrians. Rapson also provided walkways connecting the blocks at the fourth-floor level. These linked open-air hallways in each tower to "area institutions as well as with commercial and community facilities" (Cedar-Riverside Associates 1971, 15). Freed of the obligation to use the street, Cedar-Riverside residents could move throughout the complex without touching the ground.

Rapson's design did not have its origin in Minneapolis precedents, to put it mildly. An observer versed in Modernist architectural history would have recognized Cedar-Riverside's clear programmatic and aesthetic debt to Swiss architect Le Corbusier's "total designs" for dwelling, which he called "Unités d'Habitation." The Unité, several of which were built in Europe, was a unified residential, commercial, and recreational environment in which multiple uses shared an eighteen-story horizontal apartment block, rather than occupying separate buildings or spaces as they did in older cities. Rapson's material choice of unpainted concrete also mirrored the Unités, right down to Cedar-Riverside's brightly painted yellow, red, and blue window panels, which added a Corbusian palette to an otherwise unornamented, stark structure. Cedar-Riverside's aboveground walkways also showed the influence of British architects Alison and Peter Smithson's "streets in the sky" idea, first seen in their 1952 design for Golden Lane in London. In this unbuilt scheme, the Smithsons translated the traditional

Figure 1.1. The concrete megastructure of Minneapolis's Cedar-Riverside was one of the last gasps of urban renewal. Community protest and the Nixon administration's decentralization of funding for urban development stopped additional construction in 1974. *AIA Journal* 66 (November 1977): 27. Courtesy Hanley Wood.

urban street with its mixed uses and open spaces into a three-dimensional network of dwelling units and open-air hallways that functioned as both public and recreational spaces. Rapson designed Cedar-Riverside twenty years after Corbusier's and the Smithsons' projects, but he left their ideas more or less intact.

In every way—scale, program, material, esthetic references—Cedar-Riverside was alien to the low-rise, wooden neighborhood fabric of Minneapolis. Rapson's design was formally sophisticated, but it also emphasized the project's complete distinction from its host city. Given that there was nothing that remotely resembled Cedar-Riverside anywhere else in the city, Rapson took a substantial risk that this obvious difference from the rest of the city would be taken as a positive, not a negative, feature. "We wanted the physical expression to show choice and richness," Rapson stated in 1976. Architectural critics for the most part agreed, but many residents did not. On a human level, Cedar-Riverside quickly showed failings sadly typical of high-rise Modern architecture. Families with young children eager to play outside found high-rise living a difficult proposition, and low-income households found the development's nonstandard features—oversized glass windows, narrow balconies—irritating and dysfunctional (Goldberger 1976).

Even as phase I of Cedar-Riverside opened, events were occurring in Washington that would negatively impact the new-town-in-town program. In early 1973, the federal government indicated a change of heart about its commitment to urban renewal and to the New Communities program. On January 5, President Nixon placed an eighteen-month moratorium on the construction of subsidized housing so that the government could "recognize the errors of past Federal efforts to support community development and to move swiftly to correct them" (Nixon, "State of the Union" 1975, 172). Nixon followed this moratorium with a proposal in March to replace numerous "wasteful and obsolete" housing programs (Nixon, "Radio Address" 1975), including the New Communities program, with a single grant to increase cities' decision-making role in their redevelopment. Nixon's "Better Communities Act," which finally entered law as the Housing and Community Development Act in January 1975, eliminated the New Communities program together with seven others and replaced them with Community Development Block Grants (CDBGs) (Frej and Specht 1976). CDBGs permitted communities to "(spend) as they desire to meet their community development needs" (Nixon, "State of the Union" 1975, 173), releasing them from the particular obligations imposed by specific HUD programs. President Nixon argued that decentralizing the spending of redevelopment dollars would make things better for all:

> We are stopping programs which have failed. We are determined to get a dollar's worth of service out of every dollar's worth of taxes. The high-cost, no result boondoggling by the Federal Government must end. This means we will continue to press for greater efficiency and better management in Federal programs. But it also means giving the lead role back to grassroots governments again. The time has come to reject the patronizing notion that Federal planners, peering over the point of a pencil in Washington, can guide your lives better than you can. (Nixon, "Radio Address" 1975)

Nixon's March 1973 announcement was a death knell for centrally directed and funded redevelopment like Cedar-Riverside. Henceforth HUD, as Nixon saw it, would not tell communities how to spend their redevelopment dollars; it would let them do as they wished. But the dislike of centralized planning was bipartisan. In Minneapolis, a chorus of environmental and community activists filed suit against Cedar-Riverside in late 1973, arguing that the development's environmental impact statement was "inadequate" and that the project was both "unnecessary and socially destructive" (Goldberger 1976, 1). With environmental approval necessary for continued progress, construction of Cedar-Riverside halted soon after the lawsuit, and it would never be resumed. Nor would the other, as-yet unbuilt newtowns-in-town elsewhere in the country ever be completed. Instead, the entire New Communities Act was quietly canceled in 1976 as a part of what HUD called a "detailed re-evaluation of the 'new towns' program" (Oser 1976, 10). Ten years later, HUD would formally foreclose upon Cedar-Riverside (Miller 2006, 56), placing the entire development into federal receivership.

Today, Cedar-Riverside is little different from a traditional public housing development: it is heavily minority in racial composition, and 70 percent of its population is at or below the federal poverty level (Cedar-Riverside Adult Education Collaborative 2010). Isolated, deteriorating, socially segregated, and impoverished, Cedar-Riverside is a monumental white elephant. To most Minneapolitans, it is just another bombastic piece of architecture from the 1960s: a social and architectural experiment that failed, another nail in Modernism's coffin.

Across the United States, the "swift correction" (Nixon, "State of the Union" 1975, 172) of urban redevelopment policy in the mid-1970s brought urban renewal projects to a crashing halt. They were little missed. "The modernists promised Utopia," opined *Times* architecture critic Ada Louise Huxtable in 1976: "Their vision was of a cleaner, brighter, more efficient and orderly universe in which architecture and technology would create healthful and happy housing. It was to be free of all hypocrisy and cant and any reference to history, (but) it did not work because it promised too much, and what it promised was unreal" (Huxtable 1976, 47). Huxtable's critique of Modernism would be often repeated in the years that followed.

The Wake of Urban Renewal: Criticism, Crisis, Reform

President Nixon's devolution of federally funded urban redevelopment marked a watershed moment for American urbanism. Four decades of direct state intervention in the built environment that had begun with the Greenbelt towns of Franklin Roosevelt's Resettlement Administration (Hall 2002, 135) had ended, and with it had ended an era that many felt had generated more problems than solutions in American cities. The dubious architectural legacy of Modernist projects like Cedar-Riverside reinforced this skepticism. Such projects may have been architecturally innovative, but they were also alien in scale and form and constructed at the expense of beloved older neighborhoods. These flaws fixed Modernism in the public mind as a redevelopment approach that not only ignored citizen wishes but distorted and devalued the very professions of architecture and urban planning.

Even as the public's skepticism toward Modernism grew, the architecture and planning professions, long united in their advocacy of urban renewal's "elimination and prevention of slums, and development of urban communities" (68 Stat. 590, 1954), found that urban renewal's demise left their alliance at loose ends. With urban renewal transformed from a centerpiece federal program to a "policy backwater" (Altshuler and Luberoff 2003, 26), architects' and planners' means of cooperating on large-scale urban projects was greatly reduced, though it was not entirely eliminated: some federal funding for large-scale urban development would persist until 1989 (Dreussi and Leahy 2000). As federal policy shifts reduced large-scale development opportunities, architects and planners themselves began to believe that Modernism, the design ideology that had guided urban reconstruction since the 1940s, was as obsolete as the neighborhoods that urban renewal had condemned to the wrecking ball. Modernism's decline came so fast that Cedar-Riverside was aesthetically outdated before it was even completed.

Architects particularly found themselves questioning the stylistic and material basis of Modernism. The formerly doctrinaire Modernist notion that ornament was "crime," as Loos (1931) had succinctly put it, seemed not only outdated but inhumane, a rejection of the very "complexity and contradiction" (Venturi 1966) that had characterized architectural mastery since the Renaissance. Some architects also argued that Modernism was antiurban, that abandoning past aesthetic principles had not only generated inhuman architecture but had ignored the value of the city as a repository of human knowledge and culture (Rossi 1982). By the early 1980s, architecture critic Charles Jencks could boldly pronounce that Modernism had ended and that design had entered the era of Postmodernism: "[Late Modernism] keeps a primary commitment to such Modernist values as the expression of technology, circulation and efficiency, [but Postmodern architecture] emphasizes the city context, the values of the users and the perennial means of architectural expression such as ornament" (Jencks 1981, 6). Postmodern architecture was characterized, Jencks continued, by a modesty and popular appeal that attempted to recover the humanity that the Modernists had so arrogantly disowned.

The rapid decline of Modernism had a dramatic effect on urban design in both the United States and the United Kingdom, as the work of the Greater London Council (GLC) showed. The GLC was a powerful regional government charged by the United Kingdom's 1947 Town and Country Planning Act (Hall 2002, 356) with providing low- and moderate-cost housing to the London region, and it took its responsibility seriously. Between 1965 and 1970 the GLC constructed 26,000 new dwellings at a cost of some 150 million pounds (Greater London Council 1970, 12). The United Kingdom was unaffected by the early 1970s urban policy shifts that occurred in the United States, but the GLC Architecture Department underwent a commensurate design revolution. In the early 1970s, High Modernism still held sway: schemes for New Towns and large social housing estates were in full swing around London (Figure 1.2) (Greater London

Figure 1.2. The Newacres estate at Thamesmead New Town in the United Kingdom was a typical GLC design of the early 1970s. Its prefabricated tower blocks had the powerful, abstract, and often unappealing forms typical of High Modernism. Greater London Council, Department of Architecture and Civic Design, *GLC Architecture 1965/70: The Work of the GLC's Department of Architecture and Civic Design* (London: Greater London Council, 1970).

Council 1970, 16–20). These projects were vast in scale (Thamesmead New Town was more than three miles in length) and abstract in design, with typical Modernist building types such as fifteen- to twenty-five-story tower blocks; low "podium" buildings; broad, loosely defined expanses of open space; and widespread clearance of existing historic buildings. The design and planning ideology of the early 1970s seemed little different from that of twenty years earlier.

Any apparent similarity to the 1950s was misleading, however, for the early 1970s marked the final years of High Modernist schemes in Great Britain. By 1974 the GLC could declare that

> (this year) the architectural profession took another step forward in assessing its own position. Some called it a crisis in architecture, but it was really another stage in a major reappraisal. Central to this reappraisal was growing doubt about some of the established attitudes of the architectural profession and growing acceptance of the need for a deeper mutual understanding between architects and those for whom they build . . . the result was a low key architecture which was subtle and humane and of a character which the occupants would really enjoy. (Greater London Council 1974, 3–4).

Only three years later the GLC announced that it had comprehensively abandoned Modernism. "The image of housing has changed radically; its scale has altered completely. The monumental high-rise schemes of the past have disappeared, along with the policy of comprehensive redevelopment, which involved the wholesale destruction of vast chunks of urban fabric . . . design (is) reverting to a more orthodox English tradition. The era of self-consciously-ingenious schemes is over" (Greater London Council 1977, 10). Reflecting these changed ideals, the housing designed by the Greater London Council in the mid-1970s had little formal relationship to that constructed a only few years earlier. Instead of tall concrete towers and open plazas, mid-1970s buildings were only a few stories tall, with mixed uses, active streets and pedestrian ways, and a sense of urban enclosure similar to that provided by the traditional city. Much of High Modernism's abstraction disappeared; the buildings were constructed mostly of brick, with punched windows and private entryways evoking nineteenth-century London architecture. The quality and appeal of this architecture, particularly compared with its immediate predecessors, was often quite high (Figure 1.3).

Figure 1.3. By the late 1970s, GLC housing like the Queensferry Estate, completed along the Lea River in Tottenham in 1980, was more individualized in design, humane in scale and material, and respectful of its setting. Greater London Council, Department of Architecture and Civic Design, *GLC Architects Review 2* (London: Academy Editions, 1976).

The design "revolution" that removed High Modernism from the GLC Architecture Department's palette in the mid-1970s was not accompanied, at least for the time being, by an equivalent urban policy revolution. The powerful regional planning agency continued to construct social housing according to long-term master plans, though the housing it constructed was smaller in scale, more contextual in form, and more sensitive to the communities in which it was located than it had been before the revolution. This immunity from policy change would not last: the GLC would be abolished in 1986 by Prime Minister Thatcher as part of a wave of privatization measures sweeping Britain (Klatt 1986, 11). But the late 1970s and early 1980s marked a sort of halcyon period in which the United Kingdom applied a changed aesthetic—reformed Modernist architecture and urbanism—to a surviving liberal policy measure—social housing.

For a few short years, the GLC's reformed design strategy achieved notable success, plainly visible in the housing developments that the GLC constructed in the early 1980s. Among the most successful and best known is the project called Odhams Walk, constructed between 1978 and 1982 in the Covent Garden neighborhood. Today Covent Garden is an extremely prosperous, gentrified neighborhood with stores like Starbucks and Zara, but in the 1960s it was a depressed, central-city area with a mix of offices, residential, retailing, market, industrial, and entertainment uses, much like Scollay Square or West Greenwich Village in the United States. The planning struggle that ultimately generated Odhams Walk is similar to that of many redevelopments born in the late 1960s. Like parallel urban renewal sites in the United States, Covent Garden was proposed for extensive clearance in a 1968 GLC-authored plan, *Covent Garden's Moving.* This plan proposed clearing and rebuilding fifty-five of the area's ninety-three acres with a megastructure (Covent Garden Planning Team 1968, 49). The plan generated immediate controversy for its proposed displacement of working-class uses and housing, and resident protests raged throughout the early 1970s. As one working-class resident wrote angrily, "The main attraction in Covent Garden is THE PEOPLE . . . the market workers and the working-class tenants. Remove these and what have you got? Any other characterless area—[the plan should] replace the market workers with residents, East Enders, not Chelsea types" (Anson 1981, 39). By 1973 community activism and government pressure had obliged the GLC to abandon the plan and restart the planning process (Anson 1981, 176), an event that one author called "one of the most extraordinary sequences of events in planning history" (Home and Loew 1987, 9). In 1978 the GLC issued a much revised *Action Plan* following four years of consultation with a committee that included working-class Covent Garden residents and workers. Unsurprisingly the plan was quite different from its predecessor. Gone were the dramatic physical changes proposed in the 1969 plan: instead, the *Action Plan* suggested a mix of refurbished historic buildings and a few redeveloped vacant or underutilized sites, including the building site housing the former Odham's Press. The Odham's site was recommended by the plan for housing for "about 320" persons and space for businesses "affected by later redevelopment proposals" (Greater London Council 1978, 74). Following the plan, construction of Odhams Walk began in 1978 and was completed by 1981.

Residents demanded, and received, substantial input in the Odhams Walk design process, and the result was a project that reviewer Kenneth Campbell called "a most ingenious and satisfactory answer . . . an urban village in an area where community feeling is most strong and at the same time most threatened" (Woodward and Campbell 1982, 43). (Figure 1.4.) Odhams provided 102 units for 314 working-class Covent Garden residents, including 12 "five-person" (four-bedroom) flats and 8 "six-person" (five bedroom) flats (Woodward and Campbell 1982, 44).

As a response to the challenge of providing dense moderate-income housing in a central-city location, Odhams Walk was distinct in several ways. Perhaps its most visible feature was its scalar conformance with the surrounding neighborhood's four- and five-story buildings. This marked a notable departure from the high-rise towers of High Modernism. At the same time, Odhams' architect, Donald Ball, provided a modern analogue to the rowhouse by designing Odhams Walk as a three-dimensional matrix of buildings, garden patios, and public walkways, with semipublic stairs leading to private entrances for most units (Figure 1.4). Responding both to historic Covent Garden and to contemporary design currents, Odhams' architecture may fairly be called "responsive" or "reflective" Modernism. Today, thirty years after its completion, Odhams' plantings have grown in, and the development is a charming mix of green, light, shadow, and brick, with a private life subtly connected to a bustling public realm outside. The Academy for Sustainable Communities, recognizing Odhams Walk as a "showcase" project in 2010, praised the development as "one of the few housing developments where the original artist's impressions are not only matched but surpassed by the reality" (Academy for Sustainable Communities 2010).

Figure 1.4. Perhaps the high point of the GLC's brief period of reformed Modernism was Odhams Walk in Covent Garden, London. Odhams, which opened in 1982, was a formally complex and visually delightful mix of innovative urbanism and socially responsible planning. The GLC was disbanded by the Thatcher administration only a few years later, and social housing construction ceased. Greater London Council, *GLC/ILEA Architecture 1976–1986* (London: Architectural Press, 1986).

Transcending the planning and community controversies that preceded its construction, Odhams Walk is a paragon of social housing and architectural innovation generated by centralized planning. Responding both to the architectural shifts of late Modernism and to the social reaction against large-scale clearance and displacement, the GLC responded with a development that combines liberal housing policy with a sense of pride in contemporary design. Odhams Walk was only one of many such developments constructed by the GLC between the fall of High Modernism around 1974 and before the fall of the GLC itself in 1986. In this too-brief period, the United Kingdom applied the resources of the state to augment the housing and community needs of lower-income city residents with high-quality architecture and urban design.

Despite its qualities, Odhams Walk is only a partial paradigm of social policy and urban design. Over time its social provisions have been severely eroded as housing has come onto the open market through the "Right to Buy" program instituted by the Conservative government in the 1980s. This program permitted original tenants, most of whom were working-class area residents, to purchase their units at subsidized prices and then resell them at market rates. Under Right to Buy, the state sacrificed fiscal gains that its property may have accrued even as it foreclosed upon that housing continuing in future as social housing. As a result, Odhams Walk is mostly luxury housing today. Though the project still houses "many original residents" (Academy for Sustainable Communities 2010), a one-bedroom apartment in Odhams Walk sells for £500,000, or more than $700,000. This high value is doubtless a result of the development's location in the heart of London, and the GLC's original intent to provide a haven of affordability for the working class in the expensive London property market is long gone.

Odhams Walk's cannot be replicated in its surroundings today. The GLC is gone, and social housing would be impossibly expensive to provide in twenty-first century Covent Garden. But both its architectural and planning lessons are worth considering elsewhere. Working within a state planning apparatus dedicated to providing low-cost housing, Donald Ball designed a modestly scaled project that manifested both humane, vernacular design features and a notable degree of abstraction. One would have great difficulty finding projects of equivalent social and formal generosity in the overpriced London environment of today.

Planning's Parallel Crisis

In the United Kingdom, reformed High Modernism and state-directed social planning could correct, at least for a short time, the urban errors of High Modernism. But in the United States, as design innovation and social planning went their separate ways after 1975, such corrections would prove difficult to undertake. Even as architects distanced themselves from Modernism to design "low-key," "orthodox," and "humane" buildings, planners concerned with urban problems found themselves severed from the federal funding and initiatives that had shaped redevelopment activity for decades. Across the country, municipal planning departments, redevelopment agencies, and architects had worked hand in hand for decades to implement federal mandates and spend federal funds to rebuild older American cities. This relationship changed dramatically when urban renewal disappeared.

For thirty years after 1945, urban planning was closely associated with the project of urban modernization and large-scale slum clearance. The latter enterprise had long preceded Modernism: nonprofit actors constructed "model tenements" for the poor in New York City as early as the 1870s (Plunz 1990, 88–121), and the Regional Planning Association of America's housing efforts of the 1920s, guided by housing pioneer Edith Elmer Wood, were shaped by Garden City rather than Radiant City formal ideals (Birch 1976). As Modernism's influence grew in the 1930s, social housing became closely associated with Modernist design, particularly in New York, where all of the city's public housing after the Williamsburg Houses of 1938 was Modernist in design (Plunz 1990, 217). By the 1950s, following the Federal Housing Acts of 1949 and 1954 that required conformance of redevelopment to a "comprehensive community plan" as well as to "neighborhood analysis" findings (Charles S. Ryne in Kraemer 1965, 23), urban planners had vaulted into the ranks of the best-funded, and most powerful, municipal agencies. The products of urban renewal plans were clothed in the architectural language of High Modernism. Urban renewal was, of course, supported by a "growth machine" that included politicians, legislators, and business leaders whose influence far outweighed that of planners. But the identity of urban planning with urban renewal was substantial in large cities where urban redevelopment was extensive. By the late 1950s, when both Chicago and New York City comprehensively revised their zoning resolutions to reflect Modernist principles (Schweiterman and Caspall 2006, 38; and Willis 1995, 140–42), planners not only were associated with Modernist-designed redevelopment but were legislating Modernist design.

Planning's link to Modernism began to collapse during the 1960s just as the profession's powerful role in the municipal hierarchy began to shift downward. New York planners certainly got little respect from Robert Moses, a powerful bureaucrat who had represented the public face of urban redevelopment for several decades even as he oppressed and disrespected planners themselves. Author Robert Caro describes a New York City Planning Commission so impotent that planners had to "go underground" in the 1950s to provide independent estimates of urban renewal relocations carried out by Moses (Caro 1974, 966). New York's planners may have quietly opposed Moses and his well-funded agencies, but one could not expect ordinary citizens to discern this opposition or to even distinguish between the two municipal actors. By the mid-1960s, the Planning Commission's Modernist zoning was shaping out-of-scale buildings all over the city just as Moses's "master-planned" highways and housing redevelopment were generating increasing public controversy (Klemek 2008). By 1969, when New York issued its first citywide master plan, planning's image and meaning had so declined that even a New York City Planning Commissioner, Beverly Spatt, could declare the plan to be "ineffectual—a model exercise in futility" (Spatt 1969, 174). Commissioner Spatt argued that New York planning needed "early continuous informed citizen participation whereby the community people working with the professional City planners can formulate the alternatives, sort out the problems, and come up with achievable solutions . . . only by the City and community people working together from the very beginning shall polarization be minimized and reconciliation achieved" (Spatt 1969, 175). Commissioner Spatt's dissent mirrored an increasing academic disenchantment with Modernist planning that had been growing since the early 1960s. Nixon's abandonment of centralized urban redevelopment was one culmination of this skepticism in centralized planning. What historian Christopher Klemek describes as "new left urbanism" (2009) arose in the late 1950s at the University of Pennsylvania, where social scientist Paul Davidoff, trained in law rather than architecture, began to question the foundation of a planning ideology that required large-scale plans produced by experts. Davidoff rejected both top-down planning and the idea of planning as a physical enterprise allied with architecture. Davidoff's social approach to planning would crystallize in 1965, when he wrote that "(planning) must operate so as to include rather than exclude citizens from participating in the process. 'Inclusion' means not only permitting citizens to be heard. It also means allowing them to become well-informed about the underlying reasons for planning proposals, and to respond to these in the technical language of professional planners" (Davidoff 1965, 546). Planners and citizens motivated by this vision of social justice could hardly be expected to espouse large-scale redevelopment of any sort or to support a policy infrastructure that promoted such development. Social advocates were unsurprisingly mightily displeased by ambitious Modernist urban design schemes, whose flaws were quickly elided with urban design and even with physical planning itself, heretofore the core of planning curricula and practice. Inspired by a social planning agenda, Penn abolished studio from the planning curriculum by 1965 (Scott Brown 1990, 14), a move that was soon followed at other planning schools such as MIT (Rich et al. 1970). Design's banishment from planning education and vice versa (the Yale School of Architecture closed down its planning program entirely in 1970) signaled a dramatic separation of planning and architecture that the federal government's mid-1970s policy shifts only reiterated. In 1975, with urban renewal closed down and modernist planning being "reevaluated," as Nixon put it, Cleveland published a new version of the master plan, the socially centered *Policy Planning Report*. The report had nary an image in sight, and it codified planning's separation from design.

By the late 1970s both the planning and architecture professions had retreated from each other to confront their own dilemmas. Architecture, committed as always to innovative design but scarred by High Modernism's inhumanity, began to reconsider the validity of "vernacular and classic traditions" (Scully 1988, 262). Many architects took refuge in the past by rediscovering the value of historicism, context, and on a larger scale, the premodern city. At the same time liberal social planners disowned the Modernist enterprise of reshaping urban space in an ironic lockstep with a conservative federal government focused on decentralization and diminution of liberal policies. Both shifts left urban planning bereft of a major mode of shaping space: urban renewal.[1] Planning theorists and practitioners concerned with cities and people focused increasingly on the profession's potential to resolve contradictions and injustices in capitalist society. And neither professional nor academic planners had any interest in continuing the Modernist project of spatially reorganizing the city through state action. Architecture's and planning's new concern with history and society gave these professions a revised sense of purpose in the wake of urban renewal's demise and adjusted professional expectations to the straitened fiscal climate of the post–urban renewal era.

These reformed ideals had a critical lacuna, however. Ending Modernist social planning, architecture, and urban design efforts did not end the urban problems that had spurred these efforts in the first place. Instead, Modernism and urban renewal's simultaneous demise left declining cities without distinct policy measures, or physical strategies, to reshape their distressed neighborhoods. As Postmodern architects and social planners moved away from each other, they also became divorced from a policy agenda that could be ambitious enough in scale to confront the increasingly severe problems facing shrinking cities in the late 1970s. High Modernism was badly flawed, but it did have the advantage of being linked to a sizable federal policy agenda. The modest and responsible architecture and planning agendas of the late 1970s resolved ideological debates, but they were ill-suited to confront the seriousness of the urban crisis that afflicted America's older cities in the 1970s and the decades following.

When President Nixon announced the decentralization of federal redevelopment policy, he declared that his administration's new agenda would "[give] the lead role back to grassroots governments" and "give people a sense of control . . . in shaping the places where they live" (Nixon, "Radio Address" 1975). The late 1970s offered declining American cities their first chance to redevelop neighborhoods according to their own rather than federal agendas. One of the earliest examples of such decentralized redevelopment would come from New York City's troubled South Bronx.

A New Beginning in the South Bronx

Critics charged the urban renewal of the 1950s and 1960s with numerous sins. One of the worst was that urban planners confused healthy, if congested and poor, urban neighborhoods with desperate slums that required rejuvenation. The condemnation of ethnic neighborhoods such as Boston's West and North Ends signaled to critics like Jane Jacobs a professional delusion with modernization at the expense of ordinary city life: "'Why in the world are you down in the North End?' [a Boston planner] said. . . . 'That's a slum! . . . of course we have to rebuild it eventually. We've got to get those people off the streets.' . . . Here was a curious thing. My friend's instincts told him the North End was a good place, and his social statistics confirmed it. But everything he had learned as a physical planner about what is good for people and good for city neighborhoods, everything that made him an expert, told him the North End had to be a bad place" (Jacobs 1961, 10–11). Jacobs's condemnation of planning and slum clearance was polemical and in some ways accurate, but it was also an exaggeration. Not all planners supported slum clearance; as Caro (1974, 966) documented, many planners instead attempted to resist the powerful urban renewal machine supported by municipal politicians and moneyed private interest groups. But city planners employed by the public sector could hardly be expected to confront such a coalition, and often they did not even have the opportunity. Political scientist Douglas Rae's study of New Haven redevelopment politics in the 1950s (2003, 316–25) describes a mayor (Richard Lee) so well funded and confident that he could not only marginalize the city's plan commission but replicate it twice over, funding both a redevelopment commission and a private consultancy to undertake many of the urban renewal tasks that city planners were unable or unwilling to perform. City planning as a city agency per se clearly had little to do with the damage wrought in older cities by such destructive agents as the interstate highway program. But large-scale neighborhood clearance and the problems that ensued unarguably resulted from an urban policy agenda that enlisted urban planning as one of its principal participants. It was this urban policy agenda for which critics like Jane Jacobs and Paul Davidoff came to hold the planning profession accountable.

If urban renewal could be elided with urban planning, so too could urban decline. Throughout the 1960s American cities suffered from increasingly serious social problems as ethnic groups clashed over scarce resources, shrinking economic opportunities, and, some argued, punitive urban renewal policies. The federally organized Kerner Commission, appointed in 1967 to look into the nation's summer of riots, concluded that "[urban renewal] has sometimes been poorly implemented, but we believe that the concept is sound" (U.S. National Advisory Commission on Civil Disorders 1968, 480), but Robert Caro, condemning the effects of highway construction in the South Bronx only a few years later, was less kind:

The one mile of the Cross-Bronx Expressway through East Tremont was completed by 1960. By 1965 . . . the apartment buildings that

had been so precious to the people that had lived in them were
ravaged hulks. (Glassless) windows . . . stared out on the street like
sightless eyes. (Building entrances) were carpeted with shards of
glass from what had been the doors to their lobbies. In those lobbies
. . . not much remained. Plaster . . . lay in heaps . . . the pipes . . .
were gone . . . elevators no longer worked . . . staircases were broken
and shattered. (Caro 1975, 893)

Caro's depiction of a causal connection between urban renewal and urban
decline (urban renewal caused population upheaval, upheaval led to social
disorder) was something of an exaggeration, as Chapter 2's review of urban
decline in Detroit and Philadelphia will show. As much or more urban
decline occurred in neighborhoods with no experience of urban renewal
than in places where urban renewal had occurred. In reality, urban neighborhoods in older cities were declining across the United States in the 1960s
and 1970s, and neither urban renewal nor urban planning had much to do
with it.

The period after urban renewal's demise in the early 1970s marked a
particularly dark time for declining neighborhoods like the South Bronx. A
neighborhood packed tight with tenements, apartments, and immigrants,
the South Bronx had welcomed the poor and lower middle class since the
1870s (White and Willensky 1968, 218). As Caro documented, urban renewal had indeed wrought some destruction: the Cross-Bronx and Bruck-
ner Expressways were constructed through the neighborhood in the early
1960s, and more than nine hundred public housing units were constructed
in scattered locations in the Mott Haven area of the South Bronx ("Bronx
Housing Slated" 1960, 34).

The South Bronx's real problems began in the mid-1970s in the neighborhood's northern reaches near Crotona Park (Figure 1.5). Like many
other cities during this time, the South Bronx's population transitioned
racially from 78 percent white in 1960 to 76 percent black and Latino by
1980 (*CensusCD 1960*; *Census CD 1980*). Approximately 376,000 people,
almost all of them white, moved out of the neighborhood during this period,[2] replaced by a smaller number of newcomers who were much poorer
than the departing residents. This voluntary population exchange dramatically destabilized the South Bronx's real estate market. As older white residents fled their South Bronx apartments for neighborhoods further from
Manhattan, their landlords faced catastrophic fiscal difficulties. With less

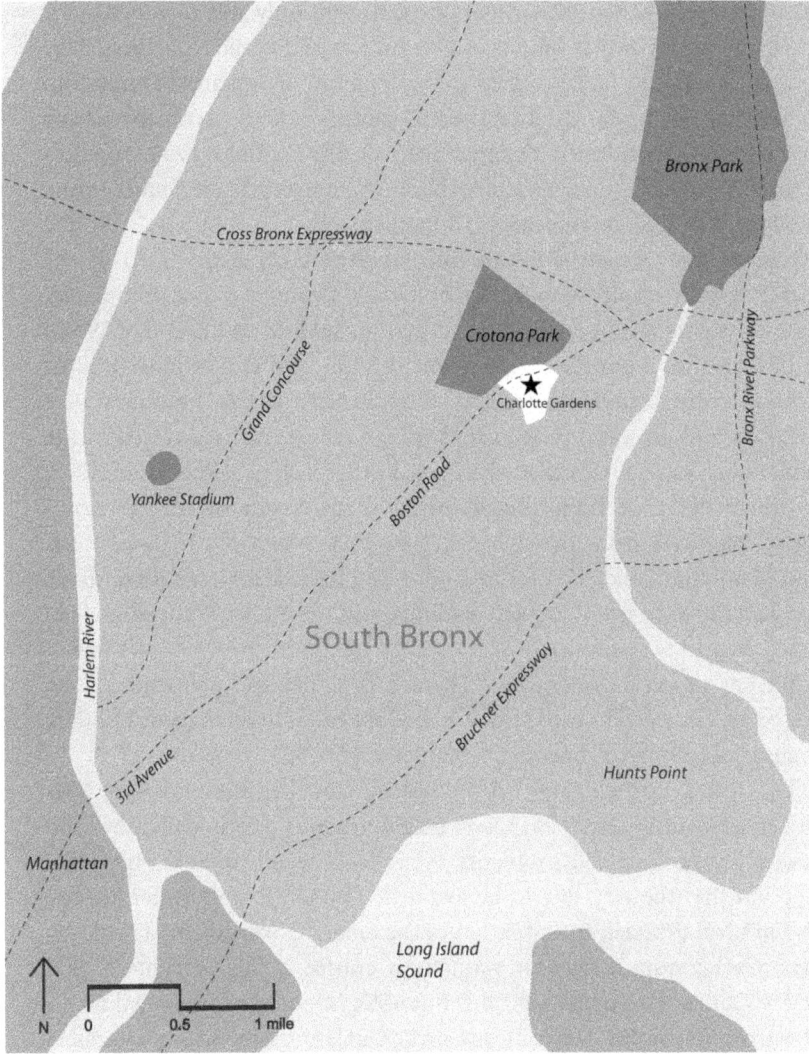

Figure 1.5. Charlotte Gardens is located in the northern South Bronx. Most of this part of New York City experienced severe depopulation, racial transition, and housing abandonment in the 1960s and 1970s. Map by author. Map illustration by Sarah Spicer.

demand for apartments, and with available tenants only able to afford lower rents, many South Bronx landlords saw no future for their business. Like their former tenants, many walked away, abandoning remaining tenants to their fates. Some landlords attempted to capture a final payout by setting their buildings, abandoned or inhabited, on fire (Rooney 1995, 56); this caused additional displacement and began to transform the South Bronx into what was called picturesquely, if insensitively, "Fort Apache". "In the thirty years that [ninety-two-year-old resident Geza Kun] lived in the Hunts Point-Intervale section of the South Bronx, he saw his placid, middle-class neighborhood, populated by 100,000 Jews at the end of World War II, turn into a bombed-out horror. Doctors and clinics moved away, groceries, kosher, butchers, drugstores closed their doors, buildings were abandoned and set afire, youth gangs spread terror, garbage rotted in the streets. Police have long called the area 'Fort Apache'" (Robertson 1977, 48). Unlike many declining neighborhoods, the South Bronx was not a marginal place far from the sights of New York's wealthy. It directly adjoined Manhattan, and the fires of its burning buildings were visible to all. It was also the location of Yankee Stadium, and the Yankees' appearance in the 1977 World Series brought the arson of the South Bronx to the television screens of every American. "There it is, ladies and gentlemen," announced newscaster Howard Cosell as he looked at an apartment building in flames, "the Bronx is burning" (Mahler 2005, 338).

The South Bronx's highly visible problems soon became a crisis for New York City's government. With many neighborhoods clearly collapsing and bedeviled by severe fiscal problems, New York began to suffer from the perception that the city should be avoided if possible. This larger "urban crisis" in turn attracted the attention of the federal government. The newly elected Carter administration wanted to confront the perception that America's cities were dying, and this domestic imperative motivated President Carter to visit the South Bronx in 1977. Carter selected a place called Charlotte Street for his visit. This was a short street near Crotona Park formerly occupied by five-story tenements, most of which were abandoned and/or burned by the time of the president's visit (see Figure 1.5). The physical appearance of the neighborhood was distressing, and the president seemed somewhat at odds about what to do: "'See which areas can still be salvaged,' the President said. 'Maybe we can create a recreation area and turn it around. Get a whole map of the whole area and show me what could be done'" (Dembart 1977, 66). New York City took Carter at his word. In

1978 Mayor Ed Koch announced that the as-yet-unredeveloped Charlotte Street project would be "the linchpin of the redevelopment of the South Bronx" (Von Hoffman 2004, 35). Koch hired a scion of urban renewal, Edward Logue, to direct the effort, an ironic action given that Logue had supervised substantial neighborhood clearance in both New Haven and Boston. But Koch's decision was not ill-conceived. No one knew better than Logue how to capture federal dollars to generate new development for distressed cities. Under Logue's leadership New Haven and Boston had two of the top three highest federal redevelopment funding per capita of any city in the United States (Rae 2003, 324). But Logue in 1978 was a scion without a funding stream, for urban renewal was gone, and even President Carter's promise was a fiscally empty one. Logue's boldly titled South Bronx Development Organization (SBDO) (Oser 1983, A17) was left without a means of accomplishing the rebirth that the president himself had promised to the people of New York City.

But Logue was innovative as well as dedicated, and he refused to walk away from the problem of Charlotte Street. Something had to be built there: the city had committed to it, and expectations were high. But that something had to be extremely cheap, as well as effective. What could be built? A New Town-In-Town or the like was obviously impossible: infrastructure and construction costs would be tremendous, and there was no time for the complex planning and design that would be required for an ambitious project. Inspiration for Logue came instead from the unlikeliest of sources: "[As I drove around the Bronx] I'd see this abandoned five-story walk-up, and the rubble-strewn streets, and then I'd see a little three-story house in the middle of this. . . . I saw that homeowner surviving in the worst of conditions. I said if home ownership works in the rest of America, it can work in the South Bronx" (Logue, quoted in Yardley 1997). Logue was true to his word. The SBDO rebuilt Charlotte Street, not as a New Town In-Town, but as a tract of ninety single-family homes called Charlotte Gardens, prefabricated in Pennsylvania and trucked into New York City over the George Washington Bridge in the dead of night (Oser 1983, A17) (Figures 1.6 and 1.7). The symbolism was obvious: as Logue asked rhetorically, "What is the American dream? A home of your own with a white picket fence. [On Charlotte Street] I want white" (Logue, quoted in Shenon 1983, 1). Charlotte Gardens homes were identical one-story ranches containing 1,152 square feet and a palette of suburban amenities, including "three bedrooms, a cathedral-ceiling living room, a dining room and fully

Figure 1.6. Charlotte Gardens site plan atop site plan of former apartment buildings. Its ninety single-family houses had 6.8 units per acre, about the same as Levittown, but the former buildings had almost 290 units per acre. Charlotte Gardens' population density is only 2 percent of the former neighborhood's. Map by author. Map illustration by Sarah Spicer. Data derived from Bromley and Google maps.

Figure 1.7. Charlotte Gardens' ninety prefabricated tract homes were constructed as cheaply as possible by a nearly bankrupt New York City in the late 1970s. Although most saw the project as a redevelopment victory and it is popular with residents, it marked a separation between urban design and social planning and set the aesthetic tone for post-renewal redevelopment. Author photo.

equipped kitchen, custom wood kitchen cabinets, one and a half baths, carpeting in the living room, dining room, hall and bedrooms, washer and dryer hookups, gas stove, security window grilles and an alarm system" (Shenon 1983, 1).

In 1976, architect Robert A. M. Stern had presciently proposed that valueless inner-city land adjacent to subways be rebuilt with low-density single-family houses with yards and driveways equivalent to those in the suburbs. He called these "subway suburbs" (Stern 1981, 92) and in true Postmodern fashion did not reveal whether or not his proposal was to be taken seriously. Charlotte Gardens made it clear that Stern's seemingly flippant proposal was not only feasible but a best-case scenario for the depressed South Bronx.

Viewed within the fiscal and conceptual constraints of the early 1980s, the SBDO's decision to construct Charlotte Gardens with the blessing of both community consultants and the city was a logical one. In an era of diminished expectations, inflation, and rampant white flight from the city, introducing suburban homes into inner-city blight provided an image of pastoral refuge that was appealing to both policy makers and potential buyers. Urban blight might destroy apartment buildings, but how could it harm a hardy homeowner neighborhood of ranch houses? Stern was right: suburbia seemed the perfect design strategy for solving the intractable difficulties of the inner city.

Charlotte Gardens was also shaped by harsher realities. Ronald Reagan's 1980 election to the presidency placed in power an avowed conservative who opposed urban policy even more than Nixon had. Carter's impoverished administration looked good by comparison. In a 1985 essay, Rebecca Lee, the former director of project development for the SBDO, detailed the fiscal creativity that allowed Charlotte Gardens to be built under Reagan's conservative regime (Lee 1985, 277–82). For four years following its creation in 1979, the SBDO flailed as it sought a funding stream for implementation of its homeownership vision on Charlotte Street. Logue's decision to construct manufactured single-family homes was made in 1980, but funding did not finally become available until 1983, when the city received a Federal Urban Development Action grant for $1.35 million. Even with this funding, the costs for preparing a complicated urban site were so high that the development cost of $71,900 per house could be reduced by only $20,000 per unit. The ninety homeowners of Charlotte Gardens ultimately paid just under $52,000 each for their homes.

As with many affordable housing projects, Charlotte Gardens' funding difficulties evaporated in the political rhetoric that surrounded its development. New York Mayor Ed Koch saw the project as a sign that the South Bronx was "on the way back": "There were those who said you cannot build in the South Bronx. We dismissed that. There were those who said that you have to build only in the strong areas . . . and shore up the peripheral areas. And we said we're going to do that too, but we're not going to write off any section of the city. And here is this area of Charlotte Street, psychologically—the President stood here—it means something" (Mayor Koch, quoted in "South Bronx Debate" 1979, E7). Other politicians saw the project as a welcome end to the troubles of the late 1970s. "'Charlotte Gardens was a noble experiment,' said Robert Esnard, a deputy mayor and chairman of the [South Bronx] development organization. 'It's more than a symbol. It means the burden has passed'" (Roberts 1987, B1).

Unsurprisingly, the 90 mostly black and Latino families (Lee 1985, 281) who were able to purchase a home out of a pool of 520 applicants were also overjoyed with Charlotte Gardens. Its suburban imagery was not lost on them. "When I come to my house, it's so different [from the rest of the Bronx]. It's just like living in Long Island," exclaimed one owner ("The Bronx Is Up," telecast, February 10, 1988, quoted in Plunz 1990, 334). Other owners believed that the Bronx's social ills would be palliated by Charlotte Gardens. "It's a whole new community. . . . I won't be worried about my girls . . . they're not going to be Bronx kids, they're going to be Charlotte Gardens kids," said one (Stewart 1997).

Ten years earlier, Cedar-Riverside's concrete megastructure had attracted architectural accolades but resident resentment. Charlotte Gardens evoked an opposite reaction: its residents exulted that the single-family suburban dream was theirs at last. But from the architectural establishment, there was only silence: Charlotte Gardens was not reviewed by a single architectural publication of the time. How could it be? There was no design to review. For in the short space of ten years New York's social housing had detached from urban design as neatly as urban design had separated from social housing in contemporary high-income projects such as Battery Park City. Only a few architectural surveys mentioned Charlotte Gardens, and their laconic critiques were predictably at odds with resident opinions. "The reconstruction [of Charlotte Street] with ticky-tacky suburban dwellings reveals another kind of destruction—that of valuable, close-in land through underutilization. Silly," opined the authors of the *AIA Guide to New York* (White and Willensky 2000, 562). Urban designer Richard Plunz was hardly more complimentary, labeling the development "a surreal contrast to the burned-out shells nearby" (Plunz 1990, 334).

In retrospect, Charlotte Gardens' legacy was mixed. Certainly the development marked the beginning of a new era of nonprofit-driven social housing in New York City (Von Hoffman 2003, 19–76). Advocates of community empowerment praise the decentralized, nonprofit-driven planning process that followed Charlotte Gardens and that produced a new landscape of affordable houses in the South Bronx. From a physical perspective, there is little doubt that the Bronx's new social housing is modest, humane, and appropriate to residents' aspirations. Yet the architecture of these developments is overwhelmingly mediocre, and their cumulative urban effect is negligible. At best these projects' architecture has a wan, vernacular historicism whose aggregation indicates little more than a semisuburbanization of the landscape. The formal insubstantiality of post-1985 social housing is perhaps Charlotte Gardens' most damaging legacy. In the Bronx, Charlotte Gardens and its peers essentially removed social housing from the realm of architecture, and from urban design as well. As Chapter 4 discusses, other cities' social housing design trajectory has been little different.

But perhaps the market should have the last word on Charlotte Gardens. The original homebuyers' confidence has certainly paid off. In 2009, 1545 Charlotte Street, a typical Charlotte Gardens home, was listed for sale at $459,000.[3] This is an approximately 900 percent increase in value in the home's twenty-five years of existence and a sobering reminder that design is far from the only variable that determines value, particularly in a boom economy like that of twenty-first-century New York.

The Revolution: Urban Design After Urban Renewal

Virginia Woolf claimed in 1924 that "human relations change(d) . . . about the year 1910," bringing a subsequent "change in religion, conduct, politics, and literature" (Woolf 1924). On a less all-encompassing level, one may also say that the design and social philosophy of urban reconstruction shifted in or about the year 1982. That year, the Greater London Council completed its mixed-use housing development for 314 working-class London residents at Odhams Walk, and the SBDO neared the date when it could plant ninety prefabricated homes on Charlotte Street. On the European side of the Atlantic, on the one hand, Odhams marked the end of a short period after 1974 when responsive Modernism, state planning, and social housing briefly merged in a benevolent hybrid. In New York, on the other hand, Charlotte Gardens initiated an era when modest Postmodern or vernacular architecture and equally modest, decentralized social planning arrived indecorously into city fabrics devastated by building and population loss. The revolution of 1982 was different from the one Woolf wrote about, but in America's declining cities it was no less momentous.

Both Odhams Walk and Charlotte Gardens were hailed as successes at the time, and both have high values in the marketplace today, but in every other respect the two housing developments have little to do with each other. Architecturally, Odhams signaled, as previously noted, a newly responsive, or "reformed" (Rowe 1993, 264) modernism. Odhams' design simultaneously expressed a relationship to Covent Garden and a new way of living in the "pueblo" of its piled-up housing units. Its materials, scale, personalization, and domestic image marked it as a project concerned with *being* (Rowe 1993, 271) in the present-day city, while its abstraction, minimalism, massing, and spatial novelty declared the project as *becoming* (Rowe 1993, 271) something else—a vision of the future—as well.

At the same time, Odhams marked a *reformed social planning process*. It took form only after a multiyear consultation with affected residents, and its program (before the advent of Right to Buy) was social, composed of low-cost housing and commercial uses. Odhams marked the reform, not abandonment, of centralized, top-down planning; the welfare state's commitment to social housing in the city core changed to respect resident concerns, incorporate their input, and serve their needs. It was exemplary both as architecture and as planning.

Charlotte Gardens also met resident needs, but it had very few of Odhams' other qualities. Its "design" was reductivist; the housing was vernacular and its site planning was similarly unsophisticated. Charlotte Gardens could not be said to be either being or becoming, in the sense that Rowe (1993, 271) described; the housing had no relation with its current environment, and its vision of the future city was hardly promising. Fortunately this vision did not come to pass; nearby 1990s rowhouse developments such as Melrose Court (White, Willensky, and Leadon 2010, 831) are much higher density, reflecting higher land costs resulting from New York's recovering economy. Charlotte Gardens marked the abandonment, not the reform, of Modernism's future orientation. At the same time it also reflected the disappointing built results of decentralized social planning policy. Later nonprofit-sponsored Bronx housing would be equally responsive to its residents, but with equally unsophisticated design (e.g., Von Hoffman 2003, 64). Logue's pragmatic project was ultimately little more than a coping strategy in an era of conservative assault on urban redevelopment. Charlotte Gardens' achievement also marked the funeral of the formal and scalar optimism that had characterized urban redevelopment as recently as Roosevelt Island.

Odhams and Charlotte Gardens are single developments that aptly represent the urban design revolution of the mid and late 1970s. This revolution has four dimensions: in urban dynamics, urban policy, architecture, and the design and planning professions. And the revolution would have particularly significant effects in underprivileged urban settings, particularly "shrinking" (Oswalt 2005), deindustrializing cities. The remainder of this book will explore these consequences for shrinking cities.

Perhaps the most damaging dimension of the urban design revolution was that the end of federally funded rebuilding in 1974 coincided with the beginning of severe population losses and economic decline in shrinking cities. The lack of any federal policy, apart from the bewildered walk-throughs of politicians, able to respond to Charlotte Street's abandonment is no coincidence. Federal policy did not cause Charlotte Street's problems, but its absence certainly made the problem worse. The absence of policy would have even starker effects in cities with much steeper problems and worse economies than New York. While one might argue, as Robert Caro did, that the destruction of urban renewal destabilized entire communities, it is impossible to elide renewal with decline in places like Detroit or Philadelphia, where far larger areas lost population than were ever affected by urban renewal.

The second dimension of the revolution was the shift from large-scale state planning to locally driven, decentralized planning. Decentralization fulfilled both conservative and liberal hopes, providing less government and more local decision making, and in American cities the consequences were clear: the federal government saved money, HUD stopped making big mistakes, and communities could decide what they wanted for themselves. On the skyline, the oversized towers of late urban renewal suddenly stopped proliferating, sometimes in midconstruction, as at Cedar-Riverside. In their place came, slowly and spasmodically, small-scale projects with nonprofit or private sponsors. These modest projects were satisfying to their developers, but they were regrettably scarce in shrinking cities, where massive decline left far larger areas of the city desolate than could ever be renewed by nonprofit action. Policy decentralization in shrinking cities constituted abandonment more than it constituted empowerment.

The urban design revolution's third dimension was architectural, as Modernism was first reformed, then abandoned in favor of Postmodernism. In urban neighborhoods High Modernism's abandonment ended the "spatial pathology" (Plunz 1990, 268–69) of abstract towers within a vernacular context. At the same time, Modernism's demise ended most spatial innovation, both architectural or urbanistic. Postmodern redevelopment was hobbled not only by the policy vagaries of decentralization but by their buildings' seeming desire for invisibility. The Postmodern concern with "context and responsibility" (Polshek 1988) stood, at its best, for the acknowledgment of history with verve and wit, but at its worst it stood for poor-quality vernacular design excused only by a pretense to contextuality. Postmodernism also ended the sometimes disastrous Modernist attempts to reimagine cities' neighborhood fabrics. In shrinking cities, Postmodernism offered at best restoration of the historical fabric, at worst a casual suburbanization of a deteriorated landscape, all under the aegis of contextuality. The end of Modernism returned needed respect for the vernacular urban environment, but it also largely marked the end of invention, of Rowe's sense of *becoming*.

The fourth consequence of urban design's revolution was the break between the professions of planning and architecture. As discussed earlier, both planning and architecture were both closely associated with state-sponsored High Modernism and damaged and altered by its demise. As planning shifted wholeheartedly toward social equity and democratic process and away from reshaping urban space, planners' desire and ability to contribute to urban design diminished markedly, though it did not vanish: design remained a remedial part of planning throughout the 1980s and 1990s (Howe in Rodwin and Sanyal, 2000). Simultaneously architecture, divorced (at least in America) from state and social planning, adopted urban design as its own, first through the lens of Postmodernism, and increasingly during the 1990s through approaches derived both from landscape architecture and, surprisingly, from the resurgence of Modernism. But planning for the most part stayed out of these formal discussions; the role of "place" in planning was mostly limited to familiar issues such as historic preservation, context, and suburban sprawl. As Postmodernism waned in architectural circles after the 1990s, it remained alive in planning, where community concerns and social practice still mattered, even if innovative design did not.

Questioning Conventional Wisdoms

Urban design's trajectory in the American shrinking city after the demise of urban renewal provides a different perspective on urban redevelopment and also permits us to question closely held beliefs in both the design and planning fields. Today, a dominant narrative in planning (e.g., Hall 2002,

283–93) argues that redevelopment's transformation after High Modernism constitutes a sort of "redemption narrative" where the sins of demolition and inhumanity are replaced with preservation and responsiveness. This narrative not only reduces Modernism to the post-1960 extremes of Chicago's Cabrini-Green or St. Louis's Pruitt-Igoe (both of which were atypical examples of public housing), but ignores the optimism and even utopianism with which those same projects, as well as arguably much better ones like Cedar-Riverside, attempted to address social needs through design. Today, conventional planning wisdom represents late Modern projects as signal trespasses and welcomes the modest projects that followed as a form of recovery. This conventional wisdom is reinforced by the now apocryphal tale of the bold homeowners in a disinvested neighborhood who stuck it out through the worst times, organized to save their community, and are now reaping the fiscal benefits of a market resurgence. In this conventional wisdom, the end of Modernism is for the best.

This conventional wisdom is flawed, for it suppresses many aspects of Modernist social planning and its decentralized successors. Instead of a dystopian failure, one might alternatively see Cedar-Riverside as a flawed but bold and generous public policy initiative with ambitious design and social goals, realized through the sincere collaboration of government, philanthropy, and design, and unfortunately colliding with economic crisis when its principal backer walked away from the project rather than attempting to reform it as the GLC did at Covent Garden. In our alternative narrative, the federal government abandoned both social planning and urban reconstruction, transferring the burden to smaller-scale actors whose coping strategies were to achieve social goals the best they could in modest projects heavily constrained by funding and capacity. Some modest projects like Charlotte Gardens were lucky enough to be in prosperous cities where they could catch a wave of rising values, but projects located in declining cities were not. The heavily promoted coincidence of modest projects and rising market values in cities like Boston, New York, or San Francisco made this new strategy of modesty look successful, even if it failed in many other places, while the former approach was slandered by the unfortunate coincidence of late Modernism and severe economic crisis.

Both narratives, conventional and alternative, are to some extent true; urban renewal was often brutal and insensitive, just as High Modernism was often overly abstract and alienating. Yet we will see in upcoming chapters that urban renewal and Modernism also produced exemplary projects of great social and physical sensitivity, stabilizing rather than destroying desperate neighborhoods. This book's reassessment of responsive Modernism as an urban design approach is not alone. Not only is Modernist architecture and urbanism coming to be reappreciated more broadly (e.g., Risselada and van den Heuvel 2006; Waldheim 2004), but historians have also come to recognize that urban renewal sometimes provided social benefits, as in New York City's public housing (Bloom 2008). Even Robert Moses, the public face of urban renewal since Caro's scathing biography (1974), has been reappraised (Ballon and Jackson 2008). The postrenewal redevelopment of shrinking cities provides additional evidence that Modernist centralized planning was not always bad and that postmodern, decentralized planning was not always good.

From the perspective of political economy, we may also view the conventional wisdom on redevelopment as a centrist acceptance of neoliberalism. This conventional wisdom sees the state's withdrawal from urban design and the consequent turn toward privately financed projects as not entirely a bad thing. Optimistic thinkers (e.g., Frieden and Sagalyn 1991, 15–38; Garvin 1996, 3) argue that physical planning can achieve its public or social agenda within the framework of profitable private development. Neoliberal urbanism has certainly achieved salutary effects in cities with very strong real estate markets and liberal political instincts, such as those in Boston, New York, San Francisco, or even Los Angeles. In these prosperous, liberal environments, public goods such as open space, low- or moderate-income housing, and properly maintained business districts can be achieved through private action and celebrated as "planning" accomplishments, even as property prices otherwise rise uncontrollably, as they did in the 1990s and 2000s in all of the above cities.

But market-based urban design and planning is by definition harder to implement in places where the market is unhealthy and unable to function. Unfortunately, many areas of shrinking cities have such low property values that any private construction, even with substantial public subsidies, is uneconomic. This is the case in shrinking cities like Baltimore or Philadelphia with healthy downtowns, and in cities like Detroit and Cleveland without them. In both cases, most of these cities' neighborhoods have failing markets and are losing population and housing units. Social needs in these cities' distressed neighborhoods are great, but the market is unable to provide for these needs. Market-driven urbanism has left most shrinking cities behind. Consequently urban designers who wish to improve these places must find ways to act where the market cannot. Doing so will necessitate a reform of both urban design approach and outcome, as well as a reconsideration of nonmarket urban design approaches from the past, including elements of urban renewal.

Any argument to reexamine urban design in depressed and shrinking areas may find little traction with skeptics doubtful of the relevance of urban design's link between the planning and design professions. Difference between the two fields is a long-standing problem: decades ago, Kevin Lynch noted (1981, 102–3) that any call for improved urban design can be countered by arguments that "physical form is not the key variable whose manipulation will induce change . . . change the environment and you change nothing." Lynch clearly intended his words for social planners skeptical of design after the fall of Modernism, but his words also may be seen as a warning to designers unaware, or uncaring, of the social consequences of their actions.

As the following chapters detail, the thirty-five years since 1975 have proved the skeptics right, in a sense, for neither Modernist urban design and planning nor its smaller-scale, Postmodern successors have reversed the problems facing shrinking cities. Yet this should not prevent optimism. Lynch countered skeptics of urban design in his day by saying that this skepticism "is a common view, one held even by most physical planning professionals, and reinforced by the history of the design professions and by the nature of normal (planning) decisions. It is a reflection of the way things are. . . . We will try to show that this [skepticism] is false . . . on this point, the reader is asked to hold his breath and suspend his judgment" (Lynch 1981, 103). We too should for a time suspend judgment, particularly in places where both design and planning have manifestly encountered difficulties. As Philipp Oswalt, an architect whose exhibits on deindustrializing cities popularized the term "shrinking city," has stated, "previous attempts to shape the process of shrinkage . . . have often failed because the conventional tools of city planning and development . . . are not able to tackle the problem" (Oswalt 2005, 15). Shrinking cities are difficult problems, and the dramatic decline of most older American cities in the latter half of the twentieth century made policy makers' jobs even more difficult.

Chapter 2

Shrinkage or Renewal?
The Fate of Older Cities, 1950–90

A Grim Half-century for Cities

In 1950, few of the many passersby on Detroit's Woodward Avenue could have predicted the ruinous condition of the street fifty years later. The street's postwar vibrancy made Woodward's future demise seem both improbable and impossible. How could Woodward's passersby have known that Detroit's central shopping street—the nexus of retailing and office trade in the great industrial state of Michigan—would be a dusty, abandoned valley of empty buildings and vacant lots in 2000? How could they have known that the mighty Hudson's department store—the largest in the United States after Macy's New York ("Vast Shopping Center" 1950, R1; Grutzner 1951, 149), featuring 2.2 million square feet of shopping (Palm 1998, 39) as well as "an auditorium, a circulating library, dining rooms, barber shops, a photo studio, holiday exhibits, a magnificent place called Toytown, and the world's largest American flag" (Hauser and Weldon 2004)—would be spectacularly imploded in 1998 to great acclaim and relief? Could passersby leaving a film at the four-thousand-seat Michigan Theater (Kleinmen 1997, 31) a few blocks away have foreseen the theater's startling and brutal conversion into a parking garage in the 1980s? And could they ever possibly have imagined that the city of Detroit itself, the home of approximately two out of three metropolitan residents in 1950, would be a burned-out shell of its former self, with only half as many residents (Table 2.1) still living in the city fifty years later?[1]

Detroit was not alone in its postwar wreckage. Across the Northeast and Midwest of the United States, dense, active cities emptied out during the second half of the twentieth century, leaving only shells of their former selves behind. Industrial cities suffered particularly badly. Industry was the lifeblood of a city like Philadelphia, supporting both its economy and its working-class residential neighborhoods. As jobs vanished—between 1950 and 1980 Philadelphia's share of regional employment dropped from nearly 68 percent to only 39 percent (Adams et al. 1991, 17)—the city's neighborhood fabric began to vanish in turn. Much of the former self-proclaimed "workshop of the world," which had more than sixty thousand textile workers alone in the early twentieth century (Scranton and Licht 1986, 113), was by 2000 a wasteland of ruined factories, parking lots, successional landscapes, and impoverished working-class communities (Campo 2010). Almost without exception, the industrial powerhouses that had made mid-century Philadelphia America's fourth-largest city had evaporated by 2000, as if into thin air.

The catastrophic changes that occurred in America's older cities after 1950 contrast starkly with their former vibrancy. The post-1950 decades saw most of America's largest cities (Table 2.2) lose population. Population decline in turn caused shrinkage of the built environment as empty, abandoned houses were demolished. Older cities assumed a war-torn look as they were first cleared by highways and urban renewal and then by the disappearance of housing and the disintegration of neighborhoods. Looking back, it is probably a good thing that city residents and politicians in 1950 could not have foreseen this ruin. The problems faced by older cities after 1950 were both severe and chronic, and they plague policy makers to this day.

The causes of the negative changes afflicting older cities after 1950 cannot be easily or completely explained, but most of the components of these changes are well known. Economically, much of these cities' reason for being vanished as businesses and industries relocated to the suburbs or to cheaper states in warmer climates; demographically, most of their white residents relocated to the suburbs or moved away, replaced in most cases by minority populations, often African American, with lower income levels and much less economic opportunity. Fiscally, cities entered a crescendo of crises as the departure of enterprises and jobs, together with the skyrocketing social costs of their poor populations, shook urban budgets to their cores. This "deindustrialization of America" (Bluestone and Harrison 1982), which caused what Rae (2003) called the "end of urbanism," was a principal force, but other technological, social, and infrastructural changes also acted in concert, driving industries, commerce, and city residents out of older cities, via rising incomes, growing automobile ownership, better roadway infrastructure, and cheap suburban land (Bluestone and Harrison 1982; Jackson 1985; Fogelson 2001; Bruegmann 2005; Wilson 1987, 1996; Bradbury 1982).

The inexorable trends driving commerce and people out of older cities left urban policy little power to influence these events. Studies that examine the relationship between decline and policy in detail, such as political scientist Douglas Rae's history of politics and urban renewal in New Haven, Connecticut (2003), have found policy to be more or less impotent. New Haven was one of many older cities that took advantage of urban renewal funds made available by the 1949 Housing Act to reverse retail housing obsolescence. With only 150,000 people in 1950, politically astute New Haven would become the largest per capita recipient of urban renewal dollars in the United States. Rae's study illustrates New Haven mayor Richard Lee's ultimately quixotic attempt to pit spectacular amounts of federal money against much larger, deleterious forces causing decline. Rae looks at Lee's urban renewal efforts and concludes that

> the tectonic forces that pressed themselves against the city, and against the major features of urbanism within it, were so powerful as to dwarf even the remarkable resources that Dick Lee had amassed during his eight terms of office. What had been a convergence of forces favoring urbanism had turned into a convergence of accidents against it. These changes of underlying structure ran far beyond Lee's reach—even when he had the benefit of large federal funding and the gifts of superb talent—his own and that of his lieutenants . . . forces like these were largely beyond the reach of City Hall, even with a titan in the mayor's office. (2003, 313–14)

Rae also argued that urban policy was not the principal driver of population and housing decline in New Haven. He found that urban renewal may have displaced approximately ten thousand households (2003, 339–43), approximately one-fifth of the city's total in 1950. This extremely high figure gives some credence to the canard that urban renewal destroyed cities, but then again New Haven had far more urban renewal than most. But Rae also found that many families, particularly whites, left the city for reasons other than urban renewal while, conversely, minorities were constrained from leaving the city by poverty and discrimination. Rae concluded that "urban renewal and highway construction [did not] cause these [population] shifts in any simple way. These changes were underway long before 1954 and have continued since" (2003, 342–43).

New Haven was not alone in using urban renewal to reverse urban decline. Older cities dominated urban renewal policy: of the ten largest recipients of federal reconstruction dollars during the 1950s, eight were located in the Northeast or Midwest; and of the twelve largest recipients of reconstruction dollars per capita as calculated in 1966, eleven were cities located in the Northeast or Midwest (Rae 2003, 324). But these tremendous expenditures of federal funds could not reengineer urban economies. Both Richard Lee's New Haven and Robert Moses's New York avidly rebuilt themselves to modernize transport, attract commerce, and rehouse their citizens. By 1959 New Haven had spent $27.4 million on urban renewal against New York's $89.9 million, and its per capita expenditures in 1966 ($745.38) were twenty times higher than New York's ($36.77). But New York's population grew after 1980 while New Haven continued to shrink, a clear sign that these very different cities were subject to very different economic, social, and physical forces. Ultimately New Haven's tremendous expenditures of federal dollars operated in vain against the city's inexorable shrinkage.

The revolt against urban renewal that resulted in its early 1970s cancellation occurred amid a field of much larger urban transformations. In this light, even megalomaniacal urban renewal projects like Cedar-Riverside can be seen in a different light. Urban renewal developments were indeed destructive—one-fifth of New Haven's residents were directly displaced!—but these policies occurred within cities that were losing much more population to unrelated forces. The disconnect of urban renewal from urban shrinkage became clearer in the late 1970s as neighborhoods like Charlotte Street continued to empty out and burn, long after the urban renewal bulldozers had gone away. One might try to argue that this abandonment was an aftereffect of urban renewal, but it is just as likely, as Rae concluded, that urban renewal per se was "unrelated" to the shrinkage that occurred after 1975.

The failure of the dramatic renewal efforts of the 1950s and 1960s to reverse economic decline and urban abandonment is sobering. Is urban policy of any scale useful against the larger forces driving urban change? This is a difficult question that we should keep in mind as we look at the rebuilding efforts illustrated in the next three chapters. This chapter will show that population and housing loss did not stop with the end of urban renewal: in several large declining cities such as Philadelphia and Detroit, shrinkage continued uninterrupted to century's end. And after 1975, these cities were left more or less to their own policy devices when federal monies devolved to municipalities. In Chapters 3 and 4, we will explore the courses that two shrinking cities, Detroit and Philadelphia, pursued in this era of decentralization. But before we do that, let us examine the population and housing trends in older cities after midcentury.

Population and Housing Change in America's Older Cities: 1950 to 2000

Almost every American city experienced significant population change between 1950 and 2000. Change patterns were consistent: the largest cities in 1950, almost all of which were located in the East or Midwest, shrank dramatically in the decades following (Table 2.2). At the same time, a new generation of cities located in the South and West rose to replace these older cities in the population rankings (Table 2.1). These changes occurred rapidly, and cities shifted quickly in the rankings during these fifty years. In 1950, only one top-ten city (Los Angeles) was located in the Sunbelt. By 1980, five of the top ten were from the Sunbelt, as Cleveland, St. Louis, Washington, D.C., and Boston left the top ten, and by 2000 seven of the top ten cities were from the Sunbelt, as Baltimore and Detroit left the top ten. Of the nine Northeastern and Midwestern cities in the 1950 top ten, only New York, Chicago, and Philadelphia remained by 2000, while rapidly growing Sunbelt cities such as Phoenix, Houston, and San Jose became some of the largest cities in the country.

The older cities that fell out of the top ten between 1950 and 2000 did so not just because newer cities gained population but because these older cities also lost population. These losses were nearly ubiquitous: of the twenty largest cities in 1950, eighteen lost population between that year and 1980, some dramatically, as Table 2.2 shows. Eight of these cities lost so much population that they fell out of the top twenty. Only two of the 1950 top twenty cities—Los Angeles and Houston—gained population between 1950 and 1980. By 2000 only half of the cities that were in the top twenty in 1950 were still there.

Table 2.1. Population Figures for the Twenty Largest U.S. Cities 1950–2000
(Ranked by 1980 population)

City Name	1950	1980	1990	2000	Change, 1950–2000
New York	7,891,957	7,071,639	*7,322,564*	**8,008,278**	+1%
Chicago	**3,620,962**	3,005,072	2,783,276	*2,896,016*	−20%
Los Angeles	1,970,358	2,966,850	3,485,398	**3,694,820**	+88%
Philadelphia	**2,071,605**	1,688,210	1,585,577	1,517,550	−27%
Houston	596,163	1,595,138	1,630,553	**1,953,631**	+227%
Detroit	**1,849,568**	1,203,339	1,027,974	951,270	−49%
Dallas	434,462	904,078	1,006,877	**1,188,580**	+174%
San Diego	334,387	875,538	1,110,549	**1,223,400**	+266%
Phoenix	106,818	789,704	983,403	**1,321,045**	+1137%
Baltimore	**949,708**	786,775	736,014	651,154	−32%
San Antonio	408,442	785,880	935,933	**1,144,646**	+180%
Indianapolis	427,143	700,807	731,327	**791,926**	+85%
San Francisco	775,357	678,974	*723,959*	**776,733**	+ <1%
Memphis	396,000	646,356	635,230	**650,100**	+64%
Washington	**802,178**	638,333	606,900	572,059	−29%
Milwaukee	**637,392**	636,212	628,088	596,974	−6%
San José	95,280	629,442	782,248	**894,943**	+839%
Cleveland	**914,808**	573,822	505,616	478,403	−47%
Columbus	375,901	564,871	632,910	**711,470**	+89%
Boston	**801,444**	562,994	*574,283*	*589,141*	−26%

Source: Data from U.S. Census.
Notes: Figures in italics indicate regained population. Figures in bold show highest
population.

While population loss was nearly ubiquitous among older cities between 1950 and 1980, this trend reversed after 1980 for a few cities. Among
the top ten 1950 cities shown in Table 2.2, two—New York and Boston—
started regaining population after 1980. A third, Chicago, gained population after 1990. But both Chicago and Boston regained only a small portion
of the population that they lost, whereas New York regained all of its lost
population. The city's 2000 population was its highest ever, with just over
8 million souls.

Cities are physical as well as demographic entities, and their geographical boundaries influenced population change. Cities could gain population
by expanding their municipal boundary to include both new people and
vacant, developable land. Or cities could add housing, and thereby people,

Table 2.2. Population Changes of Ten Largest U.S. Cities, 1950–2000
(Ranked by 1950 population)

City Name	1950 Population	2000 Population	Population Change 1950–80	Population Change 1950–2000	Annual Rate of Change, 1950–80	Annual Rate of Change, 1980–2000
New York	7,891,957	8,008,278	−10%	+1%	−0.4%	+0.7%
Chicago	3,620,962	2,896,016	−17%	−20%	−0.6%	−0.2%
Philadelphia	2,071,605	1,517,550	−19%	−27%	−0.6%	−0.5%
Los Angeles	1,970,358	3,694,820	+51%	+88%	+1.7%	+1.2%
Detroit	1,849,568	951,270	−35%	−51%	−1.2%	−1.0%
Baltimore	949,708	651,154	−17%	−32%	−0.6%	−0.9%
Cleveland	914,808	478,403	−37%	−47%	−1.2%	−0.8%
St. Louis	856,796	348,189	−47%	−59%	−2.0%	−1.2%
Washington	802,178	572,059	−20%	−29%	−0.7%	−0.5%
Boston	801,444	589,141	−30%	−26%	−1.0%	+0.2%
Houston	*596,163*	*1,953,631*	*+168%*	*+227%*	*+5.6%*	*+1.1%*

Source: Data from U.S. Census.
Note: Rates of change are from base population and are not compounded. Houston is provided for comparison. (Difference in population/30)/1950 population gives annual rate of change 1950–80, in other words, percent of 1950 population gained or lost each year.

within their existing boundaries. Political scientist David Rusk (1993) used the terms *elasticity* and *inelasticity* to describe cities that gained by expanding their boundary and those that gained—or lost—population within their existing boundaries. Rusk, a former Sunbelt mayor, saw elasticity as a virtue, particularly for fiscal stability, and many Sunbelt cities appear to see it as a virtue as well: annexation is rampant in Sunbelt cities. Houston, for example, grew almost fourfold in area since 1950 (Table 2.3) as it greatly increased in population. Yet the city's population density in 2000 was lower than it was in 1950 because Houston remained a low-density, suburban city. Most of the elastic cities that leapt into the top twenty between 1950 and 2000 were similarly low density, which reflects the widespread American predilection for suburban living.

Most older cities, in contrast, were inelastic, hemmed in by incorporated municipalities that resisted annexation. Boston, for example, began to become inelastic as early as 1871 when Brookline rejected the city's overtures to join it (Bolton 1897). Boston was ultimately frustrated by many resistant neighbors, and as a result it was the smallest of the nation's

Table 2.3. Municipal Inelasticity and Population Density of Ten Largest U.S.
Cities (Ranked by 1950 population)

City Name	Municipal Area, 1950 (Square miles)	1950 Density (Pop./ sq. mi.)	Municipal Area, 2000 (Square miles)	2000 Density (Pop./ sq. mi.)	Density Change, 1950–2000	Population Change, 1950–2000
New York	315.1	25,046	303.3	26,404	+5%	+1%
Chicago	207.5	17,450	227.1	12,752	−27%	−20%
Philadelphia	127.5	16,286	135.1	11,233	−31%	−27%
Los Angeles	450.9	4,370	469.1	7,876	+80%	+88%
Detroit	139.6	13,249	138.8	6,854	−48%	−51%
Baltimore	78.7	12,067	80.8	8,059	−33%	−32%
Cleveland	75.0	12,197	77.6	6,165	−49%	−47%
St. Louis	61.0	14,046	61.9	5,625	−60%	−59%
Washington	61.4	13,065	61.4	9,317	−29%	−29%
Boston	47.8	16,767	48.4	12,172	−27%	−26%
Houston	160.0	3,726	579.5	3,372	−10%	+227%

Source: Data from U.S. Census.
Note: Houston is provided for comparison.

large cities in 1950, less than one-sixth the size of New York. In fact, all
of the top ten 1950 cities were inelastic, including New York and Los
Angeles (Table 2.3). These were the only of these cities to gain population
more or less within their existing 1950 borders. While New York grew
only slightly, Los Angeles nearly doubled its population between 1950
and 2000.

Inelastic cities were unsurprisingly big population losers. Six of the top
ten large 1950 cities lost population every decade between 1950 and 2000.
These cities—Philadelphia, Detroit, Baltimore, Cleveland, St. Louis, and
Washington—may be called *persistent losers*. All of the persistent losers lost
over 25 percent of their populations between 1950 and 2000 (Table 2.2),
and three—Detroit, Cleveland, and St. Louis—each lost upward of 50 percent of their populations. These latter cities declined so steeply during this
period that they lost 1 percent or more of their 1950 populations per year
for three decades. St. Louis actually lost 2 percent of its 1950 population
every year between 1950 and 1980, and an additional 1.2 percent of its 1980
population every year between 1980 and 2000. In fifty years this greatly
suffering city shrank in population by almost 60 percent, by far the greatest
population loss of any large 1950 city.

Older cities mostly developed before widespread automobile use, and as a result they had high population densities (Table 2.3). Almost every top ten 1950 city had more than twelve thousand persons per square mile in 1950, with Los Angeles coming in last with just over four thousand persons per square mile. But conditions nearly reversed themselves during the next fifty years as all of these inelastic cities except New York lost population. By 2000, only three of the top ten 1950 cities—New York, Chicago, and Boston—still had densities over twelve thousand persons per square mile, with two more—Philadelphia and Washington, D.C.—between ten thousand and eleven thousand. Los Angeles's development was exactly the opposite: it densified so dramatically that by 2000 the city was nearly as dense as much-shrunken Baltimore at around eight thousand persons per square mile. Los Angeles in 2000 was denser than Detroit, Cleveland, and St. Louis, cities that fifty years earlier had been more than three times as dense as Los Angeles.

To summarize population loss, we can think of the ten largest 1950 cities as falling into three very different categories. In the first category of *steady gainers* the fortunate city of Los Angeles stands alone, increasing in size, and in density, every year between 1950 and 2000. In the second category are the *recovering cities*—New York, Boston, and arguably Chicago—that lost population before 1980 and began to regain it afterward, dramatically so in the case of New York. But the *persistent losers* are the largest category. These are the abovementioned six shrinking cities, or seven if Chicago is included, that steadily lost population every year between 1950 and 2000. This category may be divided further between those cities that lost *moderate* (27 to 32 percent) amounts of population—Philadelphia, Baltimore, and Washington, D.C.—and those cities that lost *extreme* (47 to 59 percent) amounts of population—Detroit, Cleveland, and St. Louis.

The great population losses of the persistent loser cities had dramatic impacts on their physical fabrics. Another variable, a city's number of housing units, illustrates this physical change. Housing unit counts also changed dramatically between 1950 and 2000, and they bore an interesting relationship to population change. Glaeser and Gyourko (2001) noted that houses are a durable commodity, and one would therefore expect housing changes to be somewhat different from population changes. The greatest difference, of course, is that people are more mobile than houses; if a household leaves a city, the housing unit will remain, but if a housing unit remains vacant, it will presumably vanish from the city's housing inventory in the long term when its building is demolished. Visible evidence indicates that houses in

Table 2.4. Housing Unit Changes in Ten Largest U.S. Cities, 1950-2000 (Cities ranked by 1950 population)

City Name	1950 Housing Units	1960 Housing Units	1980 Housing Units	2000 Housing Units	Housing Unit Change, 1950–2000	Housing Unit Change, Peak–2000	Pop. Change/ Housing Change
New York	2,433,465	—	—	3,200,912	—	+ 31.5%	0.03
Chicago	1,106,119	1,214,958	—	1,152,868	+ 4.2%	− 5.1%	4.0
Philadelphia	599,495	—	685,629	661,958	+ 10.4%	− 3.5%	9.0
Los Angeles	698,039	—	—	1,337,706	—	+ 91.6%	0.96
Detroit	522,430	553,199	(461,500)	375,096	− 28.3%	− 32.2%	1.53
Baltimore	277,880	—	305,800	300,477	+ 8.1%	− 1.8%	16
Cleveland	270,943	282,914	(251,000)	215,856	− 20.3%	− 23.8%	1.95
St. Louis	263,037	—	(201,800)	176,354	− 33%	− 33%	1.78
Washington	229,738	—	279,800	274,845	+ 21.8%	− 1.8%	29
Boston	222,079	—	—	251,935	—	+ 13.4%	2
Houston	191,681	—	—	782,009	—	+ 308%	0.72

Source: Data from U.S. Census.
Note: Rates of change are from base population and are not compounded. Figures in bold indicate peak unit count. Houston is provided for comparison.

shrinking cities stay around much longer than their vanished population; the sight of abandoned houses in these cities is common, indicating that empty houses remain for some time.

Table 2.4 shows housing change in 1950's ten largest cities from 1950 to 2000. It is quite different from the population changes in Tables 2.1 and 2.2. Perhaps the most obvious difference is that housing figures change more slowly than population, unless populations increased. In Los Angeles and Houston, where housing increased steadily between 1950 and 2000 in concert with population, the two behaved similarly. In the remaining nine cities, housing behaved differently. Two cities—New York and Boston—lost (and then regained) population but experienced large net gains in housing between 1950 and 2000. New York's housing stock grew more than 31 percent against a small (1 percent) population increase, but Boston's housing stock increased over 13 percent even as the city lost 26 percent of its population. In both cities, housing and population change differed by about thirty percentage points. Clearly these cities' housing stocks were unaffected, on a net level at least, by their 1950–80 population losses. But the Charlotte Street story shows that localized severe housing decline could occur in these cities, and so the net housing gains simply show that losses were outweighed by larger gains occurring elsewhere in the city. By 2000 both New York and Boston had the highest number of housing units in their history.

The remaining seven top ten 1950 cities all lost housing (and population) between 1950 and 2000, except Chicago during the 1990s. Like the recovering cities, the shrinking cities' housing losses were more moderate than their population losses and trailed these losses by about thirty percentage points. Baltimore, for example, lost almost 32 percent of its population but only 2 percent of its housing during this period. The three extreme, persistent population losers—St. Louis, Cleveland, and Detroit—also lost large net amounts of housing stock, between 24 and 33 percent of their 1950 total. Just as every two of three 1950 St. Louis residents were gone by 2000, so was one out of every three 1950 St. Louis housing units. The city's urban fabric was in many neighborhoods almost completely vacated (Figure 2.1). So cities that were extreme, persistent population losers were also extreme housing losers, whereas moderate population losers were also moderate housing losers.

Slower housing losses moderated this change. Table 2.4 shows that even as population losses were under way in older cities, their net number of housing units continued to increase, sometimes for several decades. Of 1950's ten largest cities, only St. Louis lost housing between 1950 and 1960. After 1960, Chicago, Detroit, and Cleveland also began to lose housing, as did Baltimore and Philadelphia after 1980. This led to odd juxtapositions of growth and decline. In 1980, for example, Baltimore had lost more than 160,000 people from its 1950 peak, but its housing unit count was at its highest level ever. Afterward, the city continued to lose people and also slowly began to lose housing. Behind this staggered loss and growth lie very different neighborhood-level changes. For a few decades after 1950 older cities continued to gain people and housing at their peripheries even as they began to lose people and housing in declining areas closer to the city center. In the decades after 1950, as older cities began to be "built out" within their municipal boundaries, new peripheral housing production dropped and net housing losses began to show, as we will see in the examination of Philadelphia in the next section.

Population change also differed from housing change because household sizes could change more easily than housing units. A two-bedroom

Figure 2.1. St. Louis was the largest population and housing loser of the nation's largest 1950 cities, and as a result areas like this part of north St. Louis were almost entirely abandoned by 2000 (photo from 2010). These blocks are only a short distance from the former Pruitt-Igoe public housing site. Image by Google Earth.

Table 2.5. Population per Housing Unit in Ten Largest U.S. Cities, 1950 and
2000 (Ranked by 1950 population)

City Name	1950 Population	1950 Housing Units	People per Unit, 1950	2000 Population	2000 Housing Units	People per Unit, 2000
New York	7,891,957	2,433,465	3.3	8,008,278	3,200,912	2.5
Chicago	3,620,962	1,106,119	3.3	2,896,016	1,152,868	2.5
Philadelphia	2,071,605	599,495	3.5	1,517,550	661,958	2.3
Los Angeles	1,970,358	698,039	2.8	3,694,820	1,337,706	2.8
Detroit	1,849,568	522,430	3.5	951,270	375,096	2.5
Baltimore	949,708	277,880	3.4	651,154	300,477	2.2
Cleveland	914,808	270,943	3.4	478,403	215,856	2.2
St. Louis	856,796	263,037	3.3	348,189	176,354	2.0
Washington	802,178	229,738	3.5	572,059	274,845	2.1
Boston	801,444	222,079	3.6	589,141	251,935	2.3
Houston	596,163	191,681	3.1	1,953,631	782,009	2.5

Source: Base population and housing data from U.S. Census.

apartment can hold any household size from one person (living alone) to
a couple with two children. Table 2.5 shows that the general trend during
the 1950 to 2000 period was one of uncrowding. Household sizes dropped
across almost all cities. In New York, for example, a slightly increased population could inhabit a greatly increased housing stock because the number
of people per unit citywide decreased from 3.3 in 1950 to only 2.5 in 2000.
Only Los Angeles retained a stable household size, 2.8, between 1950 and
2000. In a population of dropping household sizes, Los Angeles shifted
from being the least crowded of America's largest cities in 1950 to being its
most crowded.

In other top ten 1950 cities household sizes decreased, often dramatically. In Boston, for example, 3.6 people per unit in 1950 decreased to 2.3
people per unit in 2000. Household shrinkage was independent of population shrinkage: cities that lost large amounts of population, such as Detroit,
uncrowded their households the same as New York did. In 1950 Detroit's
population of 1.85 million lived at 3.5 people per unit, while in 2000 the
city's greatly decreased population lived more spaciously with only 2.5 people per unit. The uncrowding trend is attributable in large part to the
greatly increasing wealth and changing demography of the United States,

and indeed of all developed nations, during this time period. But uncrowding in shrinking cities is also consistent with large stocks of vacant housing. While it is difficult to say for sure, five of the six persistent losers had fewer people per unit—between 2.3 and 2.0—than New York, Houston, or Chicago, all of which had 2.5 per unit. Was the lower household size of the shrinking cities attributable to these cities' possessing many abandoned houses, thereby driving down the population per unit count?

Housing unit change is also influenced by the physical structure of the house (or apartment building). Whereas each individual person in a city is physiologically more or less identical, the same cannot be said for houses. Housing units may exist within anything from a detached, wooden, single-family house to a steel-and-glass high-rise with three hundred or more units. All cities contain a mix of different unit types, but for historical, cultural, and climactic reasons cities often have a preponderance of one housing type or another. In a city where housing is being abandoned, differences in housing types will influence rates of housing loss because certain housing types are more durable. A brick row house, for example, is less vulnerable to weathering, arson, and break-ins than a detached wooden house. In general, multifamily or attached structures are more durable than detached structures open to weathering and/or entry on all four sides.

The six persistent population losers—Philadelphia, Detroit, Cleveland, Baltimore, St. Louis, and Washington, D.C. (Table 2.6)—differed in their housing losses and in their housing stocks. The cities with the greatest housing loss were also those cities with predominantly detached single and 2–4 unit houses, whereas cities where single-family attached housing or 5 + family housing predominated had lower losses. Philadelphia, Baltimore, and to some extent Washington, D.C., were row-house cities, and as a result their housing losses were lower than Detroit, Cleveland, and St. Louis, which were lower-density cities with detached, often wooden, housing.

The fifty years after 1950 placed America's older cities on radically diverging trajectories, with rapidly growing, recovering, and shrinking cities rising and falling in the population rankings. But the fates of persistent population losers also diverged, with some cities moderating their losses and others shrinking catastrophically. Perhaps the hardest hit were smaller industrial cities that sat well outside of the top ten largest cities, but with economies heavily dependent on precisely those economic activities that were in the steepest decline during these decades. The absolute devastation of cities like

Table 2.6. Housing Types, 1980, in Persistent Loser Cities

	Phila-delphia	Balti-more	Wash-ington	Detroit	Cleveland	St. Louis
Total housing units, 1980	685,629	305,800	279,800	461,500	251,000	201,800
% single family detached	4.4	11.7	12.2	56.6	39.3	38.3
% single family attached	61.9	51.8	25.4	2.0	3.7	1.3
% 2–4 family units	16.3	18.5	14.1	23.5	36.1	41.6
% 5+ family units	17.4	17.9	48.3	17.9	20.8	18.9
Housing change, peak to 2000	−3.5%	−1.8%	−1.8%	−32.2%	−23.8%	−33%

Source: Data from U.S. Census.

Gary, Indiana, outside Chicago (Vergara 1997, 81–83); Camden, New Jersey, outside Philadelphia (Gillette 2005); East St. Louis, Illinois (Reardon 1997) and Highland Park, Michigan, outside Detroit (Marchand and Meffre 2010, 170–84) made the problems of larger cities look easy to resolve by comparison. Of America's larger cities, Detroit and Philadelphia were the two biggest persistent population losers, and their divergent fates would have a dramatic influence on their rebuilding policies after the end of urban renewal. Philadelphia, with a dropping population but more or less stable net housing figures, declined in some areas of the city but grew in others. Shrinkage in Philadelphia was a spatially confined phenomenon, while Detroit, which experienced citywide housing and population decline, was marked by widespread devastation.

Localized Shrinkage: Philadelphia's Population and Housing Change, 1970–90

In 1950 the city of Philadelphia, the third largest in the United States, had just over 2 million residents. Over the next fifty years the city would lose 500,000 residents, about one-fourth of its 1950 population. The majority of these losses occurred in a twenty-year period between 1970 and 1990, when the city lost 363,032 people, a drop from 1,948,609 to 1,585,577. This loss was almost 20 percent of the city's 1970 population. Philadelphia's change in housing units during the 1950 to 2000 period was minute by comparison: between 1970 and 1990 Philadelphia gained and then lost housing units, increasing from 674,233 to 685,629 in 1980, before dropping to 674,899 units in 1990. Philadelphia provides an excellent example of a shrinking city that was characterized by localized shrinkage, with many healthy areas of the city gaining population and housing even as other areas experienced catastrophic declines. The localized nature of Philadelphia's change can be visualized through detailed census-tract-level data available from 1970 onward (Figure 2.2).

Census-tract-level mapping shows that Philadelphia's loss of more than 360,000 people between 1970 and 1990 occurred across much of the city. This is what one might expect given the extremely large losses sustained. In this twenty-year period, almost 46 percent (167) of the city's tracts lost over 20 percent of their population ("severe loss"). An additional 30 percent (109) lost between 5 and 20 percent ("moderate loss"). Loss was worst in the neighborhoods to the immediate north, south, and west of Center City, where almost all tracts lost more than 20 percent of their population. A mere 8 percent (28) of the city's tracts gained population, and the locations of these growing tracts communicate much about the way in which cities changed after 1950. Philadelphia's tract-level change confirms that population loss was a widespread phenomenon in almost every Philadelphia neighborhood.

Philadelphia's pattern of population growth and decline during this twenty-year period forms a ring pattern analogous though not identical to Hoyt's 1939 diagram of neighborhood succession (Hoyt 1939). We may perceive Philadelphia as having three different zones: first, a population growth zone at its center, surrounded by a zone of severe population loss, this surrounded in turn by a zone of moderate population loss, and finally another growth zone at the city's periphery and in its suburbs (Figure 2.3).

The largest zone comprised the shrinking neighborhoods that surrounded Center City in a great ring. This zone included most of the neighborhoods built during the city's great era of industrial expansion in the mid- to late nineteenth century. Most of the houses in this ring were quite old by 1970; they were also densely built, and except in a few parts of West Philadelphia, they were all row houses. These were some of the poorest neighborhoods in the city. Beyond this zone of severe shrinkage was an

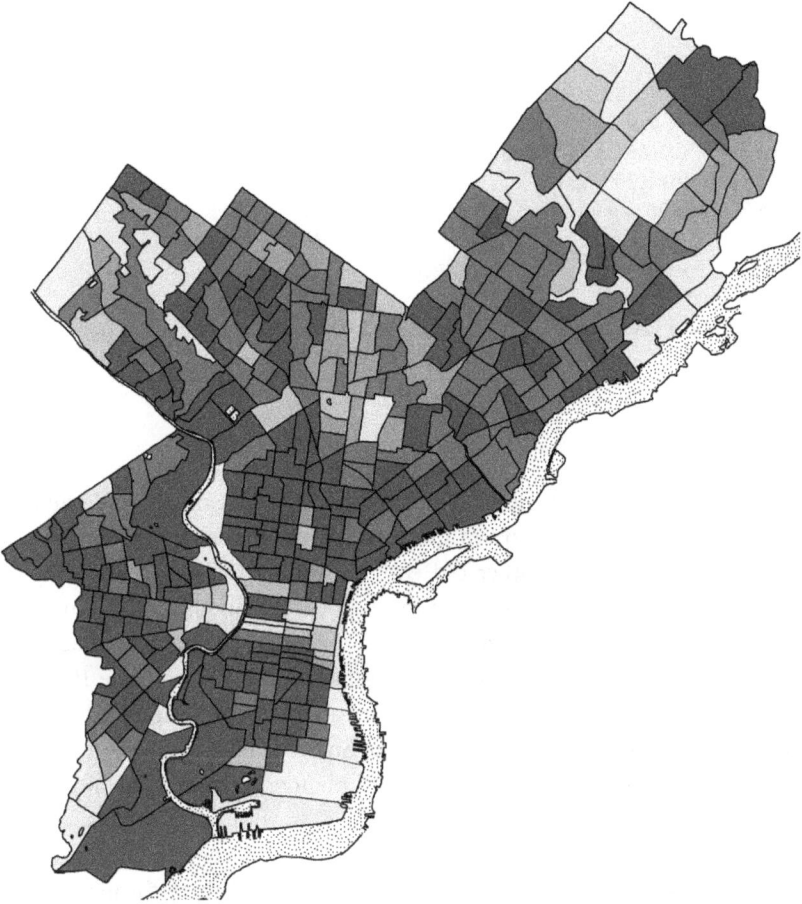

Figure 2.2. Population change in Philadelphia by census tract, 1970 to 1990. From dark to light, tones indicate > 20% population loss; 5–20% loss; +/− 5% change; 5–20% gain; > 20% population gain. Data from United States decennial censuses of 1970 and 1990. Map by author. Map illustration by Jonah Stern.

equally large zone of moderate population loss and/or population stability. These were newer neighborhoods, dating from around 1900 to around 1940, and their housing was consequently newer, in better condition, and built up with detached rows or single-family homes. These neighborhoods were also closer to the desirable suburbs, which doubtless contributed to their relative stability.

Table 2.7. Philadelphia's Census-Tract-Level Population Change, 1970–90

	Number of 1990 Census Tracts	Percent of Total Tracts
> 20% loss (90% gray)	167	46
Between 5% and 20% loss (70% gray)	109	30
+ / − 5% gain/loss (50% gray)	28	8
Between 5% and 20% gain (30% gray)	24	7
20% gain (10% gray)	28	8
No data	9	2
Total 1990 tracts	365	100
Total population loss, 1970–90	**363,032 people** (19%, 1970 total)	

Note: Percentages of gray refer to tones in Figure 2.2.

Which Philadelphia neighborhoods avoided population loss, and why? Nine of the growing tracts were in Center City, the dense, mixed-use historic core of the city. Like other old eastern seaboard cities, Center City retained a large residential population through the twentieth century. Judicious and, as we will see, relatively sensitive urban renewal efforts (Bacon 1967, 263–68) added high-income populations to Center City in the 1950s and 1960s. Philadelphia was a center of urban renewal planning, and it redeveloped some older neighborhoods like Society Hill with high-density new residential development. The city's chief planner, Edmund Bacon, also encouraged the rebuilding of Western Center City with office towers, and population drops in that area are likely due to the replacement of residential populations with the large office towers constructed there through the 1980s. All of these efforts, together with an increased interest in downtown living that began in the 1970s (Sohmer and Lang 1999; Birch 2002, 2006), attracted developers and additional residents to other parts of Center City, including Old City in the east and Rittenhouse Square in the west.

Private developers certainly contributed to land development and population increases in Center City, but institutional growth did as well. Growth near Philadelphia's two large universities, the University of Pennsylvania and Temple University, doubtless reflected new student housing in these neighborhoods. Similarly, institutional closures in Northeast Philadelphia also caused population declines in two tracts there during this period. Other population growth in Philadelphia occurred in peripheral areas, where undeveloped land was still available in the 1970s for development of

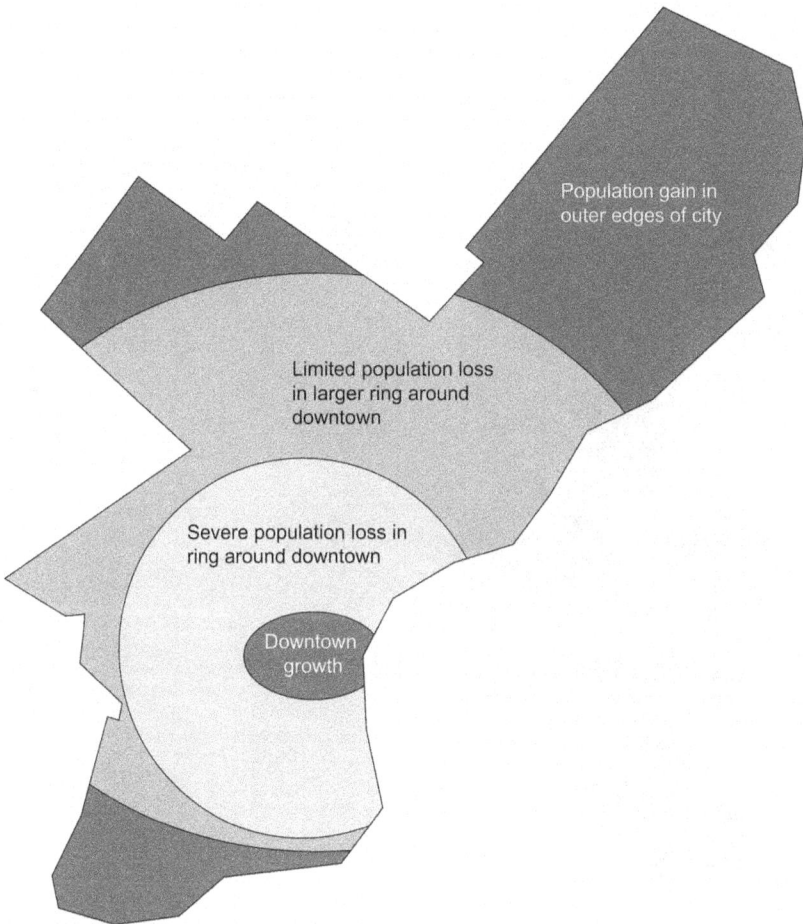

Figure 2.3. Philadelphia's population changes occurred in a series of concentric rings, with growth at the center and the periphery, severe losses adjacent to the city center, and moderate losses beyond. Illustration by author.

single-family homes at relatively low densities. These tracts were the last in the city to be converted from farmland, and their development patterns physically resembled those of neighboring suburbs. Eleven census tracts in Northeast Philadelphia gained population, including some designed by planning director Edmund Bacon but only incompletely realized (Whyte 1970, 250–52). Far northwest and far southwest Philadelphia, also more or

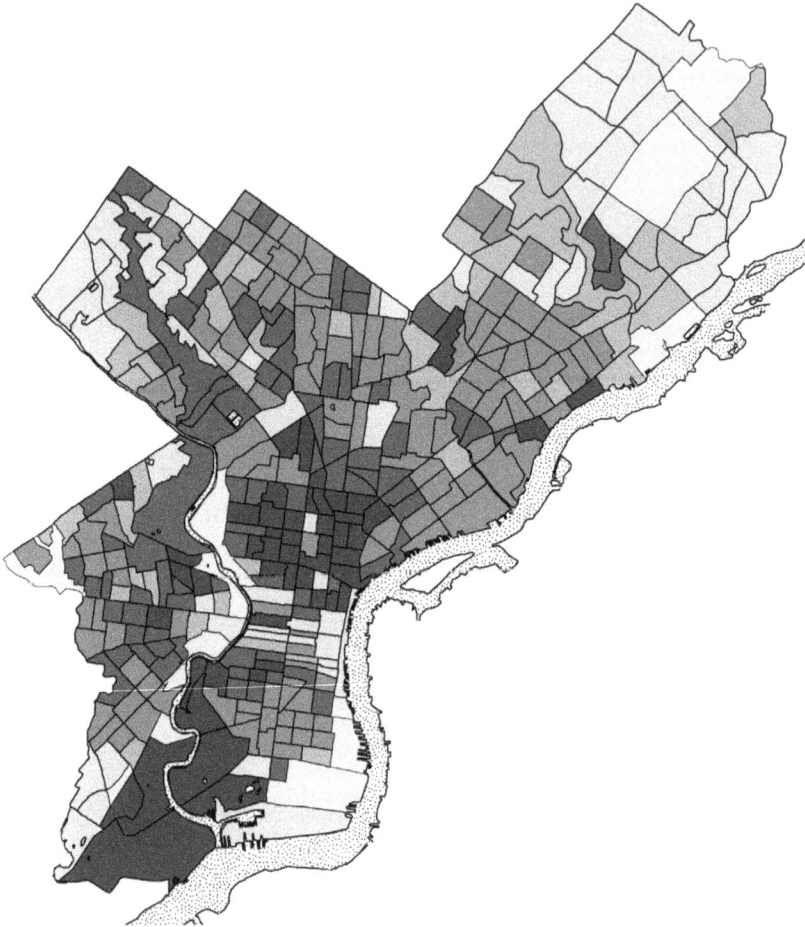

Figure 2.4. Housing unit change in Philadelphia by census tract, 1970 to 1990. From dark to light, tones indicate > 20% housing unit loss; 5–20% loss; +/− 5% change; 5–20% gain; > 20% housing unit gain. Data from United States decennial censuses of 1970 and 1990. Map by author. Map illustration by Jonah Stern.

less suburban in their development patterns, contained the remaining eight census tracts that gained population during this period.

Compared to its widespread population losses, Philadelphia's housing change was much more balanced (Table 2.8). The city gained and then lost a nearly identical number of housing units—around 10,000—between 1970

Table 2.8. Philadelphia's Census-Tract-Level Housing Unit Change, 1970–90

	Number of 1990 Census Tracts	Percent of Total Tracts
> 20% loss	53	15
5%–20% loss	74	20
+/− 5% change	128	35
5%–20% gain	42	12
> 20% gain	53	15
No data	10	3
Total 1990 tracts	365	100
Net housing change, 1970–90	+676 units (< 1% 1970 total)	
Severely distressed (> 20% loss of population and housing)	**48**	**13**

and 1990, and the tracts that gained and lost housing were also equal. Fifty-three tracts, about 15 percent of the total, gained 20 percent over their 1970 total even as the same number lost 20 percent over this total. Another seventy-four tracts, or 20 percent of the total, lost between 5 percent and 20 percent of their housing, with a plurality of tracts, about 33 percent of the total, remaining more or less stable. Like Philadelphia's population growth during this era, housing unit growth occurred both in Center City and at the suburban periphery. Northeast Philadelphia was the geographically largest area of housing gain, confirming the development of this area, the last open land in the city, with low-density housing after 1970.

While Philadelphia's housing gain was geographically consistent with its population gain, its housing loss was much less so (Figure 2.4). Although population loss was widespread across the city, housing loss was concentrated in only a few neighborhoods. Almost 60 percent of the city's steeply declining tracts (31 out of 53) were located in North Philadelphia directly north of Center City. Sixteen of the remaining steeply declining tracts were found in South and West Philadelphia, which also lost tremendous amounts of population during this period. The remaining few severely declining tracts were scattered throughout the city.

As one might expect, Philadelphia's housing loss, where it occurred, was closely coterminous with population loss. Ninety percent (48 of 53) of those tracts with severe housing loss also had severe population loss. This was unsurprising since a neighborhood with many fewer houses is almost certain to house many fewer people as well. But the reverse was not the case. Over 70 percent of the tracts that lost over 20 percent of their population either lost only moderate amounts of housing, or sustained all of their housing stock. These figures indicate that the nonhousing loss areas either uncrowded along the lines described earlier or retained a large number of vacant but stable housing units.

Those 48 census tracts with high levels of both population and housing loss, around 14 percent of the city's total, were the most troubled areas in the city of Philadelphia from a physical perspective. These tracts may be thought of as "severely distressed" (Figure 2.5). North Philadelphia was dominated by severely distressed neighborhoods: 49 percent of its tracts (29 of 59) were severely distressed. By contrast, only 20 percent of West Philadelphia tracts (7 of 35) and 35 percent of South Philadelphia tracts (9 of 26) were severely distressed.

Why did North Philadelphia lose such large amounts of housing? There is no clear answer to this question. The limited scale of post-1970 redevelopment in North Philadelphia, described later in this chapter, indicates that urban renewal was not responsible for the majority of the neighborhood's housing loss. Other public policies, however, may have contributed. North Philadelphia had very high concentrations of scattered-site public housing (Philadelphia City Planning Commission 1986, 118), and high vacancies in these units may have contributed to higher rates of housing loss. High poverty may have also have influenced North Philadelphia's severe distress, but here too there is no easy correlation. Both North and West Philadelphia, for example, had large black populations with high poverty rates, yet West Philadelphia's housing loss was much lower. Lower-income, mostly white areas of South Philadelphia and inner Northeast Philadelphia were also more stable than North Philadelphia, and they retained almost all of their housing despite high levels of population loss. Whatever the reason, by 1990 North Philadelphia was clearly Philadelphia's most highly distressed area, with the largest absolute number of severely distressed tracts as well as the highest concentrations of contiguous, distressed tracts.

Abandonment transformed the North Philadelphia landscape. One study of the early stages of abandonment in Philadelphia found a mixture of causes, including uncertainties resulting from racial transition, "filtering" of the worst units to the bottom of the real estate market where they became unsellable, inadequate public services, irresponsible absentee landlords, and

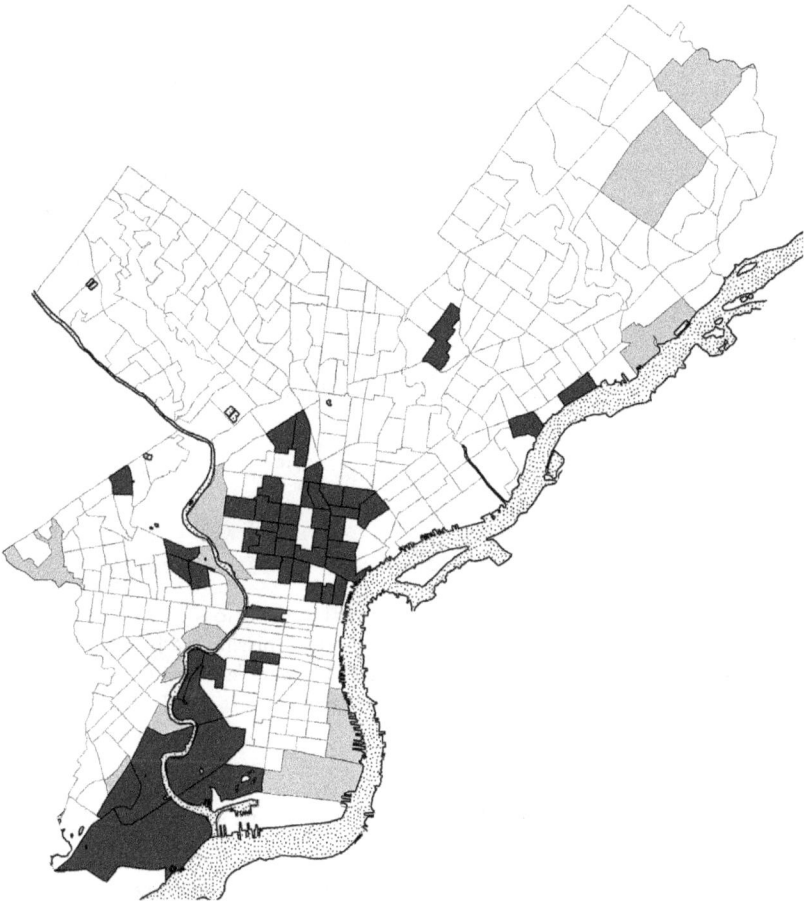

Figure 2.5. About 14 percent of the census tracts in Philadelphia lost over 20 percent of both their population and their housing between 1970 and 1990. These tracts, shown in dark tone, may be considered "severely distressed." By 1990 these areas had abundant available land for rebuilding, and North Philadelphia's concentration of severe distress made the area a magnet for rebuilding efforts in this decade. Light gray indicates very low population. Map by author. Map illustration by Jonah Stern.

Figure 2.6. North Philadelphia suffered substantial housing loss after 1970, and as a result the area's urban fabric deteriorated. Many "missing teeth" streets, such as this stretch of North Orianna Street in 2011, were left with only a few row houses on them. Photograph by Daniel Campo.

difficulties in code enforcement (Featherman 1976). This same study identified additional reasons for abandonment in neighborhoods where abandonment levels were relatively low. In these areas, a depressed real estate market made it difficult to quickly dispose of properties, and changing family situations, such as the relocation or death of older homeowners, reduced ownership responsibilities. Abandoned properties were quickly vandalized, which discouraged renovation by absentee owners. As more and more properties became abandoned and blighted, neighboring properties were abandoned in response. Through this progressive blight, marginally abandoned neighborhoods could be transformed into heavily abandoned ones within a number of years (Cohen 2000).

Abandoned areas in North Philadelphia (Figure 2.6) show the long-term effects of such abandonment. Over time, vacant buildings were seized by the city for nonpayment of property taxes. Heavily dilapidated structures were demolished. Abandonment, seizure, and clearance occurred in a piecemeal fashion, giving neighborhoods a patchwork appearance of incompleteness. In severely distressed North Philadelphia, the landscape is a fragmented network of open lots interspersed with remaining houses. The breakup of attached row houses create a "broken teeth" appearance on otherwise intact streets. By 1995, Philadelphia had approximately twenty-seven thousand vacant residential structures and fifteen thousand vacant lots citywide (Pennsylvania Horticultural Society 1998), many of which were concentrated in North Philadelphia (Figure 2.7). This concentration would make the neighborhood a natural focus for efforts to acquire, consolidate, and reuse North Philadelphia's fragmented landscape of vacant lots and vacant housing throughout the 1990s and early 2000s.

While Philadelphia experienced severe distress after the end of urban renewal, Detroit suffered much worse. Not only did the Motor City lose more population and much more housing than Philadelphia in the period after 1970, but it lost more than any other large city in the United States.

Widespread Shrinkage: Detroit's Population and Housing Loss, 1970–90

Like Philadelphia, Detroit, Michigan, experienced enormous population and housing losses after 1950. Between 1970 and 1990 the city lost a net total of 483,508 people, shrinking from 1,511,482 to 1,027,974. By 1990, an astonishing net 32 percent of Detroit 1970 population had left the city. This loss was higher than Philadelphia's in both absolute and relative terms; the city lost more than 100,000 more people than Philadelphia during these twenty years despite having only three-fourths of the larger city's population in 1970.

Between 1970 and 1990, Detroit's population loss of almost 500,000 people changed the city dramatically at the tract level (see Figure 2.8 and Table 2.9).[2] Almost every area of the city lost population. Fifty-five percent of Detroit's census tracts (175 of 320) lost over 20 percent of their population, and an additional 25 percent (83 of 320) lost between 5 and 20 percent of theirs. Figure 2.8 shows a city in demographic free fall, with population losses stretching across the city from its western to its eastern borders. Moderate population loss characterized almost all the areas of the city that did not lose more than 20 percent of their population. Population gains

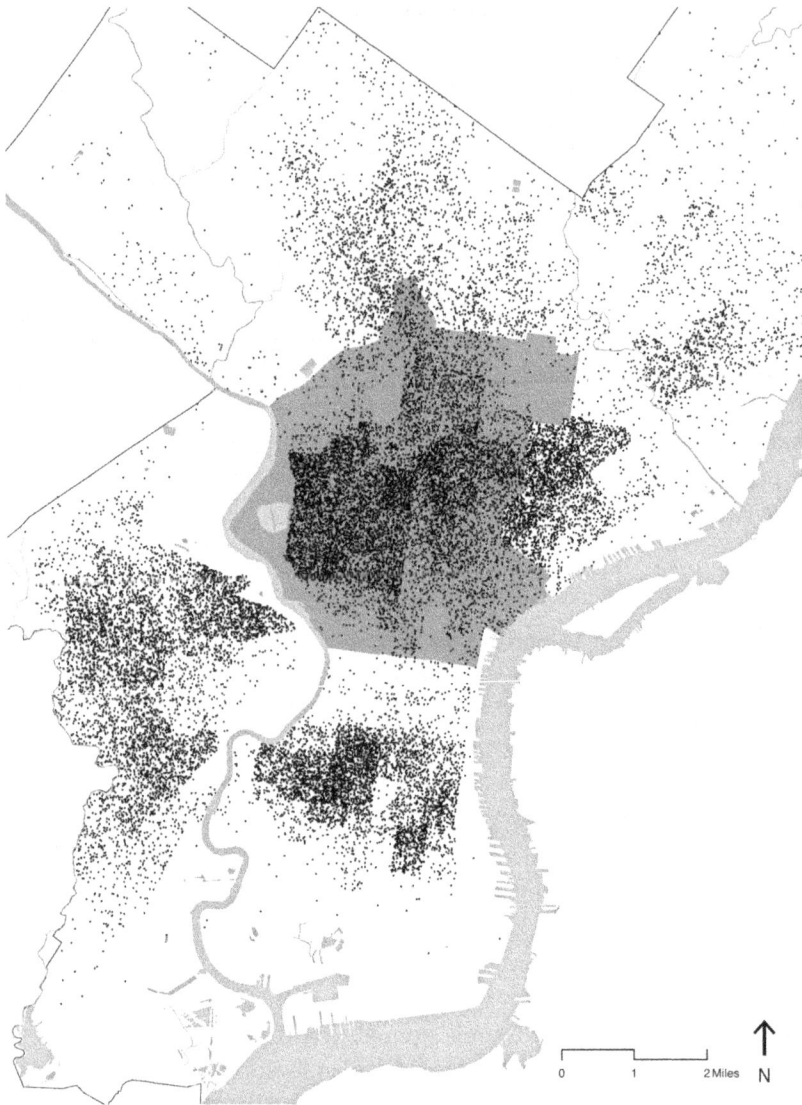

Figure 2.7. In 1999 Philadelphia had about 27,000 vacant structures, shown as black dots here. The reuse of scattered parcels vacated by a shrinking population was a major urban policy problem after 1990. Much of this vacancy was concentrated in North Philadelphia (area in dark gray). Map by author. Map illustration by Ann-Ariel Vecchio.

Figure 2.8. Population change in Detroit by census tract, 1970 to 1990. From dark to light, tones indicate > 20% population loss; 5–20% loss; +/− 5% change; 5–20% gain; > 20% population gain. Data from United States decennial censuses of 1970 and 1990. Map by author. Map illustration by Jonah Stern.

Table 2.9. Detroit's Census-Tract-Level Population Change, 1970–90

	Number of 1990 Census Tracts	Percent of Total Tracts
> 20% loss (90% gray)	175	55
5%–20% loss (70% gray)	83	26
+/− 5% gain/loss (50% gray)	38	12
5%–20% gain (30% gray)	16	5
> 20% gain (10% gray)	7	2
No data	1	<1
Total 1990 tracts	320	100
Total population loss, 1970–90	**483,508 people (32% of 1970 total)**	

Note: Percentages of gray refer to tones in Figure 2.8.

Table 2.10. Detroit's Census-Tract-Level Housing Unit Change, 1970–90

	Number of 1990 Census Tracts	Percent of Total Tracts
> 20% loss (severe)	119	37
5%–20% loss	74	23
+/− 5% change	82	26
5%–20% gain	27	8
> 20% gain	19	6
No data	1	<1
Total 1990 tracts	320	
Net housing change, 1970 to 1990	118,895 units (22% of 1970 total)	
Severely distressed (> 20% loss of population and housing)	**111**	**35**

were confined to only a few areas: Detroit's downtown had very little population growth, and most of the population growth that did occur there
could be attributed to urban renewal as sites first redeveloped in the 1950s
continued to be built out after 1970. Outside of downtown only 20 of Detroit's 320 tracts gained even moderate amounts of population. Most of
these tracts were at the periphery, indicating residual suburban expansion.
Detroit thus differed substantially from Philadelphia in that it had only two
areas of population change: severe loss and lesser loss. This was a dispiriting
situation for any city, but particularly troubling given that in 1970 Detroit
was the fifth-largest city in the United States.

Detroit differed from Philadelphia in its large loss of housing units during this same period—118,895 units, or 22 percent of its 1970 total. Housing loss was substantial in volume as well as widespread geographically
(Table 2.10): an astonishing 60 percent of the city's census tracts lost over
5 percent of their housing, with 37 percent, over one-third of the city,
losing over 20 percent. Figure 2.9 shows that housing loss was nevertheless
more restricted than population loss. Losses were steepest in the areas surrounding downtown, but some housing loss extended clear across the city,
from its eastern to its western borders. Only the northern areas of the city,
along 8 Mile Road, were unaffected by housing losses: nineteen of the
twenty-one tracts on Detroit's northern boundary lost at least 5 percent of

Figure 2.9. Housing unit change in the city of Detroit by census tract, 1970 to 1990. From dark to light, tones indicate >20% housing unit loss; 5%–20% loss; +/− 5% change; 5%–20% gain; > 20% housing unit gain. Data from United States decennial censuses of 1970 and 1990. Map by author. Map illustration by Jonah Stern.

their population during this period, but only two of them lost housing. Six tracts actually gained housing, placing them among the small minority (14 percent) of Detroit tracts that gained after 1970.

As in Philadelphia, Detroit's population loss did not always entail housing loss. But housing loss almost always correlated with population loss: 93 percent (111 of 119) of tracts with severe housing loss also lost over 20 percent of their population. This corresponded closely with Philadelphia's 90 percent figure, but Detroit's 111 tracts comprised a much larger percentage of its severe population loss tracts—63 percent—than Philadelphia's, whose 48 tracts with severe housing and population loss was only 28 percent of the severe population loss total. In other words, almost two-thirds of Detroit's population-losing tracts also lost housing against only one-third in Philadelphia, giving the former city 225 percent more severely distressed neighborhoods. Figure 2.10 shows distressed neighborhoods

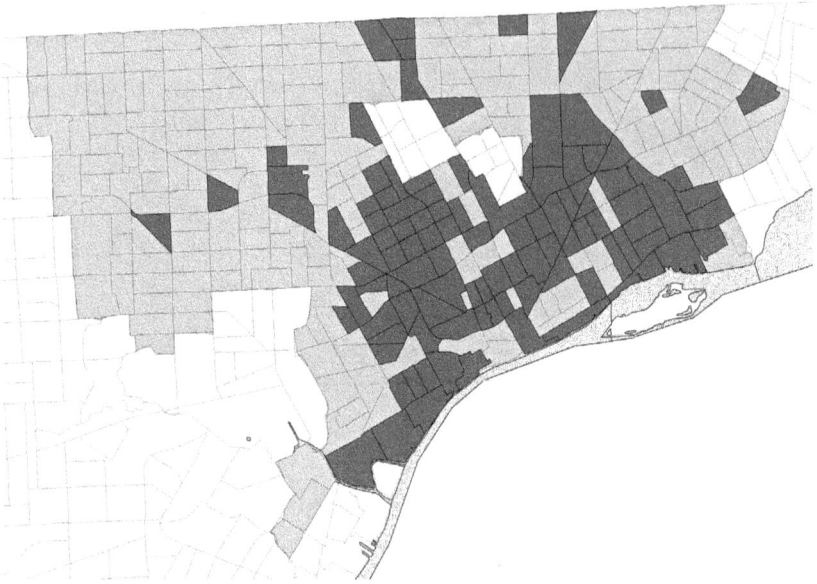

Figure 2.10. Detroit suffered a very large net loss of housing units between 1970 and 1990—22 percent of its 1970 total was gone by 1990—and as a result much of the city (approximately 35 percent of its census tracts, shown in dark gray) was severely distressed by 1990. Large areas of the city were available for rebuilding, but the city lacked both a master plan and a rebuilding policy. Map by author. Map illustration by Jonah Stern.

stretching across the city, with only the northern far western and northeastern areas of Detroit excepted. A full 35 percent of the city's census tracts were severely distressed by 1990.

Detroit lost housing in a broad belt completely surrounding downtown. By 1990, in any direction leaving the city, one passed through neighborhoods where large numbers of housing units had vanished, either through purposeful clearance or from piecemeal housing abandonment. With little residential population, Detroit's downtown, unlike Philadelphia's Center City, could not provide a psychological or fiscal counterbalance to these vast swathes of vacancy. Downtown was filled with abandoned office buildings, and the surrounding residential neighborhoods were likewise abandoned. It is easy to argue that Detroit's unfortunate reputation as a sinkhole of crime and decline, which achieved prominence during the 1980s (e.g., Chafets 1991), was a consequence of this lack of stable neighborhoods.

Much of the city resembled a carpet of empty fields interspersed with only occasional houses (Figure 2.13). Visitors to Detroit felt that the entire city was being abandoned, and to a large extent this perception was true.

Form and Policy in Detroit and Philadelphia

Detroit and Philadelphia were both large, deindustrializing cities that lost much population and housing after 1970, but they followed different shrinkage trajectories. At the citywide level Philadelphia's had less than half as many severely distressed census tracts (48 to 111). There are many possible reasons why Philadelphia's neighborhood distress was more limited than Detroit's. A likely reason is that Detroit's economy was harder hit than Philadelphia's. Detroit's economy became increasingly specialized over the course of the twentieth century (Jacobs 1969, 99). When the automobile industry was expanding, this meant explosive growth for the city, but when this industry decentralized away from the city and then began to experience problems with foreign competition, the city's economy fell into crisis. Detroit's loss was initially the gain of cities like Los Angeles (Jacobs 1969, 153–54) and subsequently that of rural areas across the United States as automobile plants moved into union-free areas beginning in the 1950s. Detroit lost 134,000 manufacturing jobs in only sixteen years between 1947 and 1963 (Sugrue 1996, 126). This was a tremendous shock for a city suffering doubly from competition in the automobile industry that disadvantaged American firms and from the decentralization of broad sectors of industry to areas outside the city (e.g., Rae 2003, 361–63).

Philadelphia was also part of the Rust Belt. The city was heavily industrialized—in 1947, the city had more than 490,000 jobs in the industrial sector—but it was also diversely industrialized, with the largest sector, textiles, occupying only 25 percent of total industrial jobs (Adams et al. 1991, 32). While this diversity may have inhibited Philadelphia from experiencing the same kind of explosive growth that Detroit had when the automobile industry boomed in the 1910s and 1920s, it also protected Philadelphia from experiencing the catastrophic economic shocks that afflicted Detroit in the decades after World War II. Philadelphia lost 115,000 industrial jobs between 1947 and 1986 (Adams et al. 1991, 31), but a larger variety of economic activities were available to take their place.

Economic factors play a significant, perhaps primary, role in the growth and decline of cities. At the same time, other harder to quantify factors also play a role. Geography and urban form also define the physical landscape of cities and shape their growth in a complex interplay with economic forces: Manhattan is a high-density city not only because of New York's dynamic economy but because its island form compresses and accentuates development. By the same token, urban design, from landscape architecture to social housing, plays a similarly deterministic role. Just as one could not imagine Manhattan without its high-density island setting, one could not imagine it without design interventions like Central Park that have shaped the city's economic growth. Cities are not just abstract economies: city form and urban policy matter, and Detroit's and Philadelphia's form and policy both differed substantially after 1950. The cities are almost the same size— 138.8 square miles (Detroit) and 135.1 (Philadelphia)—but they have unique geographies and histories that influenced the cities' form and policy during urban renewal and in the decades after its demise.

Detroit: Erasure of Context in an Unbounded City

Founded by the French as part of a series of forts around the rim of the Great Lakes, Detroit has always benefited from its convenience to this great network of waterways in the continental interior. The city's location on water initially provided easy access for fur traders and later for industry and shipping. At the same time the city's position at the edge of an industrial hinterland made it a useful entrepôt for goods manufactured there, and its location in southern Michigan made it accessible to railroads running east-west across the United States. All these advantages were mirrored by the other Great Lakes cities reaching in a long chain from Buffalo to Milwaukee.

Detroit's strategic position provides a beautiful view over the Detroit River to the Canadian shore. The land itself is unspectacular, however: a broad and featureless plain that rises gently into the equally featureless interior. This unvarying topography was convenient for communication. Not only was flat land easy to portage over, but it was easy to construct roads and railroads as well, and it was also easy to plat for commerce. Apart from a few areas platted by the French, Detroit has an unvarying street and parcel grid oriented either to the river or, further away, to the National Survey grid. The most formative urban design scheme arrived in 1804 after the

Figure 2.11. Detroit occupies a flat site along the strait connecting two of the Great Lakes. The city grew along a uniform grid developed with more or less identical housing, until urban renewal, highways, and housing loss began to erode the city's fabric. This photograph shows Detroit's downtown in the mid-1930s. Michigan State Highway Department, *Street Traffic: City of Detroit: 1936–1937* (Detroit: Michigan State Highway Department, 1937).

original French fort burned to the ground. Judge Augustus Woodward gave the city a baroque city center with broad, spoke-like radial streets reaching into the interior of Michigan. As the city grew, the baroque plan was abandoned for a uniform grid, but the spoke-like streets were retained, and they provided the principal means of access to the city center until highways came (Figure 2.11).

In 1900 Detroit was still a small city, with fewer than three hundred thousand people (Philadelphia, by comparison, had almost 1.3 million.) Over the next thirty years, the city grew by almost 1.3 million inhabitants, resulting in a cityscape of nearly identical houses (Figure 2.12). With no rivers, hills, or other geographical features to limit its growth, Detroit spread endlessly. The city was organized by its street grid, but it was visually unspectacular, broken only by rail lines and factories. This unbeautiful city was nevertheless an extremely efficient machine for housing industrial facilities and industrial workers and for shipping materials and finished parts in and out of the city (Sugrue 1996, 18–19).

Figure 2.12. Detroit's neighborhood fabric was composed of freestanding wooden or brick houses, but this did not make the city picturesque. Like many cities built quickly along rectilinear blocks, Detroit was monotonous, even dreary. Courtesy *Detroit News* archives.

Like other midwestern cities characterized by rapid growth and heavy industry, Detroit did not retain a high-income residential population downtown. The predominant pattern of development in the city was suburban: as early as the 1880s, the city had mostly freestanding single-family or two-family homes. The scale and material of homes changed from brick to wood as one moved down the socioeconomic spectrum. Detroit's rapid growth led to equally rapid shifts in high-income residential areas outward from the city center. Early high-income areas like Brush Park near downtown were soon overwhelmed by commercial and industrial growth. With an invariant residential grid and little topography, it was difficult for high-income residents to spatially segregate themselves from the masses of lower-income workers. As a result, many of Detroit's high-income residential districts clustered along the scenic Detroit River east of the city, where there were fewer railroads. This spatial growth paralleled that of Chicago along its northern lakeshore. By the 1920s Jefferson Avenue paralleling the river was lined by a mix of high-income apartments and large single-family homes. But even this high-income area, the most cohesive in the city, was interrupted by industrial facilities and rail lines. Detroit's industry predominated, and islands of high-income areas were as a result surrounded by lower-income housing. Given the city's heritage of rapid growth and rapid abandonment, one could foresee that these high-income areas might one day be abandoned in their turn.

As Detroit's economy began to decline in the post-World War II period in concert with the arrival of African Americans seeking industrial jobs in the city, the physical characteristics that had benefited rapid growth began to affect the city's decline. Historian Thomas Sugrue detailed the painful process by which white populations, paralyzed by racial fear and unprotected by geographical barriers that might dissuade population movements, attempted to "defend" neighborhood borders from black settlement with patrols and threats of violence. Dismayed by ever-growing African American populations and by the disruptive effects of highway construction, white populations fled Detroit neighborhoods in catastrophic numbers beginning in the 1950s (Sugrue 1996, 234–49).

The population and housing losses that Detroit experienced from 1970 to 1990 resulted at least in part from unique elements of its city form. The city's more or less undifferentiated geography was laced throughout by railroads and a monotonous grid. And the city's extremely rapid development meant that the majority of the city's buildings had been constructed within the relatively short time period of the first half of the twentieth century. Not only did this result in neighborhoods with few distinguishing characteristics, but the city's low-density standalone houses, mostly of wood, were singularly vulnerable to weathering and vandalism if abandoned. In addition, Detroit lacked any extensive or long-established high-income neighborhoods that might better resist decline. Finally, its excellent roadway and highway links to the periphery not only eased communication but also encouraged suburbanization into the undeveloped land available beyond the city limits on all sides except the southeast facing the Detroit River.

Just as Detroit's geography and city form brought advantages to the growing city and disadvantages to the declining one, the city pursued a series of rebuilding initiatives beginning in the 1940s that might have benefited a growing city but could not reactivate a shrinking one. These initiatives were examined in detail by Thomas (1997) and are only summarized here.

Detroit pursued urban renewal with great vigor. Not only did the city construct a great deal of highway miles per capita, but it executed massive urban renewal strategies that made other cities' efforts look minute by comparison. The first of these projects was the downtown civic center, which began design development in 1947 (Thomas 1997, 67). The civic center comprised an assortment of office buildings, assembly halls, open space, and roadway infrastructure, placed in a tabula rasa landscape that retained nothing of the former setting except a historic church.

The civic center was followed by a major urban renewal project east of downtown. The area contained by the first phase of the Gratiot urban renewal area was more than 500 acres in size (Thomas 1997, 56) and housed more than 1,900 families, almost all of whom were African American. Gratiot, later to be renamed Lafayette Park, was a signature design success under the guidance of planner Ludwig Hilbersheimer and architect Mies van der Rohe. But the project was also a signal instance of urban renewal as "Negro removal": a highly racialized, if not racist, redevelopment effort that significantly disadvantaged thousands of already singularly disadvantaged black Detroiters. Public housing was not permitted in Lafayette Park, and less than one-third of displaced families found public housing elsewhere (Thomas 1997, 60); less fortunate families were simply displaced into other neighborhoods, other slums, and they likely destabilized those neighborhoods in turn.

Detroit's urban design strategy in Lafayette Park was a complete tabula rasa approach that retained nothing of the original city fabric except a few through roads and existing railroad lines (Waldheim 2004, 128–33). No original structures were retained, and not a single historic city block remains. This urban design strategy was consistent with polemical Modernist strategies such as Corbusier's 1924 *Plan Voisin*, but it also reflected the characteristic physical qualities of the Detroit cityscape, namely its flat, unbounded quality and its carpet of identical and undistinguished houses. In other words, not only did Modernism predispose the planners of Lafayette Park to erase the Detroit cityscape in its entirety, but they were more easily permitted to do so by the cityscape itself. Detroit and urban renewal were an unfortunate match: a steeply declining city with an easy-to-redevelop cityscape combined with a redevelopment approach that saw wholesale clearance as the optimal urban design strategy. Tabula rasa urban design would continue to mark Detroit redevelopment into the twenty-first century, as Chapter 3 explores.

Urban renewal left Detroit with large amounts of cleared land that in some cases would not be redeveloped until the late 1990s. At the same time, it did little to arrest the city's economic problems, which centered around the decline of the automobile industry. Arresting industrial decline was the central urban policy agenda of Mayor Coleman Young, a long-serving executive who presided over the city from 1973 to 1993. Young could do little to reverse the disastrous population and housing losses afflicting his city, but he tried hard to retain industrial activity, even if it meant the same tabular rasa approach that had treated low-income Detroiters so brutally during urban renewal. The most notorious of these redevelopment projects was Poletown, where 465 acres of city land housing more than 3,400 people was cleared in the early 1980s for a new General Motors plant. As in New Haven twenty years earlier, the clearance could not trump economic realities. The plant on the Poletown site employed 35,000 workers in the 1950s but only 3,400 after rebuilding (Thomas 1997, 163–65). And the public costs were ruinous: land acquisition and site preparation at Poletown cost more than $200 million, much of which came from borrowing against future federal block grant funds. To construct Poletown, Detroit mortgaged years of future redevelopment monies—for just one plant.

Apart from industrial rebuilding, Young's administration concentrated its urban redevelopment energies on Detroit's downtown. This strategy differed very little from that pursued by dozens of other American cities in the 1970s and 1980s, and the products were similar: an expanded convention center, new office and shopping complexes including the visually spectacular Renaissance Center, a few residential buildings, and even an automated, elevated People Mover, all constructed through the type of public-private partnership (PPP) valorized by Frieden and Sagalyn (1989). But Detroit was a different city: PPPs might have reactivated tourism and commerce in older, better established, more attractive downtowns, but they could not leverage prosperity in a rapidly shrinking city. As Detroit's city fabric continued to evaporate, its redevelopment monuments became lonely islands amid growing areas of rubble and urban prairie (Figure 2.13).

Both Detroit's Young-dominated redevelopment era (circa 1973 to 1993) and the urban renewal era that preceded it (circa 1948 to 1973) valued Detroit land for its location but treated preexisting elements of the

Figure 2.13. In the early twenty-first century much of Detroit's landscape has come to resemble a rural environment interspersed with occasional houses, streets, and sidewalks. In places it is a beautiful, successional landscape of wildflowers. Photograph by Daniel Campo.

cityscape as disposable. Whether in urban renewal like Lafayette Park or economic-development-driven deals like Mayor Young's clearance of the Poletown neighborhood, nothing was retained on the site. Contextual considerations such as surrounding neighborhoods or significant existing buildings were irrelevant. This urban design strategy was radical and dramatic, but it was also brutally insensitive to the existing city. In the hands of talented designers like Hilbersheimer and Mies van der Rohe the tabula rasa approach could produce a new environment with urban qualities comparable to the demolished fabric, but elsewhere, postwar Detroit redevelopment usually generated banal schemes that treated the city's residents, particularly African Americans, with cruelty and completely ignored the city's existing built heritage and urbanism.

    Detroit's insouciant redevelopment approach may have provided developers with a "flexible" site, but the tabula rasa also showed a sad lack of even a moderate degree of respect for the existing city. As city officials erased the city, they also removed one of the city's principal competitive advantages in an increasingly generic world: its own built environment. In an era of rapid transport and great locational freedom, urban renewal's and Coleman Young's tabula rasa approach, together with the city's catastrophic abandonment, made the built environment of Detroit increasingly less and less attractive. By the 1990s, Detroit's redevelopment practice often behaved as if the existing city did not matter at all. Even Le Corbusier's *Plan Voisin* had never gone so far.

Philadelphia: Retention and Reflection in a Bounded City

Like other cities along the east coast of the United States, Philadelphia's site is constricted by both land and water. The city's position is a strategic one, lying at the edge of the Piedmont where the land and waters of the Appalachian plateau drop off into the flat, tidal marshlands of the outwash plain. Philadelphia's hybrid site of upland plateau and coastal plain is shared by many other cities, such as Washington, Richmond, and Paterson, along what is called the Fall Line. Being located at this topographical interface maximized the Fall Line cities' accessibility to both the ocean and the interior, and captured energy from the water dropping off the plateau. For Philadelphia, the Fall Line was a source of both energy and recreation: hilly regions to the city's west and north such as the Wissahickon Valley were early sites for mills, taverns, and hotels, and by the nineteenth century they had also become the preferred sites for suburban dwellings, as well as Philadelphia's largest park.

Philadelphia was built by idealists, but its urban design was eminently practical. The city was platted in 1683 at the narrowest part of a flat peninsula between the city's two rivers. Where the radial roads of Detroit communicated the baroque desire to extend infinitely into space, Philadelphia was a Renaissance grid of bounded, narrow streets defined by two rivers, parks at its four corners, and a larger park at its center. This ideal settlement was not only ambitious—the Philadelphia plan was larger than the actual size of London at the time—but implied completeness. Founder William Penn, apparently ignoring the urban reality of European port cities, imagined a pastoral settlement of peaceful idealists, but the real Philadelphia quickly grew into a packed, bustling port town clustered along the Delaware waterfront. The city retained Penn's plan, but urban growth had already

Figure 2.14. Philadelphia is America's greatest row-house city. This street in the city's northeast could be any one of thousands of similar streets in North, South, or West Philadelphia. Photograph by Daniel Campo.

extended beyond it before the end of the eighteenth century, and the original plan was not fully filled in until the end of the nineteenth.

As Philadelphia expanded, Center City's location amidships its peninsula made it the functional as well as geographical linchpin of the city. In an unbounded city, the downtown may become marginal, as in cities like Detroit or Los Angeles. But Philadelphia's different neighborhoods were bounded by water and were more or less mutually inaccessible. Each outlying area—North, West, and South Philadelphia—could access the other only through Center City. Their relative isolation not only increased the neighborhoods' social distinction from each other but also reinforced Center City's importance. Like New York, a city mostly confined to islands, Philadelphia developed as a compact city, and it would remain one well into the twentieth century.

As early as the mid-eighteenth century the row house was firmly established as the fundamental unit of Philadelphia's urban pattern (Warner 1968, 15–17) (Figure 2.14). This housing type would form the template of

Philadelphia's urban expansion for a full two centuries. While row houses are attractive both from a financial and an aesthetic perspective, when multiplied by hundreds or thousands they generate monotonous street-scapes. As the city expanded, developers lined its streets with row houses to such an extent that Warner (1968, 53) described nineteenth-century Phila-delphia streets as "dreary and unbroken" by any visual variety within a seemingly endless grid. In New York, the reign of the row house was broken by the apartment house, but in Philadelphia row houses remained the dom-inant residential type long after other alternatives were available. Even in 1980, after decades of suburban expansion, 62 percent of Philadelphia's housing units were single-family attached (Table 2.6), giving the city almost two row houses for every other housing unit even without counting units in subdivided row houses. None of Philadelphia's peer cities were so domi-nated by a single housing type; even Baltimore, another row house city, was only slightly over half single-family row houses. Its uniform grid and dominant rowhouse gave Philadelphia perhaps the most regular urban pat-tern of any American city as well as one of the densest.

Built by speculators on blocks that had been subdivided to the maxi-mum extent possible, Philadelphia row houses were developed at density levels that seem incredibly high today. My study of sixteen redevelopment sites in North Philadelphia (Ryan 2002, 362–71) showed North Philadel-phia residential densities in 1920 averaging fifty-one units an acre (128 u/ha). Some blocks where row houses had been subdivided had up to sixty-five units per acre, higher than many multifamily apartment buildings. With properties as little as fourteen feet wide and back streets as narrow as twenty-five (Sanborn Map Company 1984), row house amenities were few: as little as two rooms on two floors (Schade et al. 2008), no front yard, and only a few feet of yard in back. Small row houses were unacceptable for all but the very poor, and it is not surprising that such housing was vacated over the course of the twentieth century as soon as better options became available.

But Philadelphia's row houses were a diverse architectural type, not a single architectural model. While the smallest and poorest houses were only a few hundred square feet, wealthier residents inhabited spacious four-story houses up to ten times as large, with space standards as generous as those of London or New York. Many splendid row-house blocks still stand in prestigious areas of Center City or formerly prestigious parts of North Phil-adelphia such as Cecil B. Moore Avenue. As gentrification has grown apace since the 1970s, prices of row houses in parts of Center City have risen into the multiple millions of dollars. Such streets are arguably some of the finest residential streets in American cities: the mid-nineteenth-century row house provides a sense of enclosure and an architectural definition that twentieth-century housing does not equal, at least in this country. And outlying row-house districts constructed in the early to mid twentieth century have certain advantages over the older areas; housing standards are more generous, and the public realm is especially improved, with wider streets, larger yards, and shorter rows of housing. By the 1950s, developers that were still constructing row houses in places like South Philadelphia's Packer Park were building them in rows of only five or six houses along cul-de-sac streets, achieving a peculiarly Philadelphian hybrid of row-house city and single-family suburb. The hybrid amenities of these developments would be inspirational as planners redeveloped North Philadelphia in the 1960s and again in the 1990s (see Chapter 4).

The row house's overwhelming dominance guaranteed not only its place in the individual history of many a Philadelphian but also its place as an inescapable formal referent in later rebuilding efforts. In Detroit, wooden standalone houses could be scraped (or burned) clean and development could start anew, as it did at Lafayette Park and other redevelopment sites, but in Philadelphia, the row house was not so easy to eradicate. Not only were they numerous—a single fully built North Philadelphia block might contain between sixty and eighty row houses—but surrounding blocks across the narrow streets were sure to have just as many. As a result Philadelphia's redevelopment both during urban renewal and after displayed a sensitivity to the urban context guided as much by the row house's physical resistance to clearance as by its urban qualities.

Detroit's planning director Charles Blessing was a talented but modest and unassuming personality who never aspired to the role of a public figure in his twenty-one years in office between 1952 and 1973 (Thomas 1997, 120–22). Urban renewal in that city was associated less with Blessing than with the titanic scale of the city's decline and rebuilding. But Philadelphia's urban renewal history is associated as much with the outsized personality of its chief planner, Edmund Bacon, as it was with actual reconstruction. Even today, Bacon's name often comes first when discussing Philadelphia redevelopment in the 1950s and 1960s, affording him a primacy that he would very likely have enjoyed. Bacon's legacy has been discussed in detail elsewhere (e.g., Knowles 2009), but Philadelphia's (Bacon's) redevelopment approach and practice is of great interest here, both for how it compared to Detroit during the same period and for how it influenced redevelopment in the decades following urban renewal.

Philadelphia's urban renewal differed greatly from Detroit's not only because the cities differed greatly but because they pursued distinctly different renewal policies. Detroit had in 1960 a surprisingly recent fabric: most of the city was still less than forty years old. But Philadelphia was blessed, or cursed, with a downtown where many if not most buildings dated from the nineteenth century, intermingled with remaining eighteenth-century buildings and twentieth-century intrusions entangled with massive rail viaducts constructed to bring as many people as close to the city center as possible. Nothing less consistent with the low-density, auto-dependent twentieth-century city could have been imagined, so Bacon set about with great vigor to "modernize" Center City. Talented and hard-driving as Bacon was, many Center City efforts such as the South Street Expressway went unrealized, and others, such as the Interstate 95 extension along the waterfront, would have been better off so. Other infrastructure moves, such as the Center City rail connection that united the Reading and Pennsylvania Railroads and freed land for Penn Center, were salutary efforts much superior to those constructed in New York during the same era. They might have stimulated Philadelphia even more dramatically had it been healthier economically. Bacon was not solely responsible for these successes and failures: many conditions were imposed by other powerful city officials such as redevelopment director William Rafsky (Garvin 1996, 450–56; McKee 2009, 54–55).

Bacon has been criticized for being a physical determinist who depended on design to solve problems that were best solved by other means (McKee 2009, 61). This critique relies on a critique of rationalist urban planning that is almost fifty years old (e.g., Scott Brown 1990, 14), and it is unfair. Not only was Bacon an architect with fundamentally physical orientations, but he operated in an era when both federal policy and planning theory inclined toward large-scale physical projects, including the regrettable highways mentioned above. Bacon's acceptance of these roads may be a fault, but most of the neighborhood rebuilding that occurred during his tenure displayed a subtlety and respect for Philadelphia urbanism that was far ahead of its time. This may be because Philadelphia's unique neighborhood qualities obliged creative solutions, or because the city's great density and scattered ownership patterns discouraged the tabula rasa treatment of Detroit. But this assessment would be unfair to Bacon, for rebuilding efforts for which his department was directly responsible are far superior to high-rise public housing developments like Southwark Plaza, constructed between 1959 and 1963 only a few blocks away from Bacon's Society Hill project (Bauman 1987, 177).

Together with Penn Center, Society Hill was one of two redevelopment projects that established Bacon's notoriety, placing him on the cover of *Time* magazine in 1964. Acclaimed at the time for its seeming sensitivity to the historic fabric, the Society Hill project seems less so today in light of the adjoining National Historical Park's destruction of several extraordinary and irreplaceable late nineteenth-century banking buildings by pioneering architect Frank Furness, all for pallid reconstructions of colonial-era buildings and gardens. Bacon's celebration of this mostly ineffective series of open spaces as a "movement system" (1967, 252–72) seems dated today, but the urban design of the "townhouses" constructed on the blocks surrounding I. M. Pei's monumental Society Hill Towers has stood up much better. Faced with the task of constructing a new urban fabric to replace that cleared by urban renewal, Bacon and his developer's chosen architects, Pei among them, constructed a delightful series of row houses and pedestrian paths that, except for the absence of retailing space, provides a neatly Modern complement to the eighteenth-century row houses and streets that remain. There is little doubt that such exemplary architectural and urban design was a significant contributor to Society Hill's return as one of Philadelphia's highest-priced residential districts.

Were Society Hill the only residential redevelopment to emerge from urban-renewal-era Philadelphia, Bacon's office would still merit censure for social insensitivity (McKee 2009, 71). After all, Society Hill explicitly applied state power to displace low-income Philadelphians in favor of high-income ones: an act that was socially reprehensible even if it was economically advantageous to the city. But Bacon's efforts elsewhere indicate that his urbanistic approach could be not only formally innovative but socially sensitive as well. Philadelphia avoided wholesale clearance of poor neighborhoods such as that afflicting Detroit in part because Bacon, among others, argued for "scattered" rather than widespread clearance in areas adjacent to strong institutions like Temple University and the University of Pennsylvania. To simply clear areas because property values were low, argued Bacon, was nothing more than an "open spaces program" (Bauman 1987, 147).

The wisdom of this opinion could be seen in retrospect in Detroit, where areas cleared in the 1960s for the vast Elmwood urban renewal project remained vacant through the late 1990s. As a result of Bacon's more hands-off approach, the great majority of Philadelphia neighborhoods remained untouched by purposeful clearance by urban renewal, highways, or anything else. This quiet "success" amid the larger decline of the city's economy has gone little celebrated, and this purposeful neglect did not necessarily help areas like North Philadelphia, as we saw earlier in the chapter: that neighborhood remained one of the city's most distressed after 1970. But sparing North Philadelphia the urban renewal knife did leave space for smaller-scale interventions in the postrenewal era, many of which will be seen in Chapter 4. It also prevented the large-scale displacement that led to additional neighborhood destabilization in Detroit.

Row houses were an obvious formal referent around Society Hill, where the planners' aim to encourage private rehabilitation of nearby row houses succeeded tremendously. Row houses were less obviously the physical future in North Philadelphia, where conditions were worse, the population of low-income African Americans was great, and the potential for private rehabilitation was limited. Yet even in this deprived setting, equivalent in many ways to the neighborhood cleared for Lafayette Park, Philadelphia's urban renewal strategies proved that Modernist urbanism could be both innovative and sensitive. Particularly bold was Yorktown, a signal North Philadelphia housing development that will be discussed in Chapter 4. In another innovative move, the Philadelphia Housing Authority, spurred by Bacon (Heller 2009, 47), proposed in 1958 to take ownership of scattered row houses in "moderately blighted" or "conservable" neighborhoods so designated by the city's 1956 urban renewal plan. In 1967 the city was awarded federal funding to purchase five thousand homes for this purpose (Bauman 1987, 195). Philadelphia's "used house" program was pioneering both because it preserved the city's urban fabric and because it scattered, rather than concentrated, public housing residents. In time, of course, the city's well-intentioned program would experience the same maintenance and management problems that affected public housing authorities around the country. Heller (2009, 47) stated that this program was "doomed" by 1970, yet as of 2010 the Philadelphia Housing Authority owned 6,400 of these properties (Philadelphia Housing Authority 2010), a number that hardly indicates failure, at least in terms of units acquired.

By the early 1970s, urban renewal had left Detroit with monumental urban renewal projects like Lafayette Park, dozens of miles of highways, and vast swathes of empty land cleared for real estate developers who had not yet arrived. Philadelphia had built much less in its inner-city neighborhoods, and the face of the city had certainly changed less dramatically, but Philadelphia had arguably accomplished more with its novel neighborhood redevelopment approach. Publicly sponsored development in Philadelphia both retained more of the existing cityscape and reflected more of it in the design of new structures. At its best, as in parts of Society Hill, nearby Washington Square, and North Philadelphia's Yorktown, the Philadelphia approach generated a cityscape where old and new structures were interspersed within a street grid that was itself adjusted to accommodate new spatial standards, building programs, and the automobile. Philadelphia's redevelopment pragmatically acknowledged its well-established row-house cityscape, but it also reflected a design approach that valued the historic city and showed that Modernism could achieve its formal aims while respecting this past. As Modernism faded in the early 1970s, the Philadelphia precedent of responsive Modernism began to appear in other cities such as London.

Unfortunately, the Philadelphia precedent lasted only as long as Bacon himself, who left office in 1970 (Heller 2009, 49). With ex-police chief Frank Rizzo's election as mayor the following year, the city entered a phase in its urban redevelopment that has gently been described as a "planning slumber" (Steinberg 2009, 123). In November 1970 racial tensions foreclosed upon the city's largest development project, a two-mile-long "Bicentennial" megastructure to be built alongside the Schuylkill River, so there was little in Philadelphia for Nixon's 1973–74 decentralization of urban renewal to shut down. Rizzo was a particular enemy of public housing, as it alienated his core constituency of white ethnics (Daughen and Binzen 1977, 195–96). His successor in the 1980s, Wilson Goode, was much more committed to North Philadelphia, but his administration was paralyzed by the disastrous 1985 bombing of the MOVE cult in West Philadelphia (Goode 1992, 207–31) and accomplished little in the city's most blighted neighborhood beyond an assortment of modest scattered-site housing developments (Philadelphia City Planning Commission 1987, 25).

In the 1970s and 1980s, the innovative urban planning and design that had influenced rebuilding in 1950s and 1960s Philadelphia was reduced, but it did not vanish entirely. Subsidized housing construction during the

Rizzo era was low in volume, but projects like the 88-unit Dorothy Brown Homes (Philadelphia City Planning Commission 1987 113, 120–21), constructed between 1973 and 1975 at 12th and Diamond Streets, showed the influence of Bacon-era building. The Brown homes, built under the short-lived Section 236 HUD low-income rental program (Schwartz 2006, 130–31), were two-story row houses with the upper floor faced in colored siding. The homes were built both in long, rather bleak rows facing surrounding blocks and in short three-house interior rows facing parking. These homes lacked the architectural gravitas of row house streets, but they also lacked the older fabric's unremitting monotony and lack of greenery. The project attempted, albeit modestly, to both correct for and conform to Philadelphia's row house context, but its small size made this urban gesture insignificant.

The next decade's social housing production marked a subtle but significant shift in North Philadelphia. One of the largest projects shown in the 1987 *North Philadelphia Plan* was the 135-unit Montgomery Townhouses, built under the new construction Section 8 program and opened in 1984 (Philadelphia City Planning Commission 1987, 116) at 20th Street and Montgomery Avenue (Schwartz 2006, 133–34). The Montgomery Townhouses were architecturally unremarkable, resembling cut-rate versions of suburban townhouses. With their pitched roofs, uniform siding, and small yards, they resembled modest apartments at the urban fringe, an image that was probably appealing to their tenants. Montgomery was in no way significant as design, but it was noteworthy in that its vernacular suburban elements were previously unknown in North Philadelphia. Pitched roofs, vinyl siding, and other suburban signifiers marked the diminishing formal influence of the row house in Philadelphia's declining neighborhoods. The formal opposition between the urbanity of the row house and the spaciousness of the suburban dwelling would reach full fruition in the policy debate over architecture and urbanism that occurred in the 1990s with the election of Mayor Edward Rendell and the establishment of a suburban design-oriented development policy for North Philadelphia. Chapter 4 examines this debate in detail. But first, we turn to Detroit, where design after decline was driven by developers, not policy makers.

Chapter 3

"People Want These Houses": The Suburbanization of Detroit

On Detroit's far east side, along the shore of the Detroit River, lies a neighborhood called Jefferson-Chalmers. It is much like other Detroit neighborhoods, including the source of its name, prosaically derived from two neighborhood streets (Figure 3.1). Jefferson-Chalmers's very long city blocks that are located perpendicular to the river are legacies from French eighteenth-century arpent subdivisions, which permitted landowners access to the all-important strait, or *détroit*. Apart from this remnant of New France, Jefferson-Chalmers's built environment is no older than the rest of Detroit: its houses were constructed during the city's explosive early twentieth-century growth at the same time as the suburbs across the city line to the east. Like much of Detroit, Jefferson-Chalmers's homes were built at densities averaging around thirteen units per acre, twice the density of postwar Levittown. With its thousands of modest single-family homes, green lawns, and tree-filled streets, Jefferson-Chalmers was almost as suburban as Detroit's suburbs themselves.

Jefferson-Chalmers's bucolic landscape did not insulate it from the socioeconomic troubles afflicting the postwar city. Between 1970 and 1990, the neighborhood declined catastrophically, losing 55 percent of its population and over 40 percent of its housing (Table 3.1). Like other shrinking Detroit neighborhoods, Jefferson-Chalmers was emptied by both urban-renewal-driven demolition and piecemeal abandonment. Its half-empty blocks today are little different from other abandoned areas of Detroit, except for a cluster of new housing developments ranging from suburban subdivisions to a gated community at the water's edge. In the otherwise desolate landscape of Detroit, this new housing marks Jefferson-Chalmers

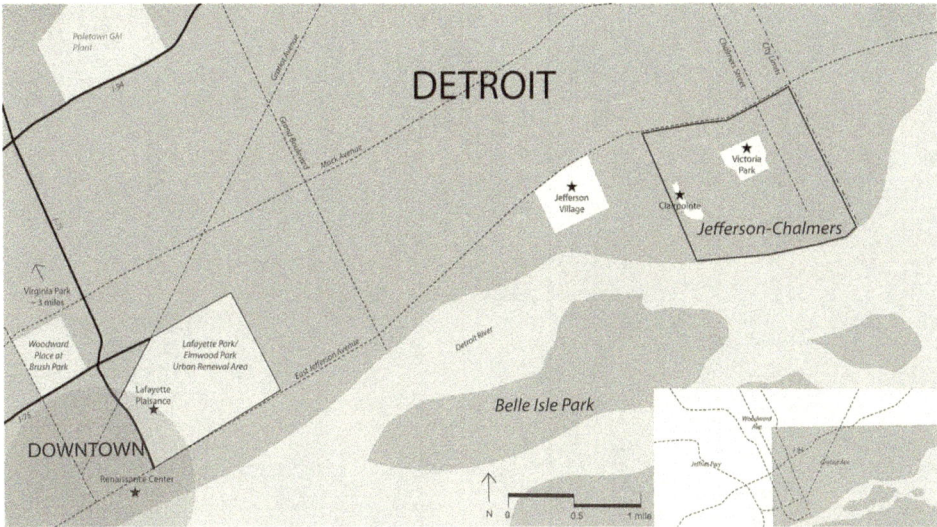

Figure 3.1. Location map of Jefferson-Chalmers. Map by author. Map illustration by Sarah Spicer.

as a locus of recent redevelopment. The sum total of these projects, however, is uninspiring, reflecting a lack of visual imagination, a lack of coordinated site planning, and the overwhelming influence of suburbia.

Jefferson-Chalmers's new suburban landscape is the epitome of Detroit's postrenewal neighborhood rebuilding, just as Lafayette Park marked the epitome of urban renewal. Jefferson-Chalmers's fragmented landscape, however, lacks its predecessor's exemplary visual unity and architectural innovation. Instead, its vernacular suburban homes, which like Charlotte Gardens are popular with their residents, speak volumes about the struggles that have afflicted postrenewal rebuilding in this largest of America's shrinking cities. This chapter explores those struggles, which began in the 1970s, and their outcomes.

The 1970s were difficult years for all older American cities, but they were particularly jarring for Detroit. The city reeled from high unemployment, racial transition, collapsing housing markets, and the unintended effects of well-meaning federal housing policies dating from Lyndon Johnson's presidency. Amid these grim events arrived the city's first African American mayor, Coleman Young, in 1973. Young would serve for twenty

Table 3.1. Population and Racial Change in Jefferson-Chalmers, Detroit, 1950–2000

	1950		1960		1970		1980		1990		2000	
Total population	24,327		22,347		20,262		12,580		9,290		8,188	
White population/percent	22,303	91.7%	17,382	77.8%	9,497	46.9%	2,578	20.5%	1,396	15.0%	846	10.3%
Black population/percent	1,913	7.9%	4,889	21.9%	10,630	52.5%	9,833	78.2%	7,807	84.0%	7,070	86.3%
Other population/percent	111	0.5%	76	0.3%	135	0.7%	169	1.3%	87	0.9%	272	3.3%*

*In 2000, 169 of "Other population" are people of two or more races.

years. He would witness the dramatic decline of Detroit but accomplish little neighborhood redevelopment success until the end of his term, when his administration would finally rebuild a Detroit neighborhood with the same pragmatism that had marked its other redevelopment efforts.

Young (1973–93) and his successors Dennis Archer (1993–2002) and Kwame Kilpatrick (2002–8) never recovered the clarity of intent and built outcomes that for better or worse had marked the tabula rasa urban renewal of 1960s planning director Charles Blessing (Thomas 1997, 89–97). Detroit's postrenewal mayors instead preferred to hand the initiative to private developers, permitting them to shape the form, location, and program of new developments. This strategy bore increasing fruit in the early 1990s as Detroit's real estate market began to recover, and for the next decade and a half developers constructed suburban-style housing on some of Detroit's most valuable neighborhood sites. Jefferson-Chalmers was of particular interest to developers for its excellent location and its abundant available land. None of Detroit's post-1973 large-scale residential projects occurred within a formal policy framework. Instead, Detroit's mayors preferred not to designate land for development until a development deal was already on the table, in a manner typical of "growth machine" politics.[1]

The great irony of Detroit's nearly planless postrenewal neighborhood development is that it was in large part guided by the ghost of urban renewal. Mayor Young's use of condemnation in the infamous Poletown industrial redevelopment is well known, but the much more modest residential redevelopment in Jefferson-Chalmers also relied on condemnation. Urban renewal clearances from the 1970s provided nearly every site for new development constructed in Jefferson-Chalmers between 1992, when the first market-rate "subdivision" opened, and 2007, when the recession cancelled further construction. And where 1970s urban renewal had not provided development sites, Detroit mayors used condemnation to provide them. Condemnation was most notable during Dennis Archer's administration, when the mayor controversially condemned 160 houses for the Jefferson Village development one mile west of Jefferson-Chalmers.

Detroit's post–urban renewal neighborhood redevelopment represented the nadir of postdecline urban design and urban policy. Detroit's new housing was constructed by suburban developers, and as a result most of it was visually banal and frankly antiurban. If developers constructing Detroit's largest residential projects had had their way, even more of the city would have been redesigned as a suburban subdivision. Their position was not ideological but pragmatic: as a developer said, "People want two-car garages, curving-streets, islands, and culs-de-sac. The market drives this kind of housing" (McDonald 2002). Mostly absent from 1990s and 2000s Detroit were sophisticated developers like Herbert Greenwald who had brought in Mies van der Rohe and his associates to design Lafayette Park in the 1950s.

Developers were hardly to blame for all of Detroit's neosuburban redevelopment. The city's new neighborhoods were shaped by reductive growth-machine politics that at their best (in the Young administration) were antipolicy and antidesign, and at their worst (in the Archer administration) were arguably corrupt. Under Archer, the growth machine reproduced urban renewal's worst features—involuntary displacement of low-income home-owners for a mostly failed attempt to attract "high-end" homes—without bringing any of the stabilizing influences that large-scale government intervention in an abandoned neighborhood might have delivered.

In Detroit's weak post-1970 market, private developers ruled. Jefferson-Chalmers's new subdivisions often required substantial subsidies as high as $150,000 per house. Only the largest projects received such subsidies: many smaller projects made do with almost no subsidies at all, and their design was often much higher quality. But the projects that received almost all of the mayors' "policy" attention—and almost all of the positive (or negative) press—also received land, infrastructure, property cleanup, and taxes at public expense. The cost to Detroit taxpayers was tremendous. Between 1991 and 2004, the two largest Jefferson-Chalmers developments—both market-rate housing—received public subsidies of approximately $50 million, an astonishing expense for projects that had generated only 250 or so homes by 2010, in a city that received only $52 million in federal CDBG funds in 2002 (U.S. Department of Housing and Urban Development 2001).

Post-1990 Detroit was marked by the city's desperate attempts to generate market-rate housing in its deteriorating neighborhoods at almost any cost. Jefferson-Chalmers's path after 1970 is a cautionary tale of Detroit in miniature, where a policy and design void intersected with the market to generate less-than-optimal outcomes.

The Fall of Jefferson-Chalmers

Detroit's industrial history planted the seeds of the social, economic, and physical transformations that enveloped Jefferson-Chalmers after 1940. The neighborhood's history was typical of Detroit, with industrial development such as the construction of the Hudson and Continental Motors Company plants around 1910 spurring residential development (Ryan and Campo 2010). During World War II, activity intensified as plants retooled to support the war effort (Flies 2002, interview with author). This war activity in turn stimulated African American migration, as workers from the South moved to the city to take advantage of relatively high-paying industrial jobs. More came afterward, and the city's black population began to grow rapidly. Although black Detroiters initially lived in a few small neighborhoods on the city's northeast side, settlement expanded after 1940 as African Americans moved to take advantage of increasingly distributed work opportunities across the city. Detroit was an overwhelmingly white city at the time, and neighborhood change was hotly contested by the dominant class. Whites met black expansion into their neighborhoods with great hostility (Sugrue 1996, 231–58), attempting to deter black settlement with threats and violence. This segregation and conflict set the stage for the even greater racial struggles of the 1960s.

Like other neighborhoods in Detroit, Jefferson-Chalmers began to gain black residents during the war, and its black population expanded rapidly afterward. In 1940 the neighborhood's four census tracts housed only 400 African Americans (Sugrue 1996, 184), but by 1950 there were around 2,600 black residents, 1,800 of whom inhabited a small area (census tract 754) bounded by Clairpointe, Jefferson, Piper, and Essex Streets (Figure 3.2). This area was adjacent to the Chrysler-Chalmers plant and contained much of the neighborhood's multifamily housing. By 1970, this "Plantside" area (Bolger 1979, 60–63) was a major locus for African Americans in Jefferson-Chalmers. Almost 9,000 African Americans crowded into tract 754 while the other three neighborhood tracts (751, 752, 753) held 7,868 whites and only 1,713 blacks (Sugrue 1996, 187; Census CD 1970, 2001). Although the Detroit News called Jefferson-Chalmers in 1970 "one of the city's oldest biracial neighborhoods," census data makes it clear that Jefferson-Chalmers was less biracial than it was segregated, a small-scale version of the city as a whole, where blacks crowded into certain neighborhoods but were discouraged or restricted from living in others.

In the 1960s and 1970s, this "biracialism" collapsed as whites fled Jefferson-Chalmers in large numbers. While Jefferson-Chalmers was 78 percent white in 1960, it was only 47 percent white in 1970 and 33 percent white in 1975 (Census CD 1970, 2001; Bolger 1979, 74). By 1980 the

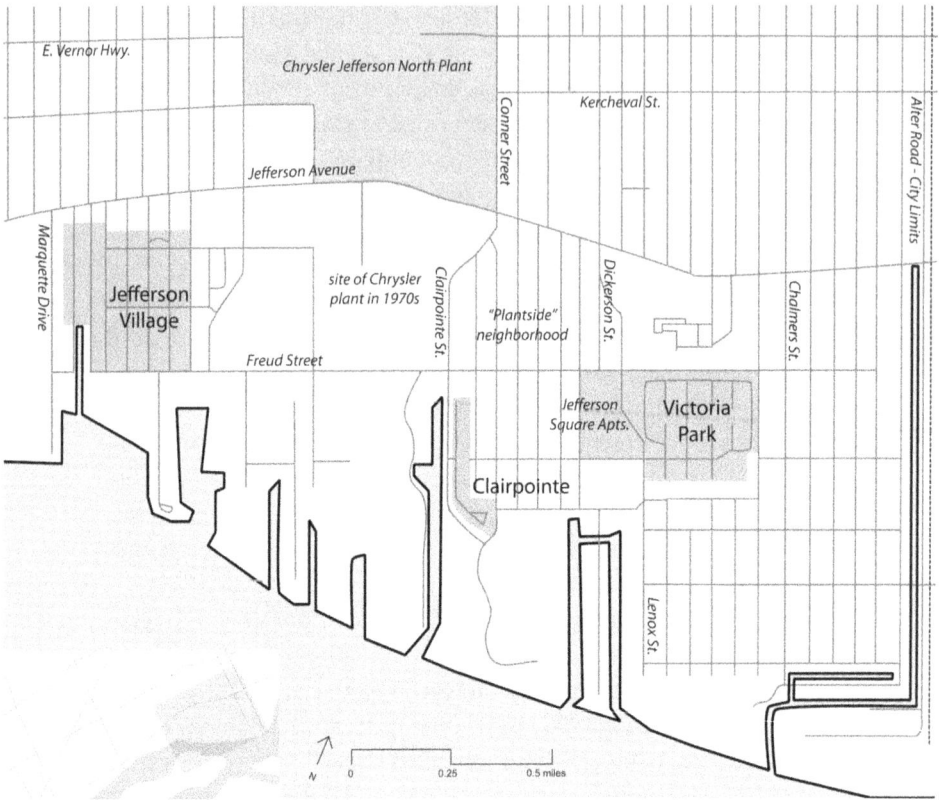

Figure 3.2. Detail map of Jefferson-Chalmers, showing the developments discussed in this chapter. Map by author. Map illustration by Sarah Spicer.

much-diminished neighborhood was only 21 percent white. The population instability in 1970s Jefferson-Chalmers was paralleled by instability in both the policy and economic spheres. A mortgage foreclosure "scandal," detailed later, seemed to place misguided federal policies at the heart of the neighborhood's problems. The reality was not quite so simple, but the unfortunate coincidence between policy failure and physical decay debased the legitimacy of ambitious public-sector plans, seeming to indicate that they could not succeed in a declining city.

Jefferson-Chalmers's decline was also closely linked to deindustrialization, as anthropologist and city planner Rory Bolger showed in a 1979

study. Bolger explained that economic blow after blow left Jefferson-
Chalmers in tatters. In the 1950s the Hudson Motor company closed. The
neighborhood's giant Chrysler-Chalmers plant also shed employment in
the 1950s and 1960s as the facility aged and the company lost market share.
By 1960, half of Jefferson-Chalmers's industrial jobs were already gone
(Sugrue 1996, 149). The neighborhood's economic base kept shrinking. In
1977 Chrysler threatened to close its Jefferson-Chalmers plant entirely, an
act that would have thrown the remaining 4,000 employees out of work
(Bolger 1979, ii). (In the late 1980s, after Chrysler threatened to close the
plant again, the city agreed to "save" 3,600 jobs by providing $200 million
to rebuild the plant [Heron 1986; Ryan and Campo 2010].) Detroit's deindustrialization caused Jefferson-Chalmers tremendous economic trauma,
and unemployment within the neighborhood rose as high as 62 percent in
1977 (Bolger 1979, 68–69). The parallel African American migration into
Detroit was devastating, both for a black population who arrived in a city
to see its low-skill job base disappear and for the city saddled with the
replacement of its white population with one suffering from high unemployment, rising crime, and social problems. These problems afflicted all
of America's older cities in the postwar era, but nowhere were they more
serious than in Detroit.

In the 1970s, Detroit policy makers could do little to stem the devastating tide of deindustrialization, rising poverty, crime, and white flight in an
era when urban policy was itself in turmoil. In Jefferson-Chalmers, the
federal government's shifting policy landscape played out as a grim tableau
in a rapidly emptying neighborhood. In 1951 Jefferson-Chalmers was still
a prosperous neighborhood, and in the city's *Master Plan* of that year it
was located far from the plan's recommended redevelopment areas centered around Lafayette Park. By 1966, with economic decline and racial
transition progressing, Jefferson-Chalmers was designated a "conservation
area" in the city's Community Renewal Program report (Thomas 1997, 92).
This designation conveyed planners' increasing concern that the neighborhood was declining, but many other areas had far more serious problems,
and Jefferson-Chalmers was thereby designated "non-assisted," meaning
that federal funding was available in the neighborhood only for home improvement loans and resident counseling (Thomas 1997, 91–92).

All this began to change in the late 1960s when well-intended federal
policies in the 1968 Housing Act that were designed to redress past wrongs

like redlining backfired badly. Most damaging for Jefferson-Chalmers was the Section 235 program, which subsidized any housing costs, including home purchase, for low-income families in excess of 20 percent of household income. Homes purchased under Section 235 were also insured by the Federal Housing Authority (FHA) under Section 223E, meaning that HUD would assume ownership of a property in the event of foreclosure (Leven et al. 1976, 175–76). Section 235 funded more than four hundred thousand home purchases by low-income buyers (Schwartz 2006, 258) within its first four years, but it was suspended by the Nixon administration in 1973 and cancelled a few years later because of massive foreclosures on Section 235 mortgages, many of them in Detroit.

How did Section 235 backfire in Jefferson-Chalmers? The key lies in the neighborhood's economic collapse. In a rising market, buyers are generally able to sell their home for more than they paid for it, guaranteeing that their mortgages can be repaid. Housing subsidies in a rising market provide low-income buyers access to valuable equity and economic security in the form of a valuable house purchased for a low price. This benevolent cycle is precisely what happened at Charlotte Gardens, where we saw that homes in 2010 were worth far in excess of what buyers paid in 1985.

But housing values fell rapidly in cities that were undergoing economic decline and racial transition, as Leven and colleagues (1976) illustrated in their study of St. Louis. Since FHA insurance under Section 235 covered as much as 95 percent of housing values, even a slight fall in housing value, combined with a default, placed a home in the hands of the federal government, saddling HUD with a large mortgage on a low-value house. Even worse, the program could be abused by speculators, who could purchase a home at a low price, conduct spurious "repairs" on the house, and resell it at a higher price to an FHA-insured buyer (Leven et al. 1976, 179). In the case of default the government would thus be responsible for an inflated mortgage on a virtually worthless property.

Precisely this disastrous scenario occurred in Jefferson-Chalmers as departing whites sold houses either directly to low-income Section 235 black homebuyers or to corrupt speculators. The second scenario seemed to be rife in Detroit: a 1972 study found that speculators held houses for 142 days on average and sold homes for twice what they paid for them (Leven et al. 1976, 183). In declining Jefferson-Chalmers, where homes in 1976 were worth only one-half to one-fifth those of adjoining Grosse Pointe (Ostmann 1976), Section 235 was doomed to failure. Unstably employed black, low-income homeowners who likely paid too much for their homes could neither make needed repairs on the homes nor repay their mortgages. As homeowners stopped making mortgage payments, many abandoned their houses, just as many homeowners did in the recent (2007 onward) sub-prime mortgage crisis. But in 1970s Jefferson-Chalmers, with a dropping population and increasing poverty, no one would purchase the newly aban-doned homes, particularly with mortgage liabilities. HUD assumed owner-ship of the houses and liability for the mortgage, and the boarded-up houses began to decay.

The same cycle of destruction, in which homes were pursued by hopeful homebuyers, abused by speculators, and then abandoned, occurred across Detroit. The disaster began to unfold in 1970. At the beginning of the year, HUD owned 900 homes in the city, but by the end of 1970 it owned 2,300, and by the end of 1971 it owned 5,000 vacant Detroit houses (Ball 1971). The vacant houses began to burn. Detroit's fire department reported 868 fires for the year as of October 1971, the majority of which were in HUD homes. Arson in abandoned houses would continue as a major problem well into the 1980s until most of the problem houses had gone. Fraud was rampant. In one reported case that may have been atypical, an investment firm purchased a house in 1968 for $4,000 but sold it to an impoverished homebuyer for $12,600 the next year. She defaulted on the house in the summer of 1969, HUD seized the house, and it was a vandalized ruin by the end of 1971. This single house cost the federal government almost $15,000 (Ball 1971). By 1976 the Justice Department had convicted more than 200 speculators, corrupt HUD officials, and FHA inspectors who had colluded to permit the purchase of low-value homes at inflated prices (Krause 1976), and HUD had lost $2.1 billion on foreclosed mortgages nationwide.

Detroit was the worst-hit city in the Section 235 disaster. By 1976 HUD owned 8,400 houses and 1,800 vacant lots in the city, more than three times as many as it did in either New York or Philadelphia (Krause 1976). Even more homes in Detroit had passed through HUD hands. Between 1970 and 1976, 25,000 homes, about 5 percent of all the housing units in the city, passed through HUD hands following mortgage default. The demoralizing effect of this "HUD scandal" on Jefferson-Chalmers and Detroit has been little researched, but the damage it caused cannot be underestimated. Crit-ics pilloried the HUD scandal as another example of liberal government's inability to get anything right. By 1979 conservative columnist Richard

Reeves could claim that the "HUD fiasco haunting liberals" in Detroit was "far worse than Watergate—it robbed the taxpayers of almost a billion dollars and nearly destroyed the city of Detroit" (Reeves 1979). The damage to Detroit from the HUD scandal has never been fully assessed, but the housing abandonment that it caused provided a sobering context—and a partial cause—for the city's disastrous housing losses in the 1970s and 1980s.

Flawed as the various 1968 Housing Act policies were in deindustrializing Detroit, Jefferson-Chalmers had a relatively small number of abandoned "HUD homes." In 1976, the *Detroit Free Press* listed only 455, one-third of which had been demolished and one-third of which were abandoned (Ostmann 1976). Urban renewal played a larger role, clearing approximately 1,000 houses in a relatively small area in the southeast corner of Plantside between 1973 and 1979 (City of Detroit City Council 1973, 1976). But all in all, the neighborhood lost many more houses than either the HUD scandal or urban renewal could possibly have caused. Between 1970 and 1977, the number of homes in Jefferson-Chalmers dropped 37 percent from 7,260 to 4,559. Housing losses were by far the worst in Tract 754, the Plantside area that had housed 8,000 African Americans in 1970. Between 1970 and 1977, this neighborhood lost 55 percent of its housing units, dropping from 3,347 to 1,514 units (Bolger 1979, 178) (Figure 3.3).

Even though many urban renewal losses were also in Tract 754, its loss of 1,833 units shows clearly that most Jefferson-Chalmers homes were destroyed neither by urban renewal nor by Section 235, but by landlords unable to rent or homeowners unable to sell. HUD-owned houses may have stimulated abandonment, but economic decline, a collapsing housing market, and racial worries were all likely to have caused as many problems in 1970s Jefferson-Chalmers as urban policy "fiascos" did. Yet federal policies were easier to blame in an era of increasing government skepticism than faceless economic change, unstoppable market forces, white bias, or social patterns. Section 235 and 223E's problems very likely stimulated, if not caused, President Nixon's urban policy reforms of late 1973. One could thus see Detroit's severe problems of the early 1970s as a primary motivation of the collapse of centralized urban policy that occurred in 1974–75. Whether or not this was the case, it certainly provides food for speculation.

Figure 3.3. In late 2010, abandoned and deteriorated houses still littered parts of the Jefferson-Chalmers neighborhood. Photograph by Drew Pompa.

Rebuilding Jefferson-Chalmers: The Rise of Victoria Park

Scattered-site housing abandonment and large, contiguous urban renewal areas present different redevelopment problems for shrinking cities. The former sites are easy for small developers to rebuild or transform precisely because they are small and scattered in between inhabited houses. But these sites also resist large-scale solutions because of the same intervening properties, whereas large, discrete parcels created by urban renewal are attractive to developers but require greater fiscal resources to be redeveloped. By the late 1970s simultaneous urban renewal and decline in Jefferson-Chalmers had generated both kinds of sites. The city was eager to see the neighborhood's larger, developable sites rebuilt, but like urban renewal sites in general, those on Detroit's far east side would prove difficult to fill, though they were limited in size and number. Jefferson-Chalmers's unspectacular postrenewal rebuilding is in part the story of how developers occupied parcels created by urban renewal amid broader scattered-site abandonment. It is also an unfinished story, for some urban renewal sites generated during the 1970s remain unfilled even today.

The beginning of rebuilding in Jefferson-Chalmers started in 1976 when a local nonprofit announced a two-hundred-unit rental complex on three urban renewal blocks in southeast Plantside (Figure 3.2). This was a subsidized project whose low- and moderate-income renters would pay only what they could afford. But the project developer backed off in the late 1970s (Chargot, "Optimism" 1980), and the site did not find a capable and willing builder until 1980, when politically connected developer Henry Hagood constructed 180 low- and moderate-income rental apartments called Jefferson Square on three urban renewal blocks in the southeast corner of Plantside (Grzech 1976; Walter 1981). These apartments occupied only a small portion of the neighborhood's available urban renewal land. Apart from a middle school developed in the late 1970s (Pawlowski 1976), the rest of the urban renewal sites remained empty.

Jefferson Square was visually unspectacular (Figure 3.4). Brick and vinyl siding and slightly pitched roofs gave the project's attached units a superficially similar relationship to the older brick and wooden one- and two-family homes remaining nearby. But Jefferson Square's site planning marked a certain improvement over the historic neighborhood, with lower densities and a more efficient arrangement of buildings. Its 180 units occupied three and a half historic blocks that had formerly been occupied by 302 units (Pawlowski 1976), and the development's aggregated units provided space for clustered parking and open space, including large interior lawns. The development's building arrangements took little advantage of this potential—interior spaces were poorly enclosed and are little used today—but the design did indicate that alternative housing designs and site amenities, like the collective green space and abundant parking, could improve upon the historic pattern.

Little other development happened in Jefferson-Chalmers in the 1980s, a period when the neighborhood's population dropped by another 3,290 people and the city's plummeted almost 200,000 (*Census CD 1990*, 2001). Development in Detroit was at a standstill: the city allegedly issued construction permits for only eleven single-family houses during the entire decade (Pepper 1991). Though Coleman Young remained in office, his administration brought few results in Jefferson-Chalmers as the mayor focused on Chrysler's plant retention and downtown improvements. New

Figure 3.4. Jefferson Square was a 1980 housing development with modest architecture, but its site plan demonstrated advantages of large-lot development, such as collective open spaces and varied building placements. Photograph by Karen Gage.

development in Jefferson-Chalmers seemed very far away, but this changed dramatically at the beginning of the 1990s when developers came back.

Coleman Young was politically astute, but the mayor could not be labeled an urban visionary. In 1986, the *Detroit Free Press* spoke with Young as he celebrated the awarding of $50 million in federal funds to rebuild the Chrysler-Chalmers plant (Edmonds 1986; Heron 1986). This was only a small portion of what would eventually cost the public $436 million, but one could hardly begrudge Young his moment of glory. When a reporter asked Young about his vision for other "reconstructed" city neighborhoods (Edmonds 1986), the mayor's response was surprising. Using the language of the long-gone New Communities program, Young stated that "we've for a long time had a plan to extend development on the east side beyond the Mount Elliott cemetery . . . the next 'new town' development, in my opinion, should be [in this area] . . . it's very logical."

Young's "new town" vision—which was not official city policy and which was never constructed—might have reflected an idea to extend the city's Lafayette and Elmwood Park urban renewal areas further to the east. But the mayor's offhand remark also revealed the lack of vision of someone who had spent little time thinking about urban planning and who consequently still thought of rebuilding in the language of urban renewal. Where his administration did rebuild neighborhoods, Mayor Young's urban vision was hardly subtle or sensitive: the Poletown and Chrysler-Chalmers projects each leveled hundreds of homes. Mayor Young would never see a "new town" on the East Side, but he would see a much-diminished version of his new town begin in Jefferson-Chalmers at the very end of his term, in a new single-family development called Victoria Park.

Despite having lost more than half of its population and more than 40 percent of its housing in the past twenty years, Jefferson-Chalmers was on the edge of a new era of rebuilding in 1990. Housing losses had slowed in the 1980s, and developers were beginning to see the large, city-owned urban renewal tracts there as "an opportunity to rebuild the city," as former city planner Ron Flies put it (Flies 2002, interview with author). Jefferson-Chalmers may have been blighted, but the neighborhood retained many of the attractions that had stimulated its development. Jefferson Avenue was convenient both to downtown and the wealthy Grosse Pointe suburbs, and the Detroit River waterfront was underdeveloped. Even the Jefferson Square apartments were a "good focal point" for new housing (Carley 2002, interview with author), as were two schools and senior housing constructed nearby. Chrysler's expensive new Jefferson North assembly plant was also nearing completion, providing a new western edge to the neighborhood. Developers had also completed new rental apartments on gated Greyhaven Island (Jackson 1989), indicating that the neighborhood had market potential.

Pleasure trips along the Detroit River have long been a favored activity for wealthy Detroiters, and on one such trip in the summer of 1990 Charles Brown, the developer of Greyhaven Island, showed his company's new homes to Garry Carley, vice president for Michigan-based Standard Federal Bank, and Charles Bonadeo, president of the Southeast Michigan Builders' Council (Markiewicz 1992). As Carley looked at Greyhaven, he thought that Detroit's underdeveloped eastern riverfront would be a "great place to do single-family housing." Carley's bank was a "home-oriented" institution that throve on mortgages, so he had a vested interest in encouraging development. Carley mentioned his idea to his friend Anthony Adams, a developer and attorney who was one of two executive assistants to Coleman Young. Following Carley's suggestion that Standard Federal "do housing" in Jefferson-Chalmers, Adams approached Young with the idea. The very next day, Adams was able to tell Carley both that "the Mayor was happy that there was a banker interested in the city" and that the city "had land that they wanted to propose for a site" (Carley and Adams 2002, interview with author). Ron Flies, head of development for the planning department, pointed out the vacant urban renewal site east of Jefferson Village.

Though Charles Brown and Joseph Slavik, the development team that had constructed Greyhaven, were initially the lead developers in the fall of 1990 for a development that they called Victoria Park (Barkholz 1990), the lead had shifted by early spring. Thereafter Carley was the lead proponent of the development, though he was not a developer himself. From the beginning, Carley envisioned a suburban subdivision identical to those in Detroit's suburbs (Figure 3.5). According to Carley, middle-class black Detroiters who could afford homes were just like anyone else. What they wanted was not necessarily to live in the suburbs, but to have houses with "all the different features" found in suburbia, such as "great rooms . . . sexy bathrooms . . . [in] a development with an identity." "We didn't do this [Victoria Park] because we wanted the suburbs," Carley said, "we [just] wanted to bring the concept here, and we thought that if we brought the concept here, then people would want to live here too. [After all], this was the first subdivision in Detroit since the Truman administration."

Carley correctly perceived that the existing cityscape of Jefferson-Chalmers, with small prewar houses interspersed with abandoned hulks, could not successfully compete with the suburbs. As he put it, "in Bloomfield Hills [a prosperous suburb] if you build a house the way it was built 50 years ago, people won't buy it. Houses are built the way they are because people want them that way." Carley thought that Jefferson-Chalmers's existing houses were insufficient for today. "I would never support a house in this city without an attached garage," he said. "People have them in the suburbs, so why would you build in Detroit without them?" Not only that, but the neighborhood's built environment was obsolete. "The old lots [in Jefferson-Chalmers] were 35 feet wide, and people didn't want that, because they didn't want their garage behind their house. We didn't want to do the old [street] grid, and the larger lots [of Victoria Park] reflect that." Carley felt that the neighborhood's rectilinear street grid was obsolete as well. "We

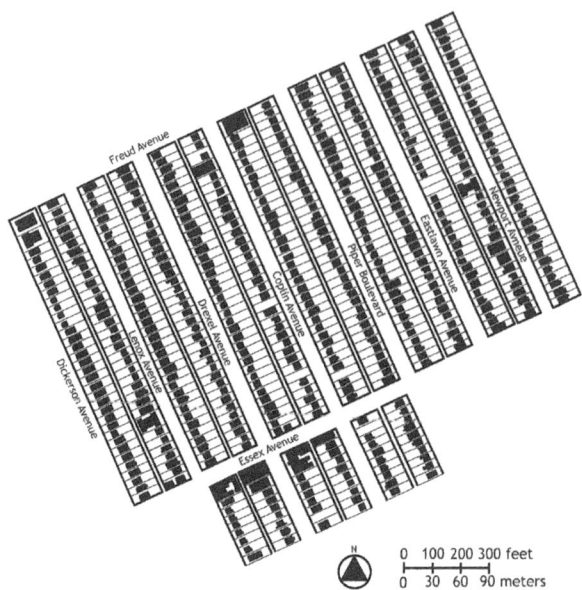

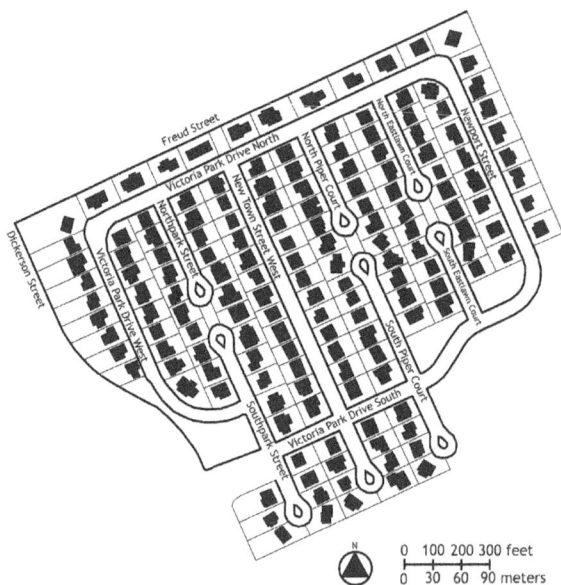

Figure 3.5. The Victoria Park site in 1950 and in 2000. Urban renewal and piecemeal abandonment devastated the original fabric before developers arrived in the early 1990s to rebuild the neighborhood as a suburban enclave. Data derived from Sanborn Map Company. Plan illustration by author and Geoffrey Moen.

eliminated the grid," he explained, "because we thought that straight streets weren't desirable, with a hundred houses in a row. Plus, there's a safety factor—people can't go so fast on shorter streets." Adams added that the developers wanted "to break up the streets so they wouldn't be runways," because Detroit's streets were especially dangerous for children.

With their vision for a suburban subdivision in Jefferson-Chalmers, Carley and Adams had grasped a fundamental reality about Detroit's residential market. While white suburbanites saw Detroit in 1990 as a dangerous ghetto and could not imagine living there, the city was less threatening for many black middle-class Detroiters already living in the city. This emerging black middle class had the same lifestyle aspirations as everyone else, but they were unable to attain them in the city's deteriorated prewar housing stock. What these Detroiters wanted more than anything else, and what a suburban subdivision in the city could provide them, was a conventional middle-class lifestyle in the middle of Jefferson-Chalmers—a "normal" life in a city whose deteriorated landscape was otherwise very far from normal. For Detroit's black middle class, Victoria Park was a development whose time had come.

The only objection to a suburban enclave in Jefferson-Chalmers came from Victoria Park's architect, Stephen Vogel, who would later become the dean of the University of Detroit-Mercy's architecture school and the founder of the school's Collaborative Design Center. Vogel's initial site plan for Victoria Park had, as he described it, attached single-family houses in a townhouse configuration. The existing Jefferson-Chalmers street grid was preserved; houses were located close to the street and built at two-thirds the density of the historic neighborhood, or about eight units per acre (Vogel 2002, interview with author). Vogel's original scheme did not literally reconstruct the cleared houses, but it evoked them, and it retained a physical connection to the adjoining remaining houses. Vogel presented this design concept to Carley but was told in response to design "suburban houses" for the site, with "curving streets" and a lower-density scheme at about four units per acre. Vogel was not proud of the resulting project: he called it "the worst project I've ever been associated with" (Vogel 2002), but at the same time he acknowledged that there was no other established neighborhood design ideal for the postdecline city. "Detroit is certainly not rural, it's not a suburb, but it's not really a city, either—what is it?" Vogel wondered in 2002. "What is the architectural typology for this landscape? I don't know yet."

Figure 3.6. Victoria Park's houses are conventionally suburban. Within the development it is impossible to tell that one is not in the suburbs. This was precisely the developer's and the city's intention. Photograph by Drew Pompa.

Such theoretical considerations played little role in the design of Victoria Park. The final design for the development, which was constructed in two phases between 1992 and 1995, was extensive and ambitious. One hundred and fifty-seven detached single-family homes occupied ten reconfigured city blocks (see Figures 3.5, 3.6, and 3.7). Victoria Park was in terms of housing units among the largest new residential developments constructed in Detroit during the 1990s (see Table 3.2), and it was by far the largest single-family home development. Out of the pieces of sixteen former city blocks, Victoria Park's developers created a single superblock accessible by a single road with an unmanned gatehouse. The superblock was enclosed from the surrounding area by a metal fence and a grassy berm. Inside the development, a loop access road provided access to houses with culs-de-sac closing the former city blocks. The single-family detached had various revivalist or vaguely historical styles complete with the numerous front gables typical of 1990s vernacular suburban housing. Inside Victoria Park, the

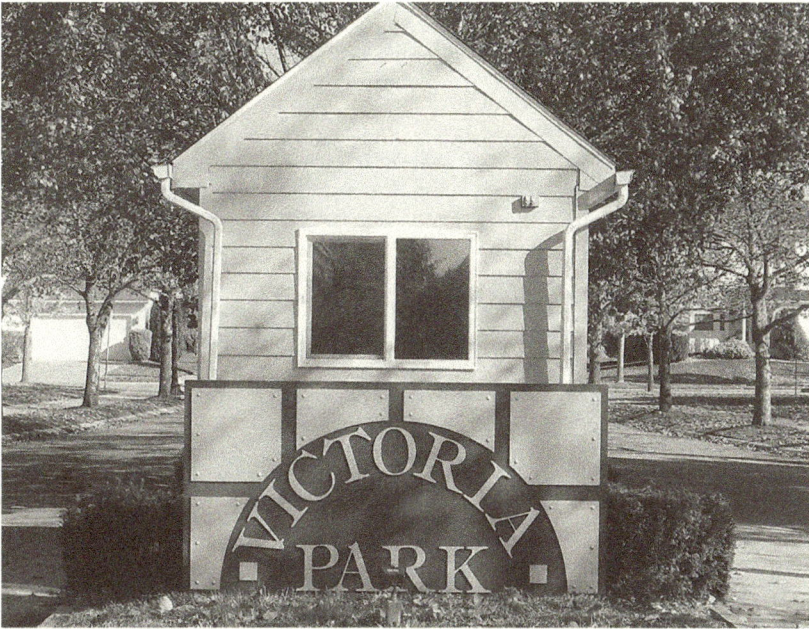

Figure 3.7. Victoria Park has a gated, but unmanned, entrance, indicating its separation from its surroundings. Photograph by Drew Pompa.

illusion was complete: the developers had created a conventional suburban subdivision located inside Detroit, but with minimal connection to the city. These suburban references and urban separation was just what Victoria Park's builders and buyers would prove to want.

For Carley, Adams, and the Young administration, the principal dilemma at Victoria Park was not what to build. In 1990 the suburban model was extremely well established, and it had a proven market. "Of course [the site plan] was suburban," Ron Flies, the former Detroit planner, said. "People want the single-family house, and they want the single-family house quality." "Suburban housing [is appropriate] where it fits," said Flies, and for him, Jefferson-Chalmers was a suburban neighborhood. The dilemma was rather how to build Victoria Park. This would be a substantial challenge. The land for the development was already cleared and city owned, but it was also unimproved; the streets and subsurface utilities were old, and parcels were filled with rubble from the foundations of the previous dwellings. Not only that, but the site was located in Detroit, an unknown

Table 3.2. Detroit Housing Developments, 1990–2001

Name	Year	Address	Type	Units
College Park Manor	2001	Puritan St. & Dexter Ave.	Apartment	30
Newberry Homes	2001	31st St. & Jackson Ave.	Single-family	120
Tri-Centennial Village (Habitat for Humanity)	2001	25th St. & Ash St.	Single-family	60
Kercheval Place	2001	Belvidere St. & Kercheval St.	Apartment	24
Puao Plaza	2001	Myrtle St. & Second Ave.	Apartment	38
Genesis Villa	2000	106 Harper Ave.	Apartment	72
Bradby Townhomes I	2000	1800 Robert Bradby Dr.	Townhouse	27
Woodward Place at Brush Park	2000	2500 Woodward Ave.	Townhouse	206
Bagley Houses II	2000	16th St. & Porter St.	Single-family	23
St. Anne's Cooperative Apartments (Bagley)	2000	18th St. & Howard St.	Apartment	65
Petoskey Place	2000	Petoskey Ave. & Collingswood St.	Apartment	96
Brush Park Senior Housing	2000	Brush St. & Alfred St.	Apartment	113
Uptown Row	1999	870 Lothrop Rd.	Townhouse	47
English Village	1999	St. Paul St. & Sheridan St.	Townhouse	95
Bagley Street Condominiums	1999	1365 Bagley St.	Condominium	20
Friendship Meadows III	1999	965–1001 Leland St.	Apartment	100
Mildred Smith Manor II	1999	1301 West Forest Ave.	Apartment	24
Brightmoor Homes	1998	14438 Braile St.	Single-family	50
Creekside Housing (Habitat for Humanity)	1998	440 Conner St.	Single-family	25
Islandview Housing	1999	1044 Townsend St.	Single-family	20
Wabash Homes (Corktown)	1998	1746 Wabash St.	Single-family	20
Clairpointe of Victoria Park	1998	620 Clairpointe St.	Single-family	42
Pablo Davis Elder Living Center/ D. J. Healy Apartments	1998	9200 West Vernor Hwy.	Apartment	80
Pilgrim Village	1998	Puritan St. & Petoskey Ave.	Apartment	24
Morningside Commons (U-SNAP-BAC)	1998	4267 Wayburn St.	Single-family	40
Bagley Houses I	1998	18th St. & Porter St.	Single-family	22
Mildred Smith Manor I	1998	1303 West Forest Ave.	Apartment	28
Alberta W. King Village	1998	Wabash St. & Myrtle St. (MLK Blvd.)	Apartment	120

Name	Year	Address	Type	Units
Ariel Square	1998	109 West Euclid St.	Condo	28
Shore Pointe Village at Grayhaven	1998	152 Keelson Dr.	Townhouse	51
Windward Court at Harbortown	1997	3400 East Jefferson Ave.	Condo	22
Lakewood Manor	1997	Lakewood St. & Kercheval St.	Apartment	30
Bethany Presbyterian Village	1996	8737 14th St.	Apartment	50
Berry Subdivision	1996	Jefferson Ave. & Parkview Dr.	Single-family	20
Eden Manor	1996	18040 Coyle St.	Apartment	65
Field Street I	1996	1458 Field St.	Two-family	49
Campau Farms in Elmwood Park	1996	2198 Prince Hall Dr. (Campau Farms Cir.)	Townhouse	180
Grayhaven	199	51 Keelson Dr.	Single-family condo	301
Virginia Park Estates	1995	1701 Seward St. (Estates Dr.)	Single-family	45
Brightmoor Homes (Habitat for Humanity)	1995	14322 Auburn St.	Single-family	35
Ida Young Gardens	1995	2250 East Vernor Hwy.	Apartment	56
Marketplace Court	1995	940–1003 Leland St.	Apartment	120
Helen Odean Butler Apartments (Elmwood VISION III)	1994	3100 East Vernor Hwy.	Apartment	97
Friendship Meadows II	1994	940–1003 Leland St.	Apartment	53
Faith Manor	1994	15321 Archdale St.	Apartment	52
McGirney-Bethune Apartments	1994	16850 Wyoming St.	Apartment	80
Ellis Manor	1993	19200 Shiawassee Rd.	Apartment	89
Victoria Park	1991	Essex Ave. & Lenox St.	Single-family	157
Circle Drive Commons	1991	1450 Robert Bradby Dr.	Apartment	128
Riverfront Towers	1990	West Jefferson & 3rd St.	Apartment	270

Sources: Data from various sources, collected by author.

market for suburban builders. Carley, Adams, and the city were committed to a middle-class development with middle-class amenities. How would this informal private-public partnership build Victoria Park?

Constructing Victoria Park would be a two-part challenge. The market was unproved: as Carley said, "[builders feared that] there was no market for new houses in Detroit. . . . [N]o one will buy anything . . . and no one can afford new housing." Given this uncertainty, Carley, with the assistance of city administration member Adams, set about convincing the city to subsidize early costs and to convince suburban builders to finance and construct the houses. The device that Carley seized upon, according to city planner Ron Flies, was a "Home-a-Rama," a Michigan housing fair occurring once per year, sponsored by the Southeast Michigan Builders' Association (today this event is called the "Parade of Homes"). Home-a-Ramas enabled different developer-builders to construct speculative homes at their own risk and to compete for sales with other builders' homes. The event distributed development risk across different builders, as no single developer was responsible for financing development. The high visibility of home-a-ramas also benefitted buyers, who could tour different "model homes" and purchase one if it struck their fancy. Carley, as vice president of a mortgage bank, committed to financing the initial stages of the Victoria Park Home-a-Rama by financing the mortgages for early buyers. Carley and Adams convinced the Builders' Association to host the 1992 Home-a-Rama at Victoria Park, with the proviso that the city would participate in subsidizing site costs. Mayor Young, eager to achieve a neighborhood redevelopment success, agreed, and in April 1991 he announced that Victoria Park would host the 1992 Home-a-rama, with at least twelve model homes open for prospective buyers ("Detroit to host," 1991).

Like many political commitments, however, Mayor Young's support for Victoria Park was an unfunded one. The city agreed to sell the existing lots on the site to builders for $1, but the land still had to be "remediated," as Carley put it, to remove debris. To pay these site preparation costs, the mayor's office had to convince the city council, who Ron Flies described as "socialist," to dedicate public funds to a project for the middle class. This was not easy to do. Although the city council approved $18.7 million in Community Development Block Grant funding for Victoria Park (Ilka 1991), some members of the city council wondered, as Flies put it, "why they should put money in for people who [already] have money." Victoria Park's middle-class market, and relatively high site costs, meant that public monies would deprive low-income housing of funding. In June 1991, the city council shifted away $2.3 million of the initial "earmark" of $9.4 million away from Victoria Park to community groups, prompting the mayor to warn publicly that the project was "seriously threatened" (Toy 1991). The city eventually made up the difference by issuing bonds, but some city council members remained skeptical of the project. "The private sector must be prepared to put in more of their own money," said one. Victoria Park is "very beautiful," said another, "[but this] is not something you can do all over the city" (Markiewicz 1992).

Throughout 1991, the city worked frantically to prepare the Victoria Park site so that builders could begin constructing homes in time for the June 1992 Home-a-Rama opening. But the suburban builders remained dubious, even though they already "had land," as Carley put it. "[The land] was almost all vacated, it was remediated, the city took out the bad soil, but they wanted more." Builders demanded an additional $5,000 cash subsidy per house to finance initial construction costs. The city would not provide this, but instead agreed to provide "remissible site improvements," including foundation and basement construction, instead. The city's final $19.4 million cost translated to $125,000 per house (Markiewicz 1992), an astronomical expense considering that this price did not even include the cost of most of the land (recall that in 1980 the city had already spent $22 million obtaining and clearing land in Jefferson-Chalmers, including the Victoria Park site [Chargot, "A nice neighborhood" 1980]). "It took this much city money to do this," argued Carley, but Mayor Young's Victoria Park subsidy model was hardly replicable, particularly since the homes were intended for a middle class already well able to afford market-rate housing.

Victoria Park can and should be seen as a showpiece project like Charlotte Gardens: a project designed to attract market interest and to demonstrate neighborhood and city viability. Given the negative perceptions of Detroit in the early 1990s—journalist Ze'ev Chafets called it a "fearsome-looking place" with "neighborhoods that appear to be the victims of a sadistic aerial bombardment" (Chafets 1991, 23–24)—the task of reversing expectations appeared equally fearsome. In this context, the excessive subsidies and lack of attention to design and planning at Victoria Park are somewhat understandable. Like Charlotte Gardens, the project reflected a city desperate to recapture the interest of a homeowning class and the respect of a skeptical suburban region. The best way to do this was to show them that the city could make a normal housing development work.

The market's reaction to Victoria Park showed that its proponents' vision of a middle-class community in Jefferson-Chalmers was correct. The response was "unbelievable," said one builder (Wowk 1993). "People want these houses," said another (Phillips 2002, interview with author). Buyers began signing purchase agreements for the homes in November 1991, before construction even began (Pepper 1991). By March 1991, seventy-one of the eighty-six homes in the first phase were spoken for, and buyers were demanding larger houses, at higher price points, than builders had originally envisioned. As one builder said, "the people, usually with dual incomes, want larger houses, and they can afford it. Prices keep going up, and that is where the marketplace is working" (Goodin 1992). Ron Flies noted in the same article that Carley and his colleagues originally had envisioned Victoria Park as a relatively modest subdivision, with 1,000- to 1,500-square-foot houses selling at $65,000 to $120,000, but that buyers were demanding 1,800- and 1,900-square-foot homes instead and were willing to pay up to $145,000 for larger homes. All the same, the homes were a bargain: the *Detroit News* estimated that equivalent houses in the suburbs would cost up to $50,000 more (Markiewicz 1992). By May 1993, the first phase of eighty-six houses was sold out, and phase II, with seventy houses, was half sold (Wowk 1993). By 1998 Victoria Park was completely built out (Colborn 1998). "About 98 percent" of the inhabitants were black, said Detroit city planner Robert Davenport (Davenport 2002, interview with author).

In the balmy real-estate years of the early 2000s, Victoria Park repeated Charlotte Gardens' rapid appreciation in home values. By mid-2002 Anthony Adams estimated that Victoria Park homes, all of which had sold for $150,000 or less, were worth "$250,000 to $300,000," providing initial buyers with a handsome profit. But Detroit was not New York, and it lacked the latter city's resilient housing market. By late 2010, in the wake of the Detroit region's post-2007 economic crash, Victoria Park homes were listed for sale for between $80,000 and $120,000, about the same prices that buyers had paid fifteen to twenty years previously. Nothing, not even heavily subsidized suburban housing, could protect real estate values in Detroit's collapsing post-bubble market.

Victoria Park set several precedents that Detroit developers would attempt to emulate after 1992. The development had received substantial public subsidies for land assembly and housing construction. It had attracted a middle-class market, and it had done so by offering a completely conventional suburban product in a desirable, convenient location within the city. City policy involvement had been minimal even as financial contributions had been large and market response had been substantial. All of these were lessons for developers, and in the 1990s they acted swiftly to follow on Victoria Park's success.

Learning from Victoria Park

Even before Victoria Park was complete, accolades began. In late 1991, with only a few houses sold, the *Detroit News* proclaimed that the development was "the most significant construction in Detroit since the Renaissance Center" (Pepper 1991). That same month, Mayor Young declared at the project groundbreaking that Victoria Park was "living proof of the fact that the city is alive and well" (Belanger 1991). The praise did not cease after construction was over. In a 2002 interview, Steve Vogel, architect of Victoria Park, credited the development with having initiated a housing boom in Detroit despite his skepticism about the project's design quality. Vogel argued further that Victoria Park had both inspired other new housing developments and made existing housing more valuable and that the homes had made it easier for other homeowners to finance improvements to *their* homes. Vogel also noted that while it had taken Garry Carley "two years" to persuade suburban builders to construct Victoria Park, many developers were eager to build further in the city once the development began to sell (Vogel 2002).

While Vogel's timeline was not precisely accurate—Young's formal Home-A-Rama announcement came less than a year after the summer 1990 boat trip—his argument that Victoria Park opened the floodgates of privately motivated development appears accurate. Between 1990 and 2000 developers constructed fourteen market-rate housing developments in Detroit (including Victoria Park), and between 2001 and 2005 they constructed a full twenty-six more, adding a total of forty-three developments to a city that had added only a few downtown residential projects in the previous decade (Thomas 1997, 157–61; Ryan 2006) (Table 3.2). Twenty-two of the post–Victoria Park projects were new construction: about half were suburban enclaves along Victoria Park lines while the other half reconstructed the Detroit neighborhood fabric along neotraditional lines. The remaining developments were rehabilitations of existing buildings, many of which reused office or industrial buildings in downtown or in the blocks along the fringes of Woodward and Jefferson Avenues.

Whether or not Victoria Park was the "cause" of Detroit's housing boom or whether it was merely well timed, the 1990s and early 2000s did see extensive building in Detroit neighborhoods. Though few of the new market-rate developments were as large as Victoria Park, the city's reconstruction activity set several precedents for rebuilding. These lessons are particularly important today as Mayor Dave Bing is preparing a new redevelopment initiative ("Detroit Works") to tackle familiar Detroit problems such as deteriorated neighborhoods, widespread vacancy, and the challenge of imagining the city's future form.

The first and probably most important precedent established by Victoria Park was public assistance for new development. In postrenewal Detroit, as in many other distressed cities, developers not only proposed projects but got the public sector to contribute substantial funds to make them happen. For developers seeking subsidies, Detroit was a seller's market, and Coleman Young would not be the only mayor to want what they were selling: market-rate housing. After Victoria Park, construction of market-rate housing consumed almost all of Detroit mayors' development attention dedicated to neighborhood rebuilding (as opposed to attention paid to stadia, industrial retention, etc.) Though Detroit's construction activity was mostly low-cost nonprofit housing, this housing remained scattered and with low visibility throughout the postrenewal period. Private enterprise was a scarce commodity in Coleman Young's and his successors' Detroit, and the city was willing to pay substantial amounts of money to attract developers and middle-class residents back to Detroit.

Coleman Young's successor, former Michigan Supreme Court judge Dennis Archer, took office in 1993. Archer personified Detroit's new suburb- and business-friendly attitude, one that Victoria Park had done much to establish. Under Archer, the city would achieve notable downtown development successes, including the construction of two new major-league sports stadia and a new office headquarters for a major corporation (Compuware). Detroit would even land the 2006 Super Bowl. None of these achievements, however, altered the basic calculus of residential redevelopment in Detroit. In the wake of Victoria Park, developers were happy to construct new housing, as long as they received city subsidies to do so. Even at the peak of the housing market in 2005–6, every developer building housing in Detroit utilized some form of subsidy (Ryan 2006). Given that no housing in Detroit was entirely privately financed, privately "motivated," or market-rate, was perhaps a more accurate term for these developer-driven projects.

Detroit's public subsidies varied widely in scale. On the one hand, many were modest: the most popular in the late 1990s and early 2000s was a state program called the Neighborhood Enterprise Zone. This was a tax abatement, similar to one in Philadelphia that Chapter 4 will describe, that waived property taxes for new home purchasers for ten years (Henderson and Ankeny 2006). Such incentives cost Detroit's government nothing, and they very likely stimulated residential development. On the other hand, large-scale capital subsidies on the order of Victoria Park were rare. But no

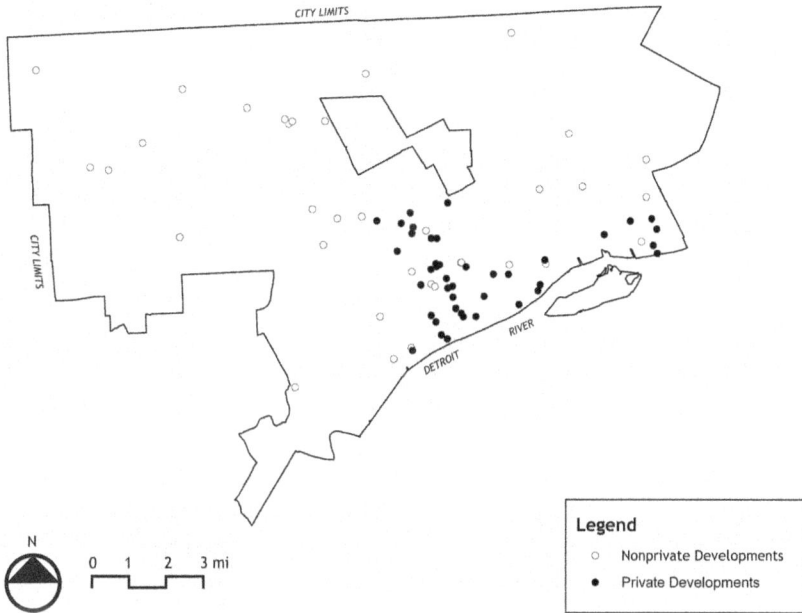

Figure 3.8. Detroit development map. In the 1990s and early 2000s, privately motivated developments stayed close to higher-value areas. Only nonprofit housing organizations constructed housing in other areas of the city. Map illustration by Geoffrey Moen.

subsidy whatsoever could incentivize developers to build market-rate housing in most Detroit neighborhoods; the market was too weak, the setting too deteriorated. The city's new market-rate housing was limited to a narrow band along Woodward and Jefferson Avenues and to the area in and around downtown. New housing in the remainder of the city was limited to scattered nonprofit projects (Figure 3.8).

Victoria Park was a large development, and this large scale had permitted it to transform its physical setting as well as market perceptions. Given the high level of vacancy in many other city neighborhoods, transformative developments were called for there as well. But Victoria Park was in a sense a paradoxical project. Large and transformative, it argued strongly for a development scale large enough to eradicate, or shelter houses from, the negative externalities of distressed, half-vacant neighborhoods. This model was clearly attractive to suburban developers, all of whom understood the benefits of a coherent, self-contained subdivision. Such transformations were also attractive to politicians, who could claim with some justification that they had not only built new housing but "remade" a neighborhood as well. Policy makers in other shrinking city neighborhoods would later be motivated by the same goals, as Chapter 4 explores. As a result, Coleman Young financed the large-scale Victoria Park development at great cost, just as his successor Archer would finance another very large residential development at even greater cost just one mile to the west. Thus Detroit's incentive to generate large, tabula rasa development was as attractive to the growth-machine-driven redevelopment model of the 1990s and 2000s as it had been to the urban renewal planners of the 1960s.

But very large residential developments presented one substantial difficulty: they were very expensive. Rebuilding Detroit's deteriorated cityscape at the scale of Victoria Park required infrastructure and site preparation costs that developers were unwilling to incur. Even in the robust market of the late 1990s developers would demand, and receive, monies from the Archer administration for similar projects. Public subsidies lowered developer costs tremendously, and where they did not exist, the additional private cost was reflected in home prices. The post–Victoria Park Clairpointe "subdivision" in Jefferson-Chalmers cost as much as $300,000 per house, and another, even more luxurious waterfront subdivision charged between $500,000 and $600,000 per house. But both of these developments occupied relatively prestigious real estate near the waterfront, where developers assumed that buyers would be willing to pay high prices.

Most Detroit neighborhoods did not enjoy this prestigious amenity. Private development in these other neighborhoods, if it were to exist at all, would require substantial city assistance, unless site and property costs could somehow be reduced. Smaller developments avoided these costs, but they were also more exposed to their neighborhoods. Small developments thus required a relatively strong neighborhood in order to be viable. This was the paradox of Victoria Park: large developments cost a lot of money, but they were relatively site independent. Small developments were inexpensive but were highly site dependent. Thus, large developments could potentially reactivate problematic neighborhoods, but they were so high cost that only a few could be built. Therefore, under Detroit's market-based, growth-machine-driven neighborhood redevelopment system, the vast majority of Detroit neighborhoods were essentially unbuildable, except to small-scale subsidized housing developers. If a redevelopment model did exist in the postrenewal era to rebuild the city's other neighborhoods at a scale larger than small clusters of infill housing, no one in Detroit identified it in the decades after 1970. So most Detroit neighborhoods, hobbled by very low housing values, continued to slowly empty out and decay, as they do to this day.

The Jefferson Village Fiasco

Apart from funding, another very important consideration for constructing a large-scale housing development in Detroit was the existence of an available site. Urban renewal had created many such sites, but what happened once these sites ran out? As discussed earlier, Victoria Park could not have existed without its site generated twenty years previous by urban renewal. Generating just such cleared, contiguous sites to stimulate large-scale private market demand was one of the primary aims of urban renewal, and Victoria Park and subsequent developments nearby showed that for-profit developers could, under the right conditions, build successfully and profitably on urban renewal sites in 1990s Detroit, just as they had in the 1960s at developments like Lafayette Park.

Though urban renewal is broadly excoriated today, Detroit planners' decision in the 1970s to clear areas of Jefferson-Chalmers brought certain benefits both then and in the 1990s. In the 1970s, the neighborhood's collapsing housing market doubtless made many homeowners eager to escape properties rapidly diminishing in value. Condemnation for urban renewal provided homeowners a way out, as a buyer (the federal government) was guaranteed. The government probably provided a higher purchase price than homeowners would have received on the open market. Detroit developers made just such an argument in 1977 as they ironically argued *against* urban renewal, claiming that condemnation artificially inflated land prices and made site assembly elsewhere more expensive as homeowners held out for additional condemnation (Neubacher and Grzech 1977). Such condemnation-based speculation did not appear to be a problem in 1970s Jefferson-Chalmers, as indicated by the neighborhood's widespread abandonment. Apparently, few homeowners outside the urban renewal area were willing to wait for the possibility of their property being condemned; instead, they were getting out no matter what.[2]

Detroit's 1970s urban renewal experience was thus very different from
the paradigmatic 1950s urban renewal disasters of places like Boston's West
End. The West End was a homogenous, stable community in an economically recovering city, making the neighborhood's urban renewal clearance
traumatic and very likely unnecessary (Boston's rising market would doubtless have revitalized the neighborhood without clearance). Jefferson-Chalmers
in the 1970s was the polar opposite of the West End: a highly unstable
neighborhood in an economically declining city, one that was racially tran-
sitioning to a poorer population and rapidly losing housing values. In this
light, urban renewal was probably among the less traumatic of the many
problems occurring in Jefferson-Chalmers, and it is therefore arguable that
more urban renewal–type intervention (and less Section 235–type intervention) was badly needed in 1970s Detroit.

The relatively small-scale urban renewal in Jefferson-Chalmers benefited Victoria Park and its successors again in the 1990s. The size of these
sites was much smaller than the older urban renewal sites closer to downtown (compare Figure 3.1 with Figure 3.2), but they were large enough to
be very attractive to developers looking for land after the construction of
Victoria Park. After 1993, developers began building on other unbuilt
Jefferson-Chalmers urban renewal sites. Some of these were quite narrow
(around 100 feet) and they directly adjoined deteriorated properties, but all
of the sites were cleared, available, and adjacent either to the river or to
Jefferson Avenue.

Housing constructed by developers on urban renewal sites in Jefferson-
Chalmers included Clairpointe of Victoria Park, a single-family home project constructed by Victoria Park developer Windham Realty between 1998
and 2001 (Figure 3.9); the Heritage Townhouses, a condominium development partially constructed between 2005 and 2007; and the Lenox Waterfront Estates, a gated single-family home development mothballed in 2007
after the housing crash (Bolger 1979; Henderson and Ankeny 2006) (Table
3.2). Each of these successor developments occupied a smaller site than
Victoria Park. Developers also built out leftover urban renewal sites elsewhere in Detroit during the late 1990s, particularly in the Elmwood urban
renewal area, where three late-1990s townhouse developments (Bradby
Townhouses, Circle Drive Commons, and Campau Farms) occupied sites
cleared in the 1960s.

Building on urban renewal sites removed developers' land assembly and
property title problems, but even cleared sites required additional subsidies

Figure 3.9. Clairpointe of Victoria Park. Built after Victoria Park, Clairpointe had fewer city subsidies and consequently much higher house prices. With a high price point and relatively limited amenities, houses were slow to sell. Photograph by Drew Pompa.

to be made buildable, as Victoria Park had demonstrated. If the city had not absorbed Victoria Park's street rebuilding and site remediation expenses, its developers would have had to pay costs in the neighborhood of $125,000 per house. This would have doubled the cost of Victoria Park homes and very likely impacted their marketability. Clairpointe's higher costs of up to $300,000 per house were compounded when Windham purchased an urban renewal site from the city and then absorbed site preparation costs for a suburban-style subdivision. The Achilles' heel of Windham's strategy came when they attempted to close a disused alley at the back of the property in order to provide larger, more secure backyards. The alley closing took two years, due to resistance from a truculent city council "fed up" with street closings following Victoria Park (Carley 2002, interview with author). This caused additional expenses and delay.

As a result of the delay enforced by the City Council, Clairpointe houses were priced high. They also sold much more slowly; Victoria Park sold out within months at prices of up to $150,000, but Clairpointe took almost five years to sell out at prices of up to twice as much (Phillips 2002, interview with author). Although developer Bill Phillips did not seem to think so, the low-value, deteriorated homes in Clairpointe's backyard may also have slowed sales. Certainly Clairpointe illustrated the twin disadvantages of developing a Detroit house for the middle class with limited subsidies, and with a small site that could not insulate the new houses from their surroundings.

In the wake of Victoria Park, developers realized that other extensive, easily buildable, publicly owned, and well-located sites in Jefferson-Chalmers existed. One such site was Maheras Park, an undeveloped, city-owned piece of property designated, but only partially used, as parkland, along the Detroit River. The site had spectacular views and full water access. In 1995, fresh from Victoria Park's success, Carley and Adams proposed to develop this parkland, which was not only undeveloped but partially zoned for single-family residences, as a suburban-style subdivision called "Victoria Woods." This "would be the ultimate extension of Victoria Park," Carley declared in 1996 (Goodin 1996) as he promoted the potential development.

From the developers' perspective, on the one hand, Victoria Woods made perfect sense: the land was undeveloped, the location was excellent, and the price would no doubt be less than equivalent suburban parcels. Some neighborhood residents, on the other hand, perceived the proposal differently, protesting what they accurately saw as a developer's land grab of public space. In the face of a likely legal challenge Carley and his partners backed off, and the city belatedly developed some of the land as recreational space. A few years later, Carley was still convinced that the project would have been good for the neighborhood, reflecting that "it's such a prime piece of property, and it would have brought people back to this area . . . [but] I'm glad to see the park fixed up this way, anyway."

Developers' willingness to build on smaller urban renewal sites in Jefferson-Chalmers, and even to propose infill developments in the intervening blocks (Phillips 2002), showed that they understood that windfall urban renewal sites were few and far between. Instead, the private market would have to rely on existing vacant residential land for new sites, much as the nonprofit market did throughout the 1990s in scattered-site projects (Ryan 2002, 145–46). Such scattered-site land was abundant in Jefferson-Chalmers, but its composition was very different from urban renewal land. Vacant residential land was often interrupted by remaining houses, either

Figure 3.10. Jefferson Village. Announced with great fanfare during the Archer administration, Jefferson Village was plagued by controversy over property condemnations and took seven years to open. Construction halted after 2007. Photograph by Drew Pompa.

inhabited or vacant, and ownership of the vacant parcels was fragmented. Some vacant parcels were owned by the city, but many were not. In Detroit and in other shrinking cities, neighborhoods with high levels of scattered, "piecemeal" abandonment may have *looked* as easy to rebuild as urban renewal sites, but this was far from being the case.

The peril of attempting to rebuild piecemeal sites with contiguous development became clear in Jefferson Village, a post-1997 development that was the "Archer version of Victoria Park," as Anthony Adams put it (Figure 3.10). Apparently inspired by Victoria Park's success, suburban developer Pulte Homes began purchasing land in 1995 in an area that was 75 percent vacant directly south of Jefferson Avenue and about half a mile west of Victoria Park. Given that the city already owned over 50 percent of the land ("Graimark Realty Advisors" 1997), the developers must have felt that creating another Victoria Park would be easy. By 1997 Pulte and its partner Graimark Associates felt confident enough to announce a planned 425-unit development of midpriced (around $140,000) single-family homes that would open in the summer of 1998 ("Graimark Realty Advisors" 1997). Dennis Archer leapt to support the proposal, much as Mayor Young had supported Victoria Park. But the Pulte property was not an urban renewal site, and neither the city nor the developers controlled all the land.

At the developers' behest, the city began in 1998 to pursue, and pay for, land acquisition and site preparation on the Jefferson Village site. Together these costs were estimated in 1998 at $32.2 million (*Michigan Chronicle* March 11, 1998), and they went up even further in 2001 (Ankeny 2001). Delays were substantial. In 2002, five years after the developers had announced Jefferson Village, and seven years after they had begun purchasing land, Anthony Adams could wryly observe that the development had cost the city "$40 million, but they haven't built a house [yet]."

Jefferson Village's site was plagued by fragmentation. The suburban-style subdivision envisioned by its developers required 100 percent ownership of the land, but even the city-owned parcels were not clearly city owned; a consultant reported in 2000 that title was unclear on 195 of the 443 city-owned parcels (Ankeny 2000). And the intervening residents would not go quietly. Even the site's renters, living in houses owned by the developers, protested the relocation payments they were offered. Many owner-occupiers of intervening houses refused to sell their homes. In a Detroit parallel to New London, Connecticut's 2005 *Kelo v. City of New London* condemnation scandal (Talley 2006), Jefferson Village owners resisted the growth machine of city and private developer attempting to shift them out of their homes. "This is an old-fashioned claim jump. They want to give my land to a developer," said one. "It's a way to steal my land," said another who had lived on her property since 1929 (Puls 2001). A third presciently commented that "I can understand condemning land for a road or a hospital, but this [Jefferson Village] isn't for public use" (*PR Newswire* January 2, 2001).

Ultimately, the city condemned 160 homes for Jefferson Village (Pristin 2006). Condemnation took so long, however, that in 2002 the initial development team had lost interest in the still-unbuilt project, and Mayor Archer left office without his costly neighborhood development having come to fruition. New mayor Kwame Kilpatrick elected to resuscitate the project, however, and a new developer, Crosswinds Communities, was soon on board. The first Jefferson Village homes finally opened in 2004, almost two years after Archer left office. But their timing was poor; Detroit's housing market slowed dramatically in 2007, before most of the development had been completed. Construction ceased with fewer than 100 of the envisioned

425 homes realized, and the rest of the site, cleared of its inhabitants with great cost and trauma ten years ago, lies quiet and empty today. In the meantime, the development's home values have collapsed. Crosswinds' Web site lists home prices ranging from $204,990 to $289,990 (Crosswinds 2010), but homes are also listed online for resale for as little as $70,000. Jefferson Village will clearly not be completed soon, and it will likely never be completed at all without additional subsidies.

Unlike Victoria Park, which was successful as redevelopment policy even if it was unprepossessing as design, Jefferson Village was a policy and design fiasco. The houses were the same old suburban product, novel in Detroit but hackneyed everywhere else. Even worse, however, was the process by which the project was realized, a process representing the worst of heavy-handed urban renewal, growth-machine politics, and insider dealing. The dubious proceedings associated with Jefferson Village were brought out clearly in a series of muckraking articles by the *Michigan Citizen*, a left-wing paper with ties to the city's African American community. Where the remainder of the Detroit press was silent or boosterish on Jefferson Village, the *Citizen* repeatedly emphasized the development's unethical aspects over a three-year period from 1997 to 2000. The paper revealed that Jefferson Village was in fact Dennis Archer's idea, not the developer's (Siegel, "Archer Hatched" 1998); that the city designated Graimark as site developer without soliciting other proposals (Siegel, "Archer Hatched" 1998); that Dennis Archer's son was in fact director of business development for the company (Siegel, "Archer's Kinfolks" 1998); and that Archer's sister-in-law had been Graimark's attorney and had subsequently become head of the Detroit Economic Growth Corporation, the public-private agency that condemned the land for Jefferson Village (Siegel, "DunCombe" 1998).

None of these revelations inhibited the Detroit City Council from approving the development in April 1998. "We may not like the way it began, but we're here," said one. Another was even more to the point, noting that "it [the development process] leaves a bad taste in the development community's mouth . . . in the long run we may be cutting off our nose to spite our face" (Siegel, "Council Members" 1998). The latter metaphor was not entirely appropriate, but the councilman was correct on the former point: Jefferson Village's insider deals, nepotism, monopolistic development, forced relocations, and lack of planning were all condemnations of the public-private development process that had characterized Detroit development since Mayor Young came to office. This project did not

indicate a promising future for large-scale neighborhood redevelopment in
Detroit, but the opposite. At Jefferson Village, Detroit got almost everything
wrong. It was doubtless little consolation to the exiled homeowners that
the development was never completed or that in the wake of the Supreme
Court's *Kelo* decision that Michigan voters ratified a constitutional amendment in 2006 forbidding economic-development-driven condemnation
(Pristin 2006).

For urban designers, the Jefferson Village fiasco emphasized the critical
importance of site control if one were to rebuild Detroit's neighborhoods.
As the project so clearly proved, 100 percent site acquisition was difficult
and expensive even with full political support and when most of a neighborhood was vacant. While the booming real estate market of the 1990s
and 2000s made site-related delays more palatable to developers, such delays cannot be borne in a weak market, where timing and absorption rates
are critical. Today, with Detroit's real estate market at a low ebb, any large
market-rate neighborhood development would likely have to accept the
existence of intervening, inhabited properties.

The post–Victoria Park period did establish some precedent for large-
scale infill development. In 2003, RAS Development, Inc., announced the
construction of "Jefferson Village North," a projected 106-unit, single-
family home development a few blocks north of Jefferson Village ("Detroit
Developers Set to Break Ground" 2003). Only two homes were constructed
before the market crashed in 2006–7. Even more ambitious was the city's
"Far East Side Plan," announced in 2000 for a two-square-mile area north
of Jefferson-Chalmers (Puls 2000) (Figure 3.11). Despite an ambitious
scheme including 1,000 to 1,200 homes (Elrick 2003) and a New-Urbanist-
inspired master plan (Pierce 2004), the Far East Side Plan never material-
ized. In 2011 the *Detroit News* labeled the area a "ghost town," blaming
everything from irresponsible developers to the market crash for the project's failure (Macdonald 2011). If Detroit's real estate values ever recover
to 2003 levels, it is possible that private developers may again evince interest
in placing luxurious new homes amid the remaining fabric of the city's
industrial past. But if market values do not recover, the city will have to
develop other strategies to reactivate these areas.

Urban Design in Postrenewal Detroit

Postrenewal development in Detroit presented policy makers, developers,
and city residents with a seemingly unending series of sad ironies. Urban

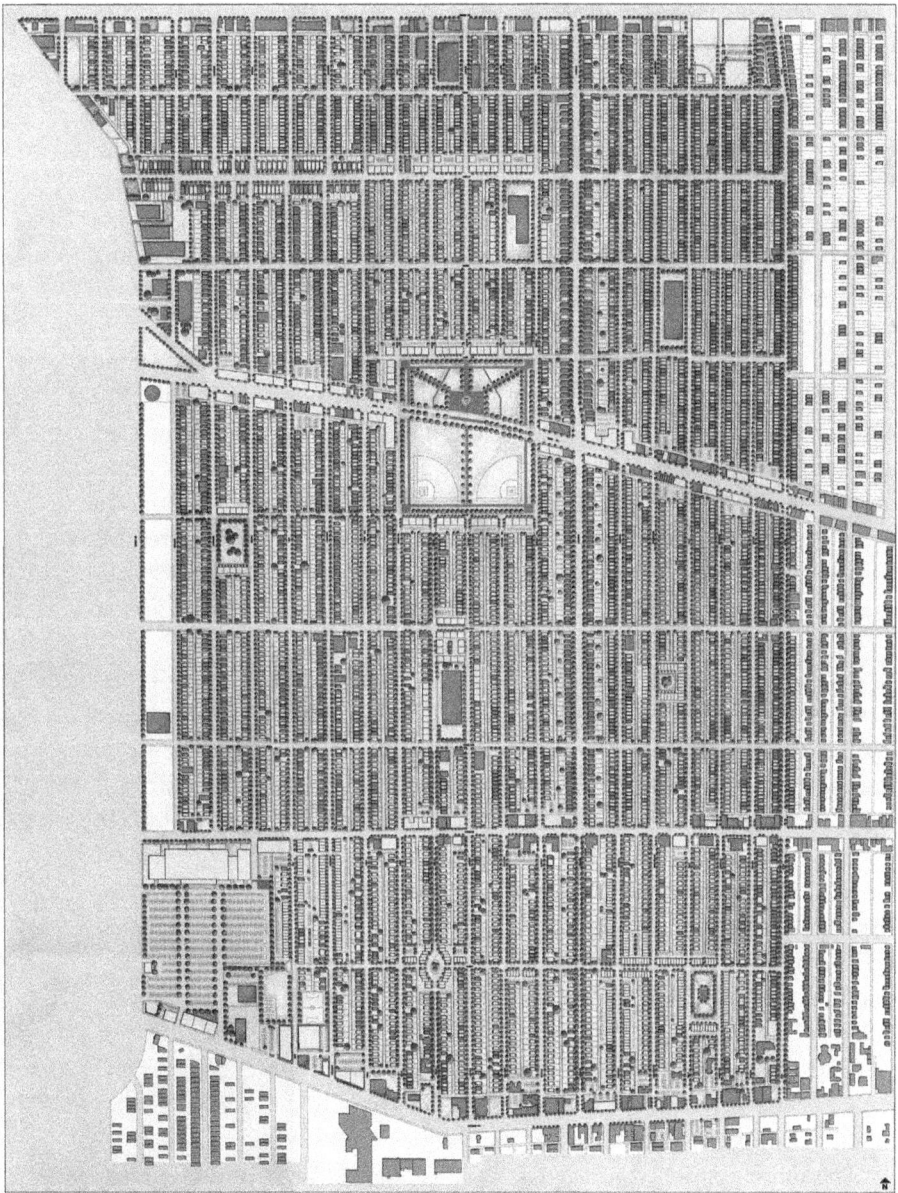

Figure 3.11. The Far East Side development as proposed to the Detroit Department of Planning and Development in 2004. The plan was too ambitious for the city's weak market and was constructed only in fragments. Courtesy Archive Design Studio, Detroit.

renewal, a redevelopment tool canceled with great fanfare in the 1970s, turned out to be the best means of providing space for new market-rate development, but its application in postrenewal Detroit proved flawed and controversial, just as it had been in the 1960s. The rest of the city continued to deteriorate, but even the emptiest-looking neighborhoods, with high levels of city ownership, resisted large-scale redevelopment. Developers were willing to consider infill development in stronger neighborhoods, but the market crashed before infill could demonstrate its validity. Everything seemed to conspire against the large-scale rebuilding that could reactivate the Detroit cityscape.

Any discussion of urban design in postrenewal Detroit was something of a misnomer, for apart from a few large downtown projects like the Renaissance Center or the Ford Field stadium that possessed an urban scale, innovative urban design qua Lafayette Park was scarce. However, in shrinking Detroit even the absence of conscious, intentional urban design had consequences for city form; the city's fabric changed and shifted irrespective of whether form-driven policies existed (they did not) or whether construction occurred. Detroit's mostly unintentional "urban design" was as much subtractive as it was additive.

At the architectural scale, Detroit's new residential construction was rarely compelling. Almost all new housing, like Woodward Place at Brush Park, had a subdued postmodern architecture, with applied historic decor such as front-end gables, Palladian windows, and colonnades. Detroit's superficial residential eclecticism resembled that of contemporary suburbia in Michigan and elsewhere in the United States, and, at a slightly greater remove, this Postmodern eclecticism also resembled the eclecticism of the city's prewar neighborhoods. One could easily argue that Detroit's postrenewal developments were simply a late phase of the historicist vernacular tradition that had characterized the city's appearance in its period of greatest growth in the work of Albert Kahn and other designers. From this perspective, midcentury, highly abstract Modernist architecture like Lafayette Park was an alien interlude in the city's architectural tradition and an aberration in a longer trajectory of historicism.

The sole exceptions to the city's architectural conservatism were rehabilitations, many of which were in former industrial or commercial buildings. The nontraditional form and generally nonresidential locations of these buildings provided designers with a certain amount of freedom that the city's residential neighborhoods did not. Like other developers in other cities, Detroit developers capitalized on the popularity of lofts with the "urbans," a demographic drawn from the upper middle class. Projects such as the Canfield Lofts off Woodward Avenue provided the finest examples of contemporary residential architecture in postrenewal Detroit, but their architecture was for the most part interior, and such projects were few in number. Apart from such rehabilitations, "contemporary" residential design in Detroit was confined to structures built before the end of the 1970s.

Detroit's post-1990 development also reflected the total dominance of the automobile. New retail was almost always automobile oriented, and automobile orientation showed even more strongly in the city's residential projects. For single-family housing, front-entry attached garages were nearly ubiquitous, reflecting Garry Carley's conviction that developers should "never support a house in this city without an attached garage. . . . [P]eople have them in the suburbs, so why would you build in Detroit without them?" Some new housing in denser areas of the city, such as Woodward Place, had one- or two-car garages in the rear of the unit (Figure 5.4). Such automobile orientation was not alien to the city's historic fabric: both before and after urban renewal, Detroit was a city of detached buildings, whether in one- and two-family houses or in apartments. After 1970, the city's increasing vacant lots made parking provision even easier. In this spacious city, providing for the automobile was the least of designers' constraints.

Automobile provision also reflected the reality of mobility in a highly decentralized metropolis, where anyone who could afford it owned a car, and where both employment and residence were highly decentralized. In this sense, the city's post-2008 plans to fund a light rail line reflected a recurring fantasy of salvation through mass transportation that had reared its head as early as the 1930s, when the city considered, but voted down, a subway, and again in the 1970s and 1980s, when the Young administration constructed a vintage trolley line and people mover, the latter of which continues to cost the public $8.3 million per year (Henion 2006). Mass transit was sure to be a boondoggle in rapidly shrinking Detroit, but this did not deter optimistic boosters like the president of the Detroit Regional Chamber from claiming that the latest light rail line would be the key to the city's rebuilding (Gray 2010).

Given the tremendous shrinkage of its physical plant after 1970, one could hardly expect Detroit to undertake the conventional public space projects that growing cities did, but this would be underestimating the city.

In the first decade of 2000, Detroit's downtown carried out many of the same open space projects that other American downtowns did, including the re-creation of the Campus Martius Park in the center of the city's business district, the first phase of an extensive downtown riverwalk, and a rail-to-trail bicycle path along a railbed called the Dequindre Cut. These attractive public space features were well used and received substantial positive press.

Outside of these conventional projects, however, Detroit's urban design at both the neighborhood and city scales was highly unusual. With an evaporating urban fabric, conventional urban design moves such as improved public space, mixed-use buildings, and dense dwellings had very limited applicability. Rampant demolition, combined with the proliferation of suburban structures, was actually the city's largest-scale urban design intervention of the postrenewal era, and by far its most radical one. As the first decade of the twenty-first century wore on and as the economic crisis brought Detroit's ruined landscape to the fore as a metaphor for America's economic woes, pundits, critics, and admirers increasingly came to see the city as an image of the future (e.g., Okrent 2009). Even historic preservation, one of the less contentious planning policies of the postrenewal period, had little traction in rapidly declining Detroit. Throughout the postrenewal period, the city steadily demolished some of its largest buildings, including the former Cadillac plant (1988), the former Hudson's Department Store (1998), and the former Statler Hotel (2006). In 2009 the Detroit City Council even voted (unsuccessfully, so far) to demolish the city's long-vacant Beaux-Arts train station.

Two trends dominated postrenewal development design in Detroit: dedensification at the development scale and concentration at the citywide scale. This was a paradoxical pairing: new development was almost always lower density than what it replaced, but its spatial distribution was also extremely limited because of the city's weak real estate market and the city's use of incentive policies to generate development. The combination of incentive-based public policy, market preferences, and a weak market generated the city form of postrenewal Detroit.

Detroit developers almost always preferred to build suburban. Whether for-profit or non-profit, developers were for the most part unconstrained by conventional urban design ideals. The frankly suburban dwellings and commercial buildings constructed in postrenewal Detroit reflected a logical, market-driven conviction that Detroiters were perfectly happy to live in suburban-style dwellings and shop in roadside shopping centers. Abundant evidence indicated that this was true. In this sense very low-density Lafayette Park proved to be prescient. While its abstract Miesian architecture had little influence on the city's architectural culture, its low-density residential realm, suburban-style shopping and extensive park space, which replaced a dense, heterogeneous fabric, was a harbinger of Detroit's future. By 1990 the deterioration of the surrounding neighborhoods that had not been cleared for urban renewal made Lafayette Park just one open place among many, "a metaphorical void surrounded by a real void," like Mies's equally abstract Illinois Institute of Technology (Koolhaas 2001, 724).

Victoria Park and successor developments did not have sophisticated design, and they did not represent a progressive planning or redevelopment policy. But projects like Jefferson Village, Victoria Park, Clairpointe, and many others did further the de-densification of Detroit that Lafayette Park and other urban renewal projects had begun. Even Woodward Place, the neotraditional development near downtown (Figure 5.4), had only eight units per acre, a density only slightly greater than suburban Levittown and only 60 percent that of pre-1970 Jefferson-Chalmers. The post-1990 suburban builders may have been unconscious of the larger-scale physical implications of their projects, but the implicit design aim of both eras of redevelopment—urban renewal and postrenewal—was the same. Ultimately, except in a few areas such as Woodward Avenue, new Detroit development rebuilt the prewar cityscape (street grid, relatively dense housing, and streetcar-oriented retail) with a suburban cityscape (disconnected residential, industrial, and commercial pods linked only by automobile).

This pressure to spatially reorganize postrenewal Detroit came both from the market and from a mostly quiescent public sector. Detroit did not have an operative city plan during this period, and there is little indication that its mayors would have followed a plan's directives in any event. In the breach, developer preferences generally held the day, except during interludes such as that of Gloria Robinson, planning director from 1993 to 1997, who squelched ideas for a third phase of Victoria Park unless it conformed to New Urbanist standards, and the city council, who were certainly not urban designers, but disfavored disruptions like street closings. In a shrinking city, de-densification seemed a best-case scenario to the majority of actors involved, including consumers, and it therefore assumed a sort of inevitability. As the story of Victoria Park makes clear, at least suburban subdivisions communicated a continued market interest in the city.

At the citywide scale, Detroit's spatial shift away from urban renewal practice was most marked. Urban-renewal-era planners had designated, condemned, and cleared large, contiguous tracts of land, mostly around downtown (Thomas 1997, 77 and 92), but postrenewal redevelopment operated at a smaller scale and in more adventitious locations. Even Jefferson-Chalmers, where so much redevelopment interest was concentrated, resembled nothing so much as a patchwork of scattered development, much like that found in growing suburbs. In this sense all of Detroit's city—and neighborhood—scale design was "unplanned": there was no coordination between different development efforts. Only urban renewal, in the form of cleared, empty parcels, provided a ghostly guiding hand from the public sector.

Though Detroit did not have strong postrenewal planning or design, many policies existed to support market-rate development, as well as low-income development. Some of these instruments, such as Community Development Block Grants, were aspatial; others, such as the Neighborhood Enterprise Zone, were spatial in that they applied only in certain areas. Given that Detroit policy supported market-rate development, development concentrated in areas where there was a strong market. Most of the city was thus left more or less alone during the postrenewal period. The only physical change that occurred in these areas was the gradual diminution of the evaporating housing stock.

The changes in Detroit's city form showed the deleterious effects of a lack of large-scale state intervention. The city's urban renewal was brutal and insensitive, as noted previously, but the great irony is that it occurred at a time when the city might have been rehabilitated rather than cleared and that urban renewal vanished precisely when the city's decline made it need reconstruction much more. "Blaming" urban renewal for city decline, as planners have done since Jacobs's 1961 polemic against clearance, was simply wrong in Detroit. Blaming renewal simplistically elided two different events—deindustrialization and public policy—and sidestepped the potentially positive role that large-scale rebuilding could have in a devastated urban fabric. The proof is that today areas that Detroit rebuilt with urban renewal often look better than those that it left alone.

It is difficult to imagine how things might be different in Detroit. Doubtless the city suffered from economic and related problems that outclassed those of any other place in the United States after 1970. Yet these very real and extensive problems should not forbid our reconsideration of the city's physical condition and the proposition of alternative physical futures. Certainly, the restorative urban design strategies espoused by some planners today (e.g., Talen 2010), have little relevance to Detroit's contemporary condition. But nor does the casual suburbanization and piecemeal abandonment that has characterized the city for most of the past twenty years seem acceptable. In 2011, the city has an able new mayor who is actively confronting the difficult conditions of the city and seeking a new physical future for Detroit. But before Detroit begins to "rightsize" it will have to confront the policy realities and physical constraints that have afflicted postrenewal rebuilding in the city and develop new formal visions that successfully encompass and transcend the grim realities of the shrinking city. One city that has done so with some degree of success is Philadelphia, and it is to postrenewal Philadelphia that we now turn.

==========

Chapter 4

"Another Tradition in Planning": The Suburbanization of North Philadelphia

Renaissance Philadelphia

On January 6, 1992, W. Wilson Goode stepped down as mayor of Philadelphia. Few, Goode not excepted, would argue that his term had been successful. In reality, the past two decades had not been good ones for the city. Polarizing mayor Frank Rizzo and Goode, the city's first African American mayor, had seen Philadelphia suffer a host of related problems: economic decline, population loss, white flight, and political fiascos such as the 1985 MOVE bombing (Goode 1992, 207–31). Philadelphia had avoided the drastic depopulation of Coleman Young's Detroit, but the city's situation looked poor in comparison to New York, only an hour and a half away. "Philadelphia is struggling to survive," said the *New York Times* in mid-1990, noting that "[As] the city shrinks and grows poorer, its problems expand" (Hinds, "After Renaissance" 1990). A few months later, the city was again in the *New York Times*, this time on the front page, as bankruptcy threatened. "Philadelphia's problems have no parallels in the nation," the paper mourned, noting pointedly that "it is substantially a political problem with an economic component" (Hinds, "Cash and Tempers" 1990). Few could have imagined a greater indictment of Mayor Goode's tenure.

North Philadelphia, the city's most distressed neighborhood, was not much better off in the 1980s. The *New York Times*, clearly interested in Philadelphia's problems, profiled North Philadelphia in 1990 as a place "struggling for a revival." The newspaper noted that the city had issued *The North Philadelphia Plan* in 1987 but that the plan had resulted in little construction because it "need(ed) a whole lot more coordination of other entities than seem to be involved," according to a Temple University professor interviewed for the article (Scism 1990). Another likely reason was that the plan had few grand ideas to pronounce. Recommendations such as "prevent neighborhood decline" (Philadelphia City Planning Commission 1987, 109) were hardly likely to inspire confidence in an area that had declined worse than any other in the city in the 1970s and 1980s. Nor did plan ideas such as "continue housing programs" (109) inspire confidence, particularly when the plan admitted in the same paragraph that "little implementation has occurred."

In one area of North Philadelphia, however, the plan was uncharacteristically forceful. Along Cecil B. Moore Avenue, a severely deteriorated commercial street, the plan's unvarnished recommendation was to "selectively use the power of eminent domain to acquire and clear sites for new development." Its reasons for this were clear: "Several blocks already have a great deal of vacant land resulting from demolition. Rehabilitation of the remaining homes would not create a good living environment inasmuch as houses would continue to be surrounded by vacant land. In such cases, the needs of the community can be best served by relocating persons . . . and making the block available for redevelopment" (Philadelphia City Planning Commission 1987, 119). The planners may have had former planning director Ed Bacon's 1956 admonition against an "open spaces program" for North Philadelphia in mind when they then recommended that construction immediately follow demolition. Vacant parcels would be "good candidates for new residential or commercial development. . . . [T]he feasibility question is how best to develop new housing on cleared sites when no significant subsidy programs exist to build new housing. [The city has] few options available to deliver new housing at a price affordable to low-moderate income households without significant public subsidy" (119). Interestingly, the plan shied away from strong recommendations in other areas of North Philadelphia. In an area known as the Ludlow neighborhood, which the plan acknowledged as "the worst neighborhood in North Philadelphia in terms of housing conditions and social problems" (138), the plan recommended only small-scale actions such as cleaning vacant lots, giving small vacant parcels to homeowners, and "developing" partnerships with various neighborhood groups. The plan's general passivity makes its activist stance for Cecil B. Moore Avenue all the more surprising, not just because the urban renewal powers that had cleared areas of North Philadelphia in the 1960s still existed, but because planners still wished to use them. In the 1980s, all that was missing was funding. But the 1990s would be different, and planners would dramatically transform the Cecil B. Moore area, among others in North Philadelphia, by the end of the decade.

The 1990s were different for Philadelphia in almost every imaginable way. In contrast to the bad news of the Goode administration in the 1980s, Philadelphia became a good news city in the 1990s under the charismatic and broadly acclaimed leadership of Edward Rendell, a former district attorney. Rendell was energetic, intelligent, and media-savvy, and his administration not only addressed the fiscal crisis left by the Goode administration but initiated a variety of policy efforts that would bear fruit both during and after he left office in 2001. Rendell was a pragmatist who did not believe in planning, according to his housing director John Kromer (2010, 88), but he supported many individuals who did, and under his tenure both Center City, an active but downtrodden business district, and North Philadelphia would be substantially redeveloped.

Rendell was capable, but he also had significant good fortune and even better timing. Soon after he entered office in 1992, a variety of previously existing downtown development initiatives reached realization. In 1993 the Pennsylvania Convention Center, a project that the Reading Railroad had promoted since the early 1980s (Stevenson 1985; Adams et al. 1991, 112) opened on land directly behind the formerly dilapidated railroad terminal. The convention center brought fifteen new hotels to Center City (Midgette 1999) and thousands of conventioneers. The same year, the Avenue of the Arts, an initiative begun in 1977 by the Central Philadelphia Development Corporation, formally incorporated as a nonprofit, in part because it was a pet project of Mayor Rendell. The Avenue soon took wing with Rendell's championing of another moribund arts project, a planned new performance hall for the Philadelphia Orchestra, an idea that had lain dormant since 1986 (Midgette 1999). The Kimmell Center opened in 2001 to initial acclaim.

Rendell had even better timing when the Center City District (CCD), a privately financed business improvement district that had also been in development since the mid-1980s, hired a new director in early 1991 (Kromer 2010, 56). Paul Levy was a talented and energetic individual who throughout the 1990s progressively increased the CCD's capacity and service delivery, transforming the organization from one that delivered the standard "clean and safe" security and sanitation services to one that performed sophisticated research, marketing, and even real estate development. By 2007, the CCD could note with pride that it had contributed to a

50 percent drop in serious crime downtown since the early 1990s and that it had constructed more than $45 million in physical improvements to the District (Center City District 2007, 6).

Mayor Rendell was also astute enough to look for bright policy ideas elsewhere. With both its budget and the nationwide economy improving, Philadelphia was well poised in the 1990s to capitalize on existing assets including its large and wealthy downtown residential population, the city's location close to New York City, and healthy and growing institutions, including several major universities and medical centers. What Philadelphia did not have was a positive development climate. No new office or market-rate residential buildings were constructed downtown throughout Rendell's two terms (1992–99.)

But Rendell's administration addressed this shortcoming as well. In 1997 the administration proposed a citywide residential tax abatement to incentivize conversion of vacant office space into apartments. This was not a new idea—New York had proposed such a policy for Lower Manhattan in late 1994 (Lueck 1994) and implemented it a year later—but again, Rendell's timing was excellent. A nationwide real estate boom was accelerating in the late 1990s, and Philadelphia's tax abatement was just the thing developers were looking for. Between 1997 and 2010 the tax abatement—which would be both extended in term and broadened in scope to include all new residential development—would generate an astonishing 12,385 new housing units within Center City (Center City District 2010). The peak of this construction wave was 2005–6, when the *Philadelphia Inquirer* could look at Center City, Philadelphia (Slobodzian 2005), and proclaim, "Renaissance!" The *Inquirer* dated Center City's rebirth "to the Rendell administration, the 1991 creation of the Center City District, and the unflagging optimism . . . of Paul Levy." Personal accolades aside, it was clear to all that when it came to downtown development, Philadelphia had done almost everything right since 1990. Center City really had experienced a renaissance, even if the convention center was a money-losing behemoth that required a $15 million annual subsidy in 2005 ("The Little Firehouse" 2008), and the Kimmel Center's acoustics were so poor that it required renovation only seven years after it opened (Dobrin 2008).

Philadelphia and Detroit were both shrinking cities, but Rendell's city was a very different one from his contemporary Archer's for many different reasons. In 1990 both cities were emerging from twenty years of flawed leadership and disastrous economic shifts, but Detroit was depressed at a citywide level, whereas much of Philadelphia, as we have already seen, was vibrant. And where Detroit was located far from other, healthier cities, Philadelphia was in the middle of Megalopolis between New York and Washington. Both Philadelphia and Detroit had severe housing and neighborhood problems, but these problems were also different in nature. Much of Detroit's housing was simply gone, but the survivors had the advantage of being on the whole much newer than Philadelphia's. Detroit's housing and its neighborhoods also conformed more closely to suburban standards because the city had always been lower-density. In contrast, Philadelphia suffered from row housing that was not only much older but also lacked most of the amenities expected in contemporary America, particularly space, privacy, and off-street parking. Conditions were particularly bad in the city's poorer neighborhoods, where families were often larger and the housing smaller.

During the course of the 1990s and early 2000s, the troubled cities of Detroit and Philadelphia diverged further as they enacted very different postrenewal rebuilding policies. Whereas Young and Archer's Detroit kept policy for the most part out of the city's rebuilding, Rendell's Philadelphia placed it at the center of its efforts to rebuild North Philadelphia. It was there that Philadelphia's rebuilding would demonstrate its most notable departures from Detroit's growth-machine-driven rebuilding, as well as some of that city's most unfortunate similarities.

OHCD's Policy Without Design

Almost immediately after Rendell took office in 1992, his administration placed a special emphasis on reinvigorating Lower North Philadelphia, the city's most chronically distressed area (Figure 4.1). Under the leadership of Office of Housing and Community Development (OHCD) director John Kromer the city would comprehensively rebuild part of Lower North Philadelphia with the guidance of a plan, something the city had not attempted since the Bacon days (Adams et al. 1991, 107–10). The centerpiece of these efforts was the 176-unit Poplar Nehemiah Houses, the largest North Philadelphia housing development since Yorktown and a resounding reminder that an interventionist public sector could comprehensively improve a depressed neighborhood. The Poplar homes were accompanied by a variety of other public-nonprofit efforts (market-rate development was not viable

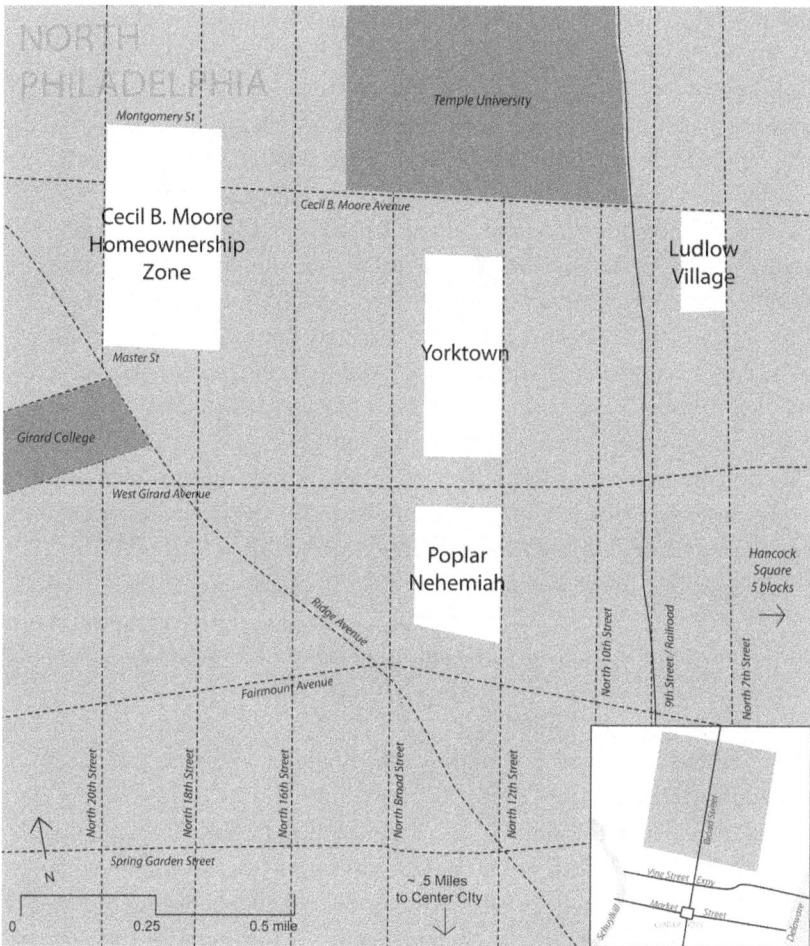

Figure 4.1. Overview map of North Philadelphia. Map by author. Map illustration by Sarah Spicer.

in North Philadelphia during the Rendell administration) between OHCD and a capable array of actors such as Asociación de Puertorriqueños en Marcha (APM) and the Ludlow Development Corporation. Late in Rendell's term OHCD was joined in its rebuilding by the Philadelphia Housing Authority, taking belated advantage of Clinton-administration HOPE VI funding to rebuild North Philadelphia's most problematic public housing. Together, as Kromer wrote, the rebuilding consortium led by OHCD made

Philadelphia's poorest neighborhood "less blighted and more attractive" (2010, 9).

OHCD's activist policy was very different from Detroit's, but the designs of the resulting new neighborhoods were distressingly similar. Ultimately, the Rendell-era rebuilding of North Philadelphia produced a series of housing developments that looked much the same and that all bore strong resemblances to postwar suburbia. Amid North Philadelphia's deteriorated row-house blocks, OHCD and its partner public and nonprofit agencies constructed standalone houses with pitched roofs, vinyl siding, attached garages, and spacious lawns. Admittedly, almost all of the houses were "twins" sharing a wall with an adjoining unit, but the iconographic intent of the homes was clear: Philadelphia was reconstructing its most distressed neighborhood in the image of the suburbs.

The process by which OHCD arrived at a suburbanization policy for North Philadelphia was also very different from Detroit's. The latter city, as we saw, more or less followed developer leads during the 1990s and early 2000s, with private or nonprofit investors initiating and designing proposals with variable amounts of public assistance. Rendell's OHCD, on the other hand, had from the beginning of the administration very clear ideas about where, when, and in what form the city would invest its limited funds in North Philadelphia. Where Detroit's suburbanization was attributable to market preferences, Philadelphia's was the direct result of public policy.

North Philadelphia's suburbanization, like that of the South Bronx, began in an era of crisis. In the early 1990s, few observers saw a development renaissance coming to North Philadelphia, or to Philadelphia in general. The private sector was particularly slow to awaken in the city: developers did not construct any privately financed housing of any size in the city until 2003, after Rendell had stepped down. In this climate, OHCD's decision to support redevelopment in North Philadelphia with publicly subsidized development was a wise decision. But where the South Bronx's development renaissance ultimately resulted in housing design shifting away from Charlotte Gardens' suburban model toward denser attached and multifamily housing, reform of subsidized housing design was slower to come to Philadelphia. Even though the market had already shifted to denser housing models, public and nonprofit builders continued to construct suburban-style housing in North Philadelphia right through the first decade of the twenty-first century.

Philadelphia initiated suburban design in its blighted neighborhoods in a moment of crisis but failed to reconsider this decision even when the crisis abated. From a pragmatic perspective one could argue that North Philadelphia's continued suburbanization hardly mattered; the homes were popular with residents, the suburban design model was a proven one, and there was little other market demand for the land, at least in the 1990s. But from either a progressive policy or a critical urban design perspective, North Philadelphia's continued suburbanization seemed both unnecessary and senseless, the more so because the city had constructed high-quality urban design models in the 1960s that provided the suburban amenities that lower-income residents wanted and deserved.

Post-1990 Philadelphia was a paradox: a city with one of the nation's most successful downtowns, a heritage of significant architecture and urbanism, and a progressive social policy apparatus operating in depressed neighborhoods with much need. From this perspective, the city's commitment to suburbanization in North Philadelphia was perhaps its most significant urban design failure of the postrenewal era. How did this failure come to pass?

Modernism's Legacy: The Rebuilding of North Philadelphia, 1940–90

The OHCD's 1990s design policy had its origin in North Philadelphia's fifty-plus-year-old history of mostly failed redevelopment programs that combined experimental design with poor postoccupancy outcomes. This association was a ghost that OHCD wished to exorcise (as did the federal government, at a much larger scale, in the HOPE VI program) as the agency once again attempted to redevelop the troubled neighborhood. This redevelopment history posed two major questions. If past projects had failed so dramatically, what should OHCD change to make redevelopment worthwhile again? And where should OHCD look for successful redevelopment precedents?

Redevelopment's beginning in North Philadelphia paralleled the area's racial transition from a white to a black neighborhood (Figure 4.1). Blacks began settling in large numbers in Lower North Philadelphia in the 1920s, and by 1950 the nonwhite population of Lower North Philadelphia comprised almost half its total. By 1980 the racial transition was complete:

Lower North Philadelphia was almost 90 percent nonwhite. As in Detroit, the new African American population was poorer than the one it had replaced, and housing abandonment and gradual population loss succeeded an initial period of overcrowding. Between 1950 and 1980, the area's population dropped 55 percent. Although most of its population was black, the eastern edge of North Philadelphia, which the city considered to be a different planning area, became the home for much of Philadelphia's Puerto Rican population.

Even in the 1930s, North Philadelphia was so clearly troubled that its redevelopment preceded that of Center City by more than ten years. In the late 1930s the city selected the neighborhood for its first two housing projects, the Glenwood and the Richard Allen Homes. These were completed in 1941 at 22nd and Diamond Streets and 11th and Poplar Streets respectively (Bauman 1987, 48). The city designated both for black tenants, which reflected the segregated policies of the era and the increasing concentration of black residents in the surrounding neighborhood.

As other authors (Vale 2000; Bauman 1987) have described, public housing was a new policy concept, and as such policy makers wished it to embody the latest design ideas. Philadelphia was no different from New York in this regard, where Bauhaus designer William Lescaze designed the city's first full-fledged public housing, the Williamsburg Houses, in 1938 along Modernist lines. Both the Glenwood and Allen Homes were inspired by the German *zeilenbau*, or "rows of buildings," principle of the Bauhaus (Bauman 1987, 25) (Figure 4.2). *Zeilenbau* designated most city streets as redundant, replacing them with pedestrian paths between buildings. To increase the amount of useful open space, *zeilenbau* concentrated houses at the periphery of superblocks, producing open spaces at the block centers. Designers intended these spaces for residents to congregate within the superblock instead of on public streets, which were often dirty, unpleasant, and filled with traffic.

Following passage of the Federal Housing Act of 1949, the Philadelphia Public Housing Authority constructed another public housing development, the Spring Garden Homes, at Spring Garden and 6th Streets between 1950 and 1952. The Spring Garden Homes and the neighboring middle-income Penn Town apartments were also *zeilenbau* designs. The projects closed all streets except major thoroughfares and sited apartment blocks along pedestrian walkways and open spaces designed for "community gatherings" (Bauman 1987, 113).

Figure 4.2. *Zeilenbau* meant "rows of buildings," and the term was certainly apt when applied to public housing, as in this development in Chicago. © 2011 Alex S. MacLean/Landslides.

One of Modernism's most notable features was its near-total rejection of the physical structure of existing cities. Le Corbusier's *Plan Voisin* was perhaps the most extreme expression of this approach, but Corbusier was not alone in despising historic fabrics: renderings of the 1920s by Mies van der Rohe and Hugh Ferriss also showed the existing city as dark and invisible amid the shining architecture of the new era. North Philadelphia's new housing developments were hardly signal examples of Modernism, but they too seemed to find little of value in the city's existing row-house neighborhoods. There were good reasons for this: existing housing in North Philadelphia was physically cramped and overcrowded, private outdoor space was minimal, and public outdoor space was scarce. It is little wonder that *zeilenbau* housing proposed the complete replacement of the row-house environment. *Zeilenbau* superblocks, with their garden apartments, green space, and pedestrian paths, introduced landscape, quiet, privacy, and space for automobiles into a neighborhood that historically had none of those features.

Zeilenbau urban design and architecture simultaneously rejected the parallel, rapidly growing built environment of the interwar and postwar years: suburbia. There was little of the picturesque in *zeilenbau*; winding paths, romantic architecture, and the mythology of the rural cottage had no place in Modernism's rationalist order. At the same time, *zeilenbau*'s focus, almost obsession, with automobile circulation, open space, and privatized community activity shared strong conceptual and physical similarities with suburbia, particularly those planned suburbs of the 1940s and 1950s such as Park Forest, Illinois, and Baldwin Hills Village, California, that fused *zeilenbau* iconography and building types with a certain picturesque attitude to landscape.

Closer at hand, North Philadelphia's *zeilenbau* blocks bore a certain resemblance to the lower-density versions of the Philadelphia row house that developers built in the outlying areas of the city in the 1950s and 1960s (Figure 4.3). The midcentury row house was a vernacular Philadelphia specialty, though other row house cities like Baltimore also had their own models. Descended from the nineteenth-century row house, such houses were popular with working-class whites in places like Packer Park, at the southern end of South Philadelphia, and in the Far Northeast in areas like Morrell Park. Midcentury row houses were also popular with developers because they were relatively dense: between 20 and 30 units to the acre. Developers constructed these houses in rows of as little as two and as many

Figure 4.3. Midcentury row houses, such as these in the Morrell Park neighborhood of Northeast Philadelphia, met expectations of both developers and aspiring working-class residents. The housing was not particularly pastoral, but it was a step up from denser, dilapidated areas of the city. Photograph by Daniel Campo.

as ten, but rows of six or eight were most common. Their concessions to suburban standards included private backyards—alleys were rare—ground floor garages and parking pads in front, as well as front yards where this space was not needed for parking. Houses were often located on short culs-de-sac, a feature that developers insisted on in Northeast Philadelphia against the wishes of the Philadelphia City Planning Commission (Heller 2009, 40). Houses were twenty to twenty-five feet wide, a great improvement over nineteenth-century standards. Midcentury row houses would not have seemed like much to a Detroiter, or to any city resident where row houses were not the vernacular, but to residents with very recent memories of the grim, crowded streets of Frankford or South Philadelphia, they were the local equivalent of Levittown.

In many ways, developers' midcentury row houses were a significant improvement over *zeilenbau* design. Density levels were equally high, and the abundant open space was mostly privatized, enhancing maintenance.

Each unit had a direct relationship to the street, with off-street auto storage, which provided convenience and safety. The only loss was public open space, which was overabundant in *zeilenbau* housing but scarce in the mid-century row house. Developments in the Far Northeast sometimes backed onto greenways, but public space within walking distance was usually rare. For its inhabitants, the greatest advantage of the midcentury row house was that it was more than the sum of its parts. It conformed to conventional social expectations of dwelling and as such was widely accepted. Row houses were part of the city's vernacular building culture and so midcentury row houses were an aspirational housing model for Philadelphians from older, poorer, lower-quality neighborhoods, a category that included the great majority of the city's African Americans.

All of the midcentury row house's advantages proved even greater when the model was transplanted into Lower North Philadelphia under the auspices of urban renewal. Between 1962 and 1972 the Philadelphia City Planning Commission (PCPC) constructed a 635-unit development called Yorktown, in partnership with suburban developer Norman Denny and William H. Grey, pastor of the Bright Hope Baptist Church. (Denny was a Revolutionary War enthusiast and named his development after the battle.) Yorktown was located at the deteriorated core of Lower North Philadelphia (Figures 4.1 and 4.4) and the site was occupied by row houses. Once planners had officially declared the site to be blighted, the federal government paid for two-thirds of its acquisition and clearance costs, totaling $5.5 million, under Title I of the 1949 Housing Act. The city cleared the dilapidated row houses by 1958, and Denny constructed the new houses over the next fifteen years. Residents occupied the last homes in the early 1970s. Pastor Grey intended the development to provide homeownership for working-class North Philadelphians, and Yorktown units ultimately sold for between $10,500 and $14,000, almost entirely to African Americans (OHCD 1996).

There is little indication that the PCPC provided any direct design guidance to Denny; Yorktown's housing, culs-de-sac, and overall appearance are all consistent with vernacular, midcentury row-house design. But in the context of North Philadelphia, and as a development alternative to *zeilenbau* or radiant-city tower blocks, Yorktown was truly revolutionary. Socially, it provided an unusual homeownership alternative for low-income African Americans, and in North Philadelphia it provided a unique design alternative to contemporary redevelopment projects. Yorktown's major design innovation was the application of the midcentury row house and

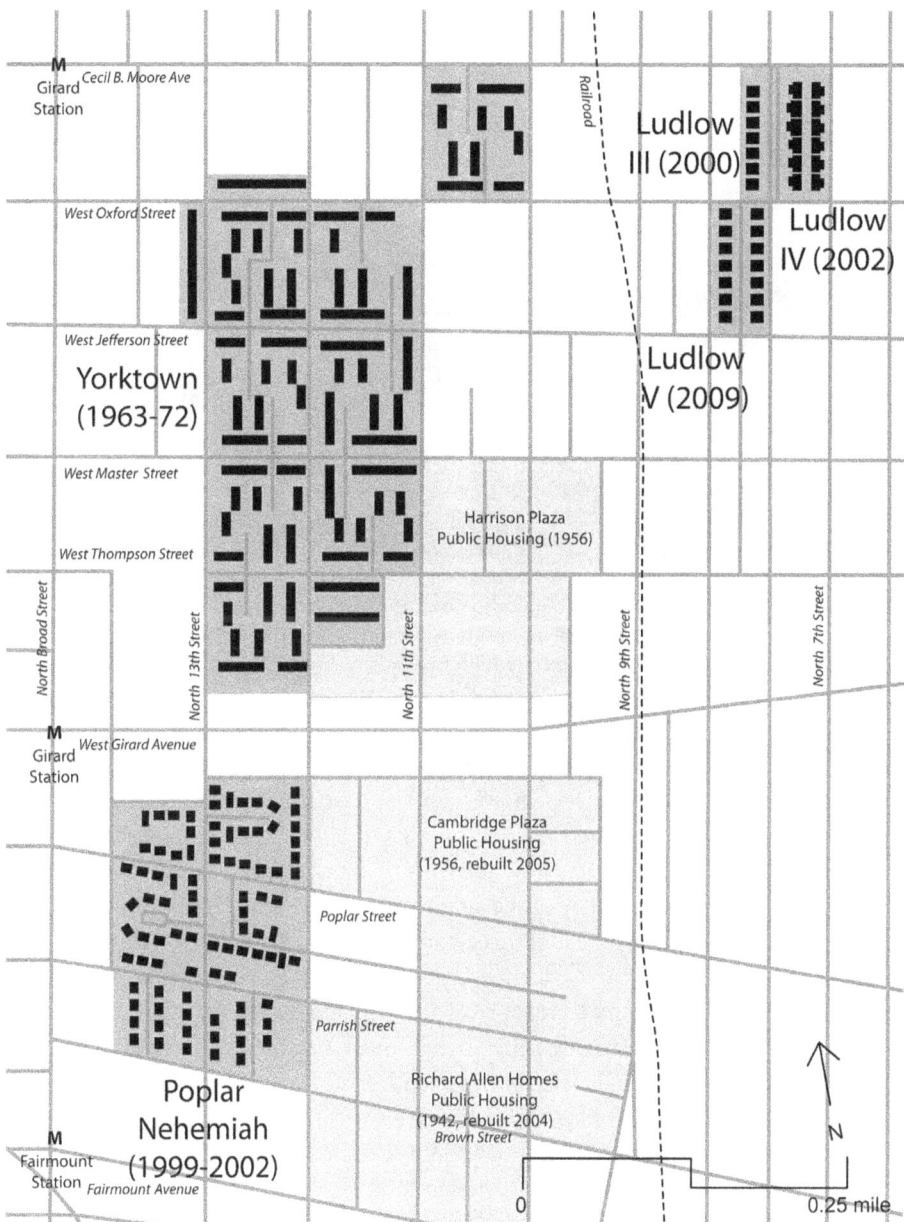

Figure 4.4. Detail map of Lower North Philadelphia, showing housing developments examined in this chapter. Map by author. Map illustration by Sarah Spicer.

Figure 4.5. Yorktown, a moderate-income development constructed in the 1960s in North Philadelphia, meshed resident aspirations with mild abstraction and sensitive urbanism. Photograph by Ellie Brown.

neighborhood model to the scale and block structure of North Philadelphia. The basic DNA of Yorktown was four- to six-unit clusters of row houses grouped around paired culs-de-sac linked by small (public) parks (Figures 4.5, 4.6). Yorktown removed the historic block structure, including minor streets and alleys, but retained major through streets. Houses were twenty feet wide and had two- and three-story models. The latter contained a garage on the first floor, the former simply a parking pad. Yorktown's urban design retained many features of North Philadelphia's historical urbanism but reduced housing densities by as much as two-thirds, from as much as 60 units per acre density in nineteenth-century row-house blocks (Ryan 2002, 362–71) to no more than 18 at Yorktown.

Unlike *zeilenbau* housing, Yorktown did not embody the latest in architectural or urban design thinking. Its design indicated the PCPC's acquiescence to suburban development standards (a battle that the commission also lost in the city's Northeast [Heller 2009, 39–42]), not the Modernist thinking that shaped projects like Society Hill. Yet it was Yorktown, not the *zeilenbau* projects nearby, that in retrospect provided a true revolution in

Figure 4.6. Yorktown houses feature attached garages, private yards, and spacious interiors, features associated more with the suburbs than with nineteenth-century Philadelphia housing. Photograph by Ellie Brown.

redevelopment thinking. In one fell swoop, the project provided nearly every physical attribute that one might hope for in social (homeownership) housing in a dense urban setting, except for mixed uses, which were banished to nearby shopping centers. Yorktown's design proffered a unique combination of multiple private spaces (cul-de-sac, backyard, local park); accessibility (nearby major streets, pedestrian connections to other culs-de-sac); spaciousness (wide house, front and back yards, and garage or parking pad); and urbanity (connection to adjoining houses, alignment with neighborhood streets and adjacent blocks, formal consistency with historic row houses).

Yorktown's urban design also possessed a systematic aspect that cemented the development's position as not only exemplary housing but exemplary urbanism. Both *zeilenbau* and the vernacular Philadelphia row house were highly systematic: building, open space, and street structure had a regular and consistent relationship that varied little by individual building. Philadelphia's historic street grid–row house combination was also a systematic element that adapted to the opportunities and constraints of the grid over a period of more than one hundred years (Ryan 1998). But both the row house and *zeilenbau* systems had flaws. Yorktown instead created a new systematic relationship between building, open space, and street in which each Philadelphia block was subdivided by two culs-de-sac and occupied by six groups of row houses ranging in length from five to eleven row houses. Like all systems, Yorktown's could be replicated by another architect, builder, or developer given approximately the same block pattern and building type. This replicability had already occurred across Philadelphia during the nineteenth century, and it firmly established Yorktown as a new urban design paradigm for the Philadelphia street grid. Yorktown's design improved upon the nineteenth-century Philadelphia row house and on Modernist design itself, providing by chance or by design an antithesis of both the *zeilenbau* public housing and the *Ville Radieuse*, all without surrendering to historicist nostalgia.

Despite these qualities, Yorktown was a redevelopment footnote during the city's 1970–90 "planning hiatus." Philadelphia did not construct any follow-up social housing of equivalent size during this period, and the housing that was constructed during this period was not as innovative as Yorktown, as we saw earlier. But Rendell's appointment of John Kromer in 1992 brought an official committed to interventionism and to constructing the sizable social housing development that the *North Philadelphia Plan* framers had called for but never realized. Upon entering office Kromer immediately initiated a policy process that explicitly reviewed goals, successes, and failures and then proposed a redevelopment strategy based on the findings. This does not sound very radical, but one has only to compare Philadelphia's approach with Detroit's rebuilding during the same era (1992–2000) to see just how unusual was Kromer's thinking.

OHCD's research and policy phase, carried out between 1993 and 1996, generated two reports with equally clear conclusions: future large-scale, publicly subsidized redevelopment in North Philadelphia should have much lower residential densities, and it should follow a design model drawn from outlying Philadelphia neighborhoods. The architectural model that OHCD chose to follow, however, was not the midcentury row house, constructed in rows of six or eight units, but the twin, conjoined, side-by-side single family houses that had no precedent in Lower North Philadelphia. Twins existed in abundance, OHCD noted, in outlying upscale Philadelphia neighborhoods such as Mount Airy and Chestnut Hill. Like the midcentury row house, twins offered privacy and off-street parking, and they offered even more space. Twins were "another tradition in planning and design . . .

[that] could be effective in inner-ring new communities," Kromer wrote later (Kromer 2000, 95).

In 1993 OHCD published a short study titled *Home in North Philadelphia* that analyzed existing redevelopment policy and suggested substantial changes. The plan drew two conclusions. First, the scattered redevelopment that had characterized North Philadelphia since the end of urban renewal (since Yorktown) was "fragmented," represented a "duplication of effort," and showed little "coherence" (OHCD 1993, 8–9). One consequence of fragmentation was that "some neighborhoods are over-funded, while most are under-funded" (12–13). This modestly stated conclusion quietly but firmly rejected the decentralized redevelopment policy that the federal government had called for in the Better Neighborhoods Act of 1974 and that Philadelphia had pursued for the past twenty years. *Home* was a call for top-down social planning as well as for greater social justice, as lower-density development provided a higher probability of more North Philadelphians having new development nearby.

Home's low-density policy was paradoxical. OHCD's plan to concentrate efforts in a single project resolved the problem of "leaving other portions [of North Philadelphia] . . . with far less funding than the amount needed to . . . lead to permanent improvement" (OHCD 1993, 13), but at the same time OHCD sought to *spread out* development to "revitalize acres—not just target blocks" (11), "generate more benefit to the acre," and "produce results over a broader area" (27). OHCD's explicit argument, in other words, was that the previously decentralized housing approach was both *too diffuse*, lacking any critical mass, and *too dense*, rebuilding row houses where they were neither desired nor useful. *Home* argued against rebuilding North Philadelphia at anywhere near its historic density, instead advocating a low density of ten units per acre for future projects.

Home's low-density housing policy clearly had North Philadelphia's major housing problems—poor condition, low values, and few amenities—in mind. Observing the steady abandonment of North Philadelphia's nineteenth-century housing, OHCD doubtless felt that row houses were unmarketable because they lacked amenities that low-income Philadelphians wanted, such as more space, privacy, security, quality, and community. These were amenities that OHCD felt were "practical and desirable" (1993, 27) in new housing. Low-density housing with the above amenities would possess more value, would be better maintained by their owners, and therefore would better merit the scarce public subsidies necessary to construct them. Reading *Home*, one senses OHCD's conviction that low-density housing was the only feasible model for future publicly subsidized new housing in North Philadelphia.

A second OHCD study, *Learning from Yorktown*, was published in 1996 and directly drew upon that earlier housing as a model. The study reviewed Yorktown's design and published the results of a survey of current Yorktown residents. The report concluded that Yorktown's low-density design provided stability and desirability, implying that Yorktown's design features should be replicated in future housing. The survey emphasized that Yorktown's residents particularly appreciated the community's "suburban" site planning and architecture, praising its "suburban style housing" in what they called a "suburb within the city." They also liked the physical features absent elsewhere in North Philadelphia, such as "less traffic [i.e., quiet streets], large yards, and play areas" and a lack of loiterer-attracting stores. Most Yorktown residents owned cars, and over 75 percent of survey respondents used automobiles to shop, an unsurprising statistic given North Philadelphia's poor retail options.

Residents also liked the way that Yorktown's design distinguished it from its (deteriorated) context. They attributed Yorktown's suburb-like design with providing a sense of community absent elsewhere in North Philadelphia. One resident emphasized that she lived "in Yorktown, not North Philadelphia." Others felt that Yorktown made "neighbors look out for children," providing "a cohesiveness of spirit" and "a sense of family and community" that made people remain in Yorktown. OHCD also noted that Yorktown homes had increased in value while the rest of North Philadelphia's values had declined. The homes' median sale price in 1991 was $54,000, and by 1997 Yorktown's values were between $60,000 and $70,000 ("Making Housing Affordable" 1997). Though these values were low in comparison to the suburbs, they were much higher than sale prices of older row houses nearby.

Yorktown's stability and success spoke volumes about the way design could make the difference in a troubled neighborhood. Its private yards, quiet culs-de-sac, garages, sense of community, and "suburban" image all seemed to have retained homeowners who might otherwise have left Lower North Philadelphia. OHCD's appreciation of Yorktown was astute. Yorktown was different from its surroundings, but unlike other Modernist developments Yorktown's residents perceived this distinctiveness as positive. Its distinction gave the development value and preserved it in an otherwise deteriorating place. Residents understood Yorktown's difference as aspirational, not stigmatizing, because it provided desirable features for working-class Philadelphians. In a row house city Yorktown's design provided a social status that had preserved the neighborhood, making it a location of choice for the working class as well as prominent Philadelphians like City Council President (and later Mayor) John Street.

OHCD clearly understood this; otherwise, *Learning from Yorktown* would never have been commissioned. But OHCD neglected the important design features that differentiated Yorktown from single-family suburbia and from row-house neighborhoods. Yorktown was dense, but unlike existing row houses it provided suburban features such as parking, privacy, a yard, and a spacious house. But Yorktown also had urban qualities such as attached housing, density, a formal link to its context, a streetwall, and pedestrian connections to the neighborhood. Yorktown's design subtly balanced the urban and suburban. Its owners understood this, just as they understood how this balance was missing in other postwar North Philadelphia developments. But OHCD did not, and as the agency embarked on its lower-density housing experiment in Lower North Philadelphia, this failure to understand Yorktown's subtleties would become clear.

Poplar Nehemiah: Suburbia Revisited

The Poplar Nehemiah Houses, or Poplar, were the largest housing development constructed in North Philadelphia in the 1990s and the showpiece project of the OHCD's low-density housing policy. Begun in 1997 and completed in 2001, Poplar's 176 homes occupied a rough quadrangle of twelve city blocks directly east of Broad Street (Figure 4.4). The development was only twelve blocks north of Center City. Poplar required substantial public spending and political will, and more than any other project it epitomized the Rendell administration's vision for the future of Philadelphia's shrinking neighborhoods. And as 1993's *Home in North Philadelphia* had promised, Poplar's design strongly differentiated the homes from its heterogeneous and deteriorated surroundings and established a distinctly suburban visual identity for the area.

The Poplar area was one of Lower North Philadelphia's most deteriorated neighborhoods, but it had once been one of its densest. In the mid-nineteenth century the area had a small-scale block pattern carpeted with row houses, with more than fifty units per acre. Each Poplar block

Figure 4.7. Poplar Nehemiah, a moderate-income development from the 1990s, followed Yorktown's precedent of lower housing densities but ignored the other architectural and urban design lessons from that earlier development.
Photograph by Ellie Brown.

contained dozens of row houses interspersed with alleys, giving the area a street network of almost medieval complexity. By the 1950s much of this housing was gone, replaced with industry and commercial uses, and by the 1990s even these uses were deteriorating.

In depressed Lower North Philadelphia, the completed Poplar homes were as surprising as Charlotte Gardens had been fifteen years earlier (Figures 4.7, 4.8). The project held 176 houses at 14 units per acre, and commercial and industrial uses were eliminated. Poplar's twin houses were conjoined single-family units sharing a party wall, with pad parking on either side of the building adjoining a gabled front porch. Homes had a nonstructural brick front facade and vinyl siding elsewhere. Poplar's yards were comparatively spacious: every house had open space on three sides. Pitched roofs completed the pastoral architectural image, reinforced by the transformation of two small east-west streets to culs-de-sac.

Poplar actually originated two years before OHCD created its low-density policy for North Philadelphia. A community group called Poplar Enterprise Development Corporation (PEDC) initiated schematic designs

Figure 4.8. Poplar Nehemiah houses were designed as attached twins with side parking pads and front and back yards. These modest amenities were unusual in North Philadelphia, yet they failed to provide the privacy and security found at Yorktown. Photograph by Ellie Brown.

for housing on the site in 1991 but lacked the resources to move the project forward. In 1992 and 1993 the city discussed the dormant project with PEDC before Rendell's OHCD committed to funding the project in mid-1993, by which time *Home*'s design policies were in effect. During 1994 OHCD and a project development team (PDT) discussed design issues, a phase that lasted several months. The development eventually began construction in 1997 and was completed in 2001.

Poplar began in 1991 when the U.S. Department of Housing and Urban Development approved the PEDC application for a $3.075 million Nehemiah Housing Opportunity Grant. HUD had created the Nehemiah Grant program in 1987 to assist nonprofit organizations with providing home-ownership opportunities (Cummings et al. 2002, 333). The HUD grant was limited to a $15,000 interest-free mortgage loan, a pittance compared to the Section 235 grants of the late 1960s and an amount that was clearly intended to minimize HUD liability in case of default. Like Yorktown, Nehemiah was intended for the "deserving poor"[1] just as the original Nehemiah program from East New York, Brooklyn, had been in the early 1980s (Plunz 1990, 330–34). In mid-1993 OHCD pledged $8.7 million in CDBG funds to match the $2.6 million in federal funds that were ultimately awarded. Total public subsidies for Poplar eventually came to $18.2 million, with the balance coming from Section 108 loans, which borrowed against future CDBG allocations (HUD 2011). The total cost of development per unit was $163,407, with public subsidies running $103,500 per unit (Cummings et al. 2002, 334–35). Eligible homebuyers had to earn between $18,900 and $30,650 per year (Northrup 1992). Homebuyers paid between $57,000 and $63,000 per house, making the mean homebuyer contribution only 37.5 percent of its total development cost. Poplar's final sales price was jointly determined by deliberations between OHCD and PEDC to make the homes affordable to householders earning approximately $22,500 per year (Kromer 1992), which was well within the range of eligible incomes for purchasers.

The Poplar grant came only after two years of grant-making efforts between the Poplar Community Development Corporation (a local CDC) and Philadelphia Neighborhood Enterprise (PNE), a local office of national affordable housing provider the Enterprise Foundation. The Nehemiah grant was modest, but that same year then-mayor Wilson Goode committed more than $8 million in city money to support a development to which the Nehemiah funds might be applied. This commitment, as Kromer would later dryly note, was premature, for the mayor had "supported . . . ventures which had not been derived from comprehensive neighborhood plans, [that] had not been substantively reviewed by City planning and development agencies . . . and [that] were not authorized by City Council" (Kromer 1993). In January 1992 PEDC, acknowledging that it needed city funds to complete the project, formally requested development assistance from OHCD for what was at the time a 205-unit development.

The Nehemiah funding determined that the Poplar homes would be entirely residential, precluding retail or other land uses, as well as "detached dwellings, townhouses, (or) condominium projects (with no more than) four units." The awarded grant did permit row houses to be interpreted as "townhouses" (Ryan 2002, 244), potentially permitting housing consistent with the row house context. PEDC's preliminary design from 1991 bore certain similarities to the neighborhood's older housing, with six-unit rows, rear parking, and the several new alleys. A public open space formed a rectangular central green at the core of the development (Figures 4.9, 4.10).

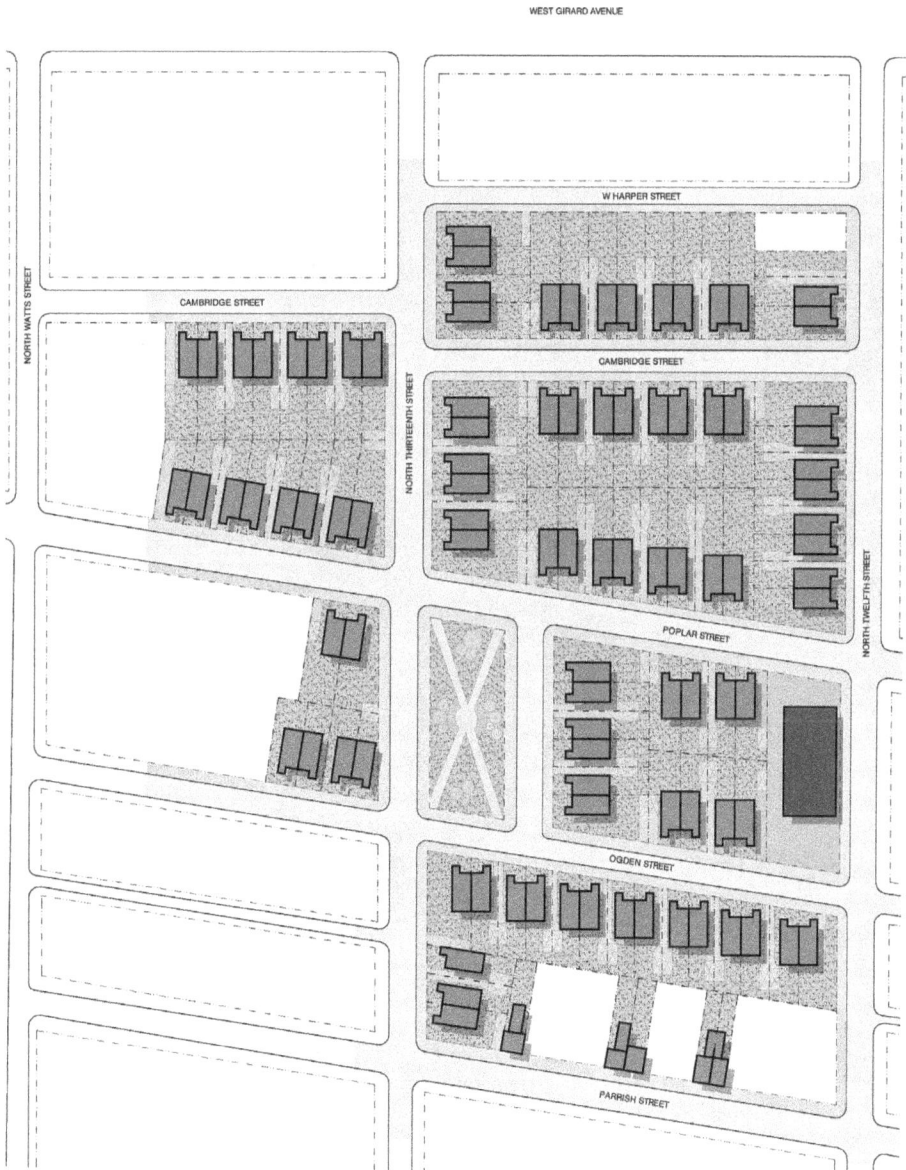

Figure 4.9. The April 1994 version of phase I of the Poplar development contained twin houses facing the street and a neighborhood open space. Courtesy KSK Architects Planners Historians, Inc.

Figure 4.10. The February 1995 final design for Poplar was similar except for the transformation of a secondary street into a cul-de-sac. Courtesy KSK Architects Planners Historians, Inc.

OHCD never seriously considered PEDC's preliminary design, for it felt that this attempt to replicate the historic neighborhood pattern would make the row houses difficult to market and that other housing types would have more value in the Poplar neighborhood. Kromer justified delaying the project on this basis (Kromer 1993). The central green space, however, would remain in the final design.

Home in North Philadelphia was published in July 1993 at a time when OHCD had just committed to funding the Poplar development, but the report's recommendations were revealed earlier in April, when Kromer noted that OHCD was "focusing on a smaller, lower-density first phase which will enable us to test the market potential for sales housing in Poplar" (Kromer 1993). In September 1993 PNE agreed to this lower-density approach, citing their desire to conform to *Home*. By the time design discussions began in earnest in 1994, Poplar's low density was already confirmed. As built, Poplar would be fifteen units an acre, higher than *Home*'s "recommended" ten units per acre but lower than the PEDC's original design of twenty-two units per acre.

Home specified that new developments should occupy several city blocks if possible. While Poplar's site met this criterion, it was partially occupied by deteriorated row houses and industrial structures. For the Poplar site to be buildable, it would have to be acquired and cleared by force. At OHCD's behest, Philadelphia's Redevelopment Authority (RDA) applied for the Poplar site to receive blight designation, which if approved would permit condemnation, forcible public purchase, and clearance of the land. In September 1993, the RDA certified to the PCPC that the Poplar neighborhood was a "blighted area." The RDA stated that the site possessed three blight criteria: "unsafe, unsanitary, inadequate, or overcrowded conditions," "faulty street or lot layouts," and "economically or socially undesirable land uses" (PCPC 1993). These urban-renewal-era blight criteria were not entirely applicable to the Poplar site in the 1990s. The overcrowding criterion was certainly no longer the case, as the area was half-abandoned, and planners in the 1990s no longer considered street layouts and mixed uses criteria for blight. The RDA therefore had to make some novel interpretations of the site, describing the area's abandoned lots and buildings as "unsafe and undesirable uses," which in a sense they were, and labeling the area's street grid as "faulty."

In February 1994 OHCD selected the architectural firm of Kise, Franks, and Straw (KFS) to design the area plan for Poplar. The firm was also

designated chair of the PDT, a group of area stakeholders with city and
community representatives including RDA, OHCD, PCPC, the Pennsylvania Horticultural Society (PHS), Enterprise Social Investment Corporation
(ESIC), and PEDC. The PDT met from March to October of 1994 to resolve
Poplar's site design. KFS then produced a final plan for the Poplar area in
February 1995, which the housing constructed between 1997 and 2001
would follow closely.

The Suburbanization of Poplar:
Urban Design Decision Making

Unlike Detroit's Victoria Park, where the development process was developer driven, OHCD's planning and design process at Poplar was public,
inclusive, and highly deliberative. While the PDT's mandate was not as
broad as it could have been, given that OHCD had already established a
low-density policy for Poplar and that a preliminary site design had already
been created, the rest of Poplar's design decisions came from the six-month
PDT process in 1994.

The PDT's design decisions ranged from large-scale site planning to
interior architectural issues (Table 4.1). The PDT first confirmed those design ideas proposed in the earliest plan for the site. PEDC and ESIC's first
scheme for Poplar from early 1992 featured a neighborhood open space, or
"village green," on 12th Street (Figure 4.9). KFS retained this open space,
though security concerns dictated low shrubs and a lack of seating. Nor did
the Philadelphia Parks Department want to commit to maintaining the
village green, so the nonprofit organization Philadelphia Green committed
to maintenance.

The PDT made several site planning decisions in April. Poplar's blocks
had alleys from the row house era. The PDT considered three street con-
figurations to make this pattern consistent with new housing. First, the
PDT eliminated alleys, citing security and sanitation problems. KFS's first
design scheme therefore removed three minor streets and several smaller
alleys. At a subsequent meeting, the PDT transformed two block-long
streets into culs-de-sac, noting that this would provide "enhance(d) security and privacy" (OHCD 1994). Kromer later stated that these culs-de-sac
sheltered Poplar both from deteriorated public housing and from busy
Broad Street traffic (Kromer 2010, 85).

Table 4.1. Design Decisions of the Poplar Nehemiah Houses Project
Development Team

Design Topic	Design Decision	Decision Discussion Dates
Street and block design	Eliminate alley streets	4/19
	Parallel parking along major streets	8/3
	Provide culs-de-sac	4/19, 4/28, 5/12, 5/25, 6/9, 7/8
Housing type	Twin houses	4/19, 4/28, 5/4
Access to houses	Front entrance facing street	4/19, 5/12, 5/18, 7/8, 8/19, 9/21, 9/22, 9/29, 10/6
Automobile access	Individual driveways	4/19, 5/4, 8/19, 9/21, 9/22
Distance of house from street	5 to 10 feet	4/19
Architectural image	Gabled, pitched roofs	4/19, 5/18, 10/6
Materials of house	Brick and stucco facades	4/19, 5/18
Internal site planning	Number, location of rooms, amenities	5/18
Neighborhood open space	Form and location of open space, relationship to neighboring houses	4/19, 4/28, 5/4, 5/12, 8/16

The PDT recognized that a lack of alleys would necessitate front parking for automobiles, and they therefore considered several parking alternatives including shared rear parking, individual front yard parking, front-access rear parking, and private side yard parking. The PDT quickly selected side yard parking to leave front and rear yards intact for lawns. PCPC members questioned this decision, for side yard parking would require a large number of curb cuts. The PDT therefore agreed that adjoining pairs of twin houses could share driveways, reducing the required number of curb cuts. Side yard parking, however, introduced another question: Would the front entrance to Poplar homes face the driveway or the street? This would prove a difficult question to answer.

Although the ten-unit-per-acre density advocated in *Home* made row houses unlikely at Poplar, the PDT considered many housing types ranging from row houses to single-family detached housing. Presented with photographs of a range of houses in different Philadelphia neighborhoods, the

PDT selected those in Mount Airy, a low-density neighborhood far from the city center. The team agreed early that twins would be Poplar's only housing type. Twins represented a clear compromise between OHCD's desired low-density level and the higher cost of individual houses. OHCD, still interested in even lower densities, requested KFS to evaluate the cost-effectiveness of detached housing, but KFS found that single-family homes would significantly increase per unit infrastructure costs, though no figures were cited.

North Philadelphia row houses generally fronted the street directly. The PDT decided to give the Poplar houses a "modest setback, 5 to 10 feet from the sidewalk." Setbacks would give each house a small front yard, an amenity found in Yorktown but otherwise rare in North Philadelphia. The PDT's stated aim for these modest front yard setbacks was to enhance privacy and security while retaining enough space for a back yard.

The PDT also discussed the architectural image that the houses should present. At its second meeting the team declared that the houses "should not look like public housing." This was a clear repudiation of the *zeilenbau* flat roofs and planar brick facades found in the nearby Richard Allen Homes public housing. The team noted that the upcoming HOPE VI reconstruction of the Allen Homes would replace its flat roofs with pitched roofs and that pitched roofs would also be appropriate for Poplar. With this decision the PDT abandoned a row-house feature that had persisted from the eighteenth century through Yorktown.

In May the PDT asked KFS to enhance the "variety" of Poplar's front facades. The PDT suggested a front porch. Variety, of course, was less typical than uniformity in row-house neighborhoods. The PDT then considered facade options, including brick, stucco, and even imitation wood siding. Area residents on the PDT selected brick and stucco as preferred materials, and KFS suggested different facade treatments—an all-brick front and a brick-and-stucco front—to provide the requested variety. The PDT selected an all-brick facade in front, with vinyl siding on the sides to save money.

Urban or Suburban? The Front Door Dispute

Little about Poplar's design was contentious. The PDT accepted the OHCD low-density mandates, and subsequent design decisions were made with little incident. But this consensus broke down over a seemingly insignificant question: What would Poplar's front doors face, the street or the driveway? To the PDT's community members, driveway-facing front doors would complement the otherwise consistent suburban feel of Poplar. But to other PDT members, particularly the city agencies, whether front doors would face the driveway or the street was a critical issue. The resulting dispute disrupted the PDT's consensus and nearly delayed the entire development.

In early PDT meetings, front door locations were the sole topic where community and city members differed strongly. City representatives stated early on their position that driveway-facing front doors would diminish houses' relationship to the street and neighborhood, while community members countered that driveway-facing front doors provided privacy and security. Given that agreement was not forthcoming, the PDT tabled this contentious issue in its early meetings, focusing on more easily resolvable items. In May 1994 OHCD suggested a second entrance facing the drive-ways to "ease the unloading of groceries." KFS did not take up this idea, and the homes were designed with a single entrance.

By summer KFS had produced detailed plans for house interiors. At this time, PDT members from the Enterprise Foundation attempted a compro-mise, again suggesting side doors to introduce OHCD's desired variety. ESIC acknowledged that side entrances would reduce the side yard size, or con-versely require more space between houses, further reducing density. They therefore suggested side doors only where "absolutely necessary." Commu-nity PDT members continued to support side entrances, and ESIC approved unit plans in late summer that featured side entrances on all homes.

The looming possibility of side entrances would have given both Poplar and the *zeilenbau* public housing entrances that did not face the street. This drove the city members of the PDT to exercise additional clout. PCPC members argued against side entrances, criticizing the infringement of side porches into the small side yards. PCPC members argued that the "somewhat-suburban" character of the homes would be lessened by side entrances, something that did not seem to trouble the PDT's community members. ESIC did not change their plans, however, so in early fall the PCPC again protested the proposed side entrances (Leonardo 1994).

The PCPC cited two reasons why front-facing entrances were preferable. The first cited defensible space theory (Newman 1972), an anti-Modernist ideology that advocated entrances facing public space to promote activity, watchfulness, and safety there. The PCPC also expressed concern that side entries would give "undue prominence to the automobile" by forcing cars further into the front yards of houses (Leonardo 1994). Other members of the PDT weighed in. The Horticultural Society joined the PCPC in speaking against side entrances, citing defensible space concerns for the "village green" and a reduction of residents' ability to create pleasant gardens in their "arrival zone" (Mishler 1994).

In the face of these concerns, PEDC emphasized community members' support for side entrances. In late September PEDC sent an open letter to the PDT explicitly stating community preferences for side entrances. Community members stated that houses "felt bigger" when entered from the side and that side entrances permitted split-level plans like suburban ranch houses. PEDC then argued that side entrances were actually more contextual. Residents stated that "front porches are not a prevalent feature in this neighborhood. . . . [Side entrances] will help to maintain the character of West Poplar" (PEDC 1994). PEDC provided more reasons, including additional privacy and the possibility for ornamental bay windows in front if entrances were removed. Finally, PEDC argued that the city's vision of defensible space was false, as much of Poplar faced deteriorated (i.e., insecure) surroundings or busy streets, including the vacant (in 1994) Richard Allen Homes. At the next PDT meeting, the PEDC attempted to refute the defensible space argument with testimony from the Philadelphia Police Department. A representative of the local police district testified that side entrances "(did not) pose a security issue." (OHCD 1994). The officer suggested that outdoor lighting, motion sensors, and window guards could adequately address security concerns.

Community's convictions did not sway the PDT's city members, who stood firm that Poplar's front doors would face the street. The PDT's final meeting in October focused solely on this final design issue. At this meeting, OHCD, RDA, and PCPC representatives stated "strong opposition, at both the staff and director level, to an all-side yard entrance site plan." To bring the point home, these members then stated that the city "would only support a plan similar to the preliminary plat plan that featured mostly front entrances" (OHCD 1994). This adamant and thinly veiled reference to the city's control of the purse strings won the day. A week later the PEDC board approved a Poplar plan with front entrances.

Like many picayune issues that disrupt design review committees everywhere, Poplar's front door dispute was shorthand for a larger, more important, and more ethereal issue. Here, the real issue was whether or not Poplar was primarily "urban" (part of its neighborhood, related to its neighbors, and part of the Philadelphia housing tradition) or "suburban" (standalone, pastoral, private, and auto oriented). The irony of the dispute was that the city's intransigence over the project's front doors had little to do with the actual urbanity of the project. At fifteen units per acre, Poplar was close to Yorktown's density as well as Detroit's Jefferson-Chalmers in 1950; Philadelphia's new neighborhood had sidewalks, streets, and front-facing houses, but the houses lacked any typological connection to the surrounding neighborhood; twins had nothing to do with the "vernacular tradition" (Rowe 1993, 281) of North Philadelphia.

Nor did the Poplar Houses possess any meaningful relationship to each other. Apart from the homes' minimal vernacular architecture, the irregularity of the site meant that almost every block was a different size and shape, with remaining structures on part of almost every block. The site's low density meant that Poplar, at least in its early years before its vegetation matured, had the feel of a lightly populated space within a bleak cityscape. The site was just small enough to lack a feeling of self-enclosedness, and the placement of the homes was irregular enough to remove the sense of Yorktown's consistent neighborhood pattern. Of course, Yorktown had an extremely regular block system; Poplar's irregularity was not the designers' fault, but the density and siting of its homes did little to alleviate the almost random nature of the neighborhood design. Houses were sited more or less casually, sometime facing north-south streets, sometimes facing east-west, and sometimes facing neither because they were oriented to culs-de-sac or to the cardinal axes instead of to the street they were facing. The result was a not-so-studied irregularity that, again, was almost unknown in Philadelphia, where dense row-house arrangements always gave first priority to the street directly in front of the house and always generated part of a larger streetscape as a result.[2]

Poplar's superficial material contexualism and formal historicism only lightly disguised the houses' true ties to suburbia. Front porches and front-end gables, as PDT residents correctly noted, did not exist in historic North Philadelphia, nor for that matter did vinyl siding, culs-de-sac, or front, side, or rear yards. Poplar's use of brick on its front facade feebly disguised its deeper anticontextualism. Residents who argued for side doors were simply recognizing this deeper quality: the houses' "contextual" street-facing doors were a red herring.

Unfortunately, the "completion" of the Poplar site with housing did not provide completion to the neighborhood at a larger scale. Instead, Poplar continued the fragmentation of Lower North Philadelphia's cityscape that abandonment had begun. With the completion of Poplar, a new vision of the Philadelphia cityscape appeared that even the *zeilenbau* housing had not achieved, in which the city as a series of bounded spaces and coherent urban facades simply ceased to exist, and where buildings became objects more or less loosely floating in space, surrounded by variably green, variably public, variably active spaces. The modestly designed houses at Poplar were ironically more Modernist in this sense than any previous buildings in North Philadelphia, with the arguable exception of the neighborhood's few public housing towers. Like Yorktown, Poplar's unexceptional design cloaked a radical urban intervention, one that would soon be joined by equally modest, equally radical developments.

No one, including John Kromer, would argue that Poplar was a design masterpiece, and he has addressed criticisms relating to "smart growth" (density) and the site's lack of mixed uses in his writings (Kromer 2010, 86–87). Admittedly, Poplar was a low-budget project produced under difficult circumstances, under a policy regime that other cities such as Detroit did not even possess. The OHCD policy process that produced Poplar was exemplary in both execution and in much of its conception, and the results were in a sense successful: the houses were constructed, after all, and today, almost ten years after their construction, they are not only well maintained but have appreciated tremendously: in 2010, one Poplar home was for sale for $250,000. The house was likely overpriced, for the house did not sell and was soon listed for rent for $1,700 per month.[3] But the value increase shows that from a market perspective there is little to criticize about Poplar, and that just as Charlotte Gardens and Victoria Park may have represented the maximum achievable results under difficult circumstances, so may have Poplar.

But Poplar, like Victoria Park, set a disturbing design precedent. The full weight of the city's policy infrastructure (together with federal funding and redevelopment powers) stood behind its 176 houses, and Poplar quite forcefully implemented the OHCD's emerging redevelopment policy. Given Poplar's signal status, it is little wonder that it would have an influence on later subsidized housing developments in Lower North Philadelphia. As a result, Poplar was far from the only "suburban-like" housing constructed in North Philadelphia during the 1990s. Two of the largest of these other developments, the Cecil B. Moore Homeownership Zone and Ludlow

Homes, illustrate how Poplar's low-density cityscape influenced the further suburbanization of North Philadelphia.

Suburbia, Continued: The Moore and Ludlow Homes

In 1991, when the Poplar CDC applied for the Nehemiah grant that ultimately generated the Poplar homes, a nearby CDC made a similar application for its own housing. National Temple CDC, a neighborhood group operating in an area northwest of Poplar along Cecil B. Moore Avenue, also wanted to revitalize their neighborhood with a Nehemiah grant, but the city delayed consideration of the Temple Nehemiah application for four years, because the city perceived organizational problems that would make it difficult for the CDC to administer the grant. By 1995 HUD had withdrawn funding from the Nehemiah program, but OHCD committed to funding the project through other means should they become available. These means became available in April 1997 when OHCD received a HUD Economic Development Initiative (EDI) grant for $5.52 million. EDI was a Clinton-administration effort to fund housing within designated "homeownership zones" that met specific economic and physical distress criteria (OHCD 1996; HUD 1996). EDI envisioned that new for-sale homes would encourage middle-income homeowners to invest in distressed neighborhoods. Unlike the Poplar homes, which were sold to relatively low-income buyers earning around $20,000 per year, HUD intended homeownership zone housing to be sold to households earning up to 20 percent more than the city's median household income ($37,090 in 2008), so as to diversify incomes in distressed neighborhoods. OHCD's 1997 award formally created the Cecil B. Moore Homeownership Zone, and the new housing constructed within that area would also be known by that name.

With EDI funding together with an additional $18 million in Section 108 loans, OHCD proposed 214 new and 82 rehabilitated houses (296 total) in the area bounded by Bouvier Street, 20th Street, Master Street, and Montgomery Avenue, Wesson Street, and Marsh Street (Johnson 1998, 3A) (Figure 4.1). OHCD and its nonprofit partner, the Philadelphia Housing Development Corporation, developed the Moore homes in several phases. Phase I, completed between 1999 and 2002, had 71 new and rehabilitated units, with a total cost of $11.3 million, or $155,000 per unit; phase II, built between 2001 and 2004, had 51 new and rehabilitated units for $11.2 million, or $220,000 per unit (PHDC 2010; OHCD 2011). Construction of these phases of the Moore Homes was financially troubled: expenses were higher than forecast because of subsurface soil problems (Wilds 2002, personal communication), and the project languished until a new developer, OKKS Development, took control of the project in 2004. Whereas phases I and II had operated on a block-by-block infill pattern, OKKS favored a Poplar-style "master plan" approach with larger, more contiguous development sites. Between 2004 and 2007 the developer assembled additional land owned by the Housing Authority and private owners (Caulfield 2009). By the development's closeout in 2010 the Homeownership Zone had cost the city $34 million, nearly twice as much as originally projected. Additional public funds came from the Neighborhood Transformation Initiative, a post-Rendell vacant space effort that is discussed in Chapter 5, as well as other federal, state, and city funds (OHCD 2011).

Phase I of the Cecil B. Moore development established that Poplar's suburban design would also shape that of the Homeownership Zone. Though the Moore site was more densely developed than Poplar, with many existing large row houses, many early Moore design features were similar to Poplar, and this relationship increased in the lower-budget phase III (Figures 4.11, 4.12). Phase I of Moore was also low density: 15 units per acre in a neighborhood that had historically had 70, covering only 21 percent of the average lot (Ryan 2002, 370–71). Also like Poplar, all 214 new Moore houses were detached twins, with the addition of attached front-entry garages. Garages were eliminated in phase II because of soil conditions (Wilds 2002, personal communication) but returned in phase III.

Reflecting their intended middle-class audience, the first two phases of the Moore houses, designed by Kise, Franks and Straw and Cassway Albert, had an architectural quality markedly higher than Poplar. Moore's architecture integrated forms and materials like pitched roofs, street-end gables, and colored brick that were more characteristic of Victorian-era railroad "suburbs" such as Germantown and Mount Airy than North Philadelphia. Gabled front porches mirrored roof gables, and diverse cladding materials alluded further to polychromatic Victorian housing. Street facades were clad in brick, and vinyl siding covered the gables and side walls. Brilliant blue front doors and porch columns made the homes colorful and cheerful. On their own, phase I and II of the Moore houses would not have been out of place as infill housing in Mount Airy or Germantown. Their architectural

Figures 4.11. Cecil B. Moore Houses phase I. The first phase of this moderate-income North Philadelphia housing attempted, with some success, to emulate the Victorian-era vernacular of outer-city neighborhoods like Mount Airy. Photograph by Ellie Brown.

detail was no worse than infill housing elsewhere in the city, and it was better than many such projects in higher-income neighborhoods. KFS's design clearly indicated Moore's residents' middle-class status, and as a result it was criticized as overelaborate by some city officials.

The "fancy" design of the first two Moore phases (Pope 1997) contributed to their cost overruns, and phase III, in the hands of a national affordable housing developer and out of the hands of KFS, was a markedly less attractive, more conventional housing model with few frills. Reflecting the problems that had bedeviled the past two phases and exhausted the original HUD funding, phase III was simple slab-on-grade construction. The ornamentation that had marked the previous two phases departed in favor of an inexpensive suburban model with a minimum of brick on the front facade and artificial shutters. No architect was required: OKKS was economical, and it showed in the homes' design, but phase III's economy was also effective: all 151 remaining units were completed within three years,

Figure 4.12. Cecil B. Moore Houses phase III. Cost overruns led to a markedly simpler and more suburban final phase. Photograph by Ellie Brown.

selling at $110,000 each. Homes sold quickly: the project was "an overwhelming success, including a rapid sell out," according to the developer (OKKS 2011).

While the budget suburban form of phase III reflected its developer's not irrational wish to complete the project on time and minimize cost overruns, the basic suburban design parameters of all three Moore phases were shaped by a project development team similar to that which had guided Poplar. Following Poplar's precedent, OHCD convened a Moore PDT for several months in 1995, before the project was even funded, to establish design policies. The PDT's composition was similar to Poplar's and included several community residents. The Moore PDT recorded meeting minutes, and their recommendations were published in the *Neighborhood Housing Strategy for the Cecil B. Moore Area* (RDA 1996) released in February 1996.

The Moore site confronted the PDT with conditions very different from those at Poplar. The Moore site was much more dispersed and included several blocks of existing row houses that were architecturally distinguished and up to four stories in height. Total site clearance was therefore out of the question. The PDT's original conception was that the contiguous new neighborhood fabric of the Poplar homes could not be re-created and that new homes would in many cases adjoin existing row houses. Despite the very different neighborhood setting, the Moore PDT's design decisions were very similar to Poplar's. The team's final report stated the following design recommendations:

- New housing would be low in density and would generally take the form of twin houses. Twins were relatively inexpensive to construct and allowed "contemporary amenities such as yards and off-street parking."
- The neighborhood's urban design would be altered to the extent possible. Where there was sufficient land, streets would be "eliminated and redesigned to provide more generous sites for new houses and to help reduce densities."
- Contextual design was not desirable. Neighborhood and building designs would "contrast with the older deteriorating fabric of the area and project a new image for the community."
- Wherever possible, new houses would be set back from the street and have side yard parking, porches, and rear yards. New homes would have pitched roofs to "contrast with the existing fabric."
- The context would in some cases be preserved. Existing row houses with "significant architectural merit" or "existing strong blocks" of occupied homeownership houses would remain. (RDA 1996, 12, 23)

The Moore team's recommendations reflected the PDT's collective wishes for a low-density neighborhood. Their decision meshed with *Home*'s low-density policy for Lower North Philadelphia, but it also meshed with community desires to "project a new image" for the neighborhood with the new houses. The desired new neighborhood was one with detached homes, private yards, off-street parking, larger lots, fewer small streets, and a different "image" from North Philadelphia's dilapidated row houses. The suburban inferences of these guidelines were clear, and in the Homeownership Zone they would be realized in both their most expressive (phase I) and reductive (phase III) form. From the perspective of Philadelphia urbanism, phase III's close resemblance to Jefferson Village and other similar suburban-type developments in Detroit was regrettable, but from its home-owners' perspective the similarity of the two inner-city suburbs would likely not have been troubling at all (compare Figure 3.6 with Figure 4.12).

Another example of Philadelphia's reductive 1990s design approach to rebuilding in Lower North Philadelphia was Ludlow Village, a series of small developments (twenty-three units in the first three phases, twenty-five in the fourth, and twenty-two in the fifth) constructed between 1997 and 2008 (Figure 4.4). As at Moore, Ludlow's last two phases were mark-edly more suburban in design than its first three. Ludlow was less ambi-tious in scale than either Poplar or Moore, which reflected its origin in the struggles of the Ludlow Development Corporation (LDC), a neigh-borhood CDC, to produce new housing for its residents in this most disinvested of North Philadelphia's many troubled neighborhoods. LDC and partner developer the Philadelphia Housing Development Corpora-tion intended Ludlow III, IV, and V for low-income homebuyers earning less than 80 percent of the Philadelphia metropolitan area's median in-come (Wilds 2002, personal communication), and the houses were priced accordingly: Ludlow Village III homes sold in 1998 for only $42,000, a price that required only $291 in mortgage payments per month, and Ludlow IV in 2001 for $45,000, with a mortgage payment of $440 per month (PHDC 1998, 2001).

Despite their small scale, Ludlow IV and V's site planning and architec-ture were distinctly suburban. Ludlow IV had a density of twenty-five units per acre, higher than either Poplar or Moore, but its design provided a spaciousness absent in other suburban-style redevelopments (Figures 4.13, 4.14). The most distinctive neighborhood design feature was a planted mall in the center of Franklin Street, Ludlow IV's western boundary. This space provided a symbolic "town green" for the Ludlow Village complex.

Ludlow IV and V's housing was unexceptional, but like Moore and Poplar it contrasted strongly with historic row houses and even with Lud-low III. Ludlow IV houses had two stories, with pitched roofs, front gables, and wraparound front and side porches. Ludlow V strongly resembled phase III of the Moore Houses, with two-story twin homes with a modest brick facing and a small front porch. Unlike Moore, Ludlow V had some neotraditional leanings: half of the homes had parking pads accessible from a rear minor street, while the other half had front parking pads like those at Poplar.

Figure 4.13. Ludlow Village phase III. An early phase of this low-income housing in eastern North Philadelphia attempted to emulate the row house while providing private outdoor space for unit owners. Photograph by Daniel Campo.

Unlike the Poplar and Moore houses, Ludlow's suburban architecture was not motivated by a PDT process. At Ludlow IV, its architects, the firm of Buell Kratzer Powell (BKP), were largely responsible for its design. BKP provided two reasons for Ludlow's suburban appearance. The first was that community residents, together with the Ludlow Development Corporation, wanted a "more suburban-like" image than earlier Ludlow phases had provided. The personal design preferences of the LDC's chairperson, Marvin Lewis, were apparently also influential in the decision to move away from a low-density, row-house-like model to a low-density, suburban model. And although LDC's instructions for Ludlow V were for BKP to design housing that looked "more like the older neighborhood fabric" than Ludlow IV did (Wilds 2002, personal communication), the constructed housing looked more suburban than ever.

Figure 4.14. Ludlow Village phase IV. The subsequent phase of this housing was markedly simpler and more suburban, with features like pitched roofs and vinyl siding. Throughout the 1990s and the first decade of the 2000s, North Philadelphia public and nonprofit housing design rejected the very architectural and urban design features that higher-income residents were moving into the neighborhood to attain. Photograph by Daniel Campo.

Modernism's Return: Lower
North Philadelphia Between Crises

In an end-of-2010 interview for the *PlanPhilly* development Web site (Kerkstra 2010), the chief of development for Asociación de Puertorriqueños en Marcha, a sister CDC to the Ludlow Development Corporation, spoke with a reporter candidly about the design choices that Lower North Philadelphia was facing. "You may look around and say this is very eclectic," she said, referring to the contrast between APM's suburban-style homes and the "cutting-edge, overtly-green" design of some new APM housing planned for the neighborhood. "It's not just eclectic. It's what our community wants. Their desires. Their ability to get a suburban style house. Their ability to get a totally green house."

APM's new awareness of "cutting-edge" architecture reflected the sea change that had occurred in Lower North Philadelphia in the twenty years since 1990. A neighborhood that housing economists described without exaggeration in 2002 as a "low quality of life community" with "some of the highest poverty census tracts in the city" (Cummings et al. 2002) had become, by 2010, the western fringe of the Northern Liberties neighborhood, one of Philadelphia's "hippest, most overpriced, and most rapidly developing neighborhoods" (Kieran 2008). Since 2000, young, wealthy Philadelphians had moved north from Center City, seeing in Northern Liberties what the creative class saw in postindustrial neighborhoods everywhere—cheap space, convenient access to downtown, and a gritty place with narrow streets, old brick row houses, and a mixed-use fabric of small shops, warehouses, and open spaces—a place to be creative or just to feel like one was escaping the everyday conformity of conventional neighborhoods. What the new Northern Liberties residents also wanted, of course, was the surviving historic fabric of lower North Philadelphia, an environment that was the antithesis of what public agencies like OHCD and nonprofit developers like APM had been shaping for the past twenty years. APM's shift to "green" housing was a savvy but belated acknowledgment that Lower North Philadelphia was changing and that the visual language of new development was changing along with the neighborhood's demographics.

By 2010 modern architecture had arrived in North Philadelphia on both its eastern and northern edges. In Northern Liberties, the "Corbusier-inspired" (Saffron 2006) Hancock Square had narrow, twelve-foot-wide one-bedroom apartments renting for $1,350 per month. While the Corbusian analogy was perhaps a stretch, Hancock Square's abstract design and substantial scale (three 200- to 400-foot-long, six- to seven-story concrete slabs) did evoke midcentury New York projects like I. M. Pei's Kips Bay Plaza more than it did the smaller-scale, rather conservative urbanism of Philadelphia. Located on a long-vacant former industrial site, Hancock Square and its associated retail and semipublic open space provided a new aesthetic and a new type of public space in a neighborhood long accustomed to modest row houses and hulking factory buildings.

Hancock Square was less than a half-mile east of the Poplar Nehemiah Houses, which as we saw were themselves renting for $1,700 per month by 2010. The *Inquirer*'s architecture critic imagined that she saw Hancock "soaked through with the calloused, working-class feel of the city's old row-house neighborhoods" (Saffron 2006), but the building's "calloused feel" did not diminish its high prices, nor did it make Hancock Square's "row-house" units large enough for the "working-class" families who still lived in Northern Liberties. Hancock Square was sophisticated design, but no one could argue that the development was anything but luxury housing.

Elsewhere, at the northern edge of Lower North Philadelphia, rapidly expanding Temple University stimulated the development of the neighborhood's first movie theater in thirty years in 2006, together with a twelve-story, eight-hundred-room "dorm-style" residence hall along Broad Street, designed as a single wall of folded glass and concrete, together with a "swoopy" two-story commercial building that housed the movie theaters. Only a few blocks east of the Cecil B. Moore Homeownership Zone, "an estimated 45 developers" hungrily eyed the "abundance of barren lots and the guaranteed clientele" (Clark 2010) that Lower North Philadelphia and Temple respectively provided.

In 2010 one era of crisis in Lower North Philadelphia—urban decline—seemed to be over, but another was perhaps beginning. Temple students were moving into Yorktown, and late-night parties, overcrowding, and trash-strewn front lawns were now residents' main concerns, together with a thinly veiled skepticism of the racial diversity that white students brought to the formerly African American development. The crime-filled Cambridge Plaza and Robert Allen public housing developments that had statistically so stigmatized the neighborhood at the beginning of the decade were gone, replaced by HOPE VI housing that was if anything more suburban than the Poplar housing directly across 12th Street (Figure 4.4). John Kromer (2010, 94) noted that the new homes appeared almost to be "a subsequent phase of the West Poplar [Poplar Nehemiah] homeownership development." Taking a cue from Poplar, the new Cambridge Plaza/Richard Allen Homes had twin houses with brick front facades, vinyl siding, side parking, and front doors with modest porches that faced the street. In all substantive respects they were identical to the Poplar homes, except for their profusion of front gables, which gave the HOPE VI project a link to vernacular suburbia that even Poplar had failed to provide.

Across Lower North Philadelphia the stage seemed set for a transition from the twentieth-century struggle against poverty, crime, and decay to a twenty-first century one against the improving, and excluding, power of the market and the upper middle class. Lower North Philadelphia, in short, seemed to be gentrifying on all sides. Were further gentrification to occur in Lower North Philadelphia, as it seemed to be at the end of the first decade of the 2000s, familiar battle lines would soon be drawn between older, lower-income, ethnic residents and younger, wealthier, mostly white residents. The terms of the struggle would also be familiar. "Affordable housing" or "inclusionary zoning" would become the battle cry, as it already was in New York, Boston, and Washington, D.C., where the market had long been making inroads into depressed neighborhoods. In a 2009 interview with the *Philadelphia Daily News* on the future of North Philadelphia, John Kromer argued that the suburban-like housing constructed by the OHCD policy process after 1993 had in fact spurred market interest, because it "helped to save the area." Subsidized housing, said Kromer, "gave developers more confidence in the area," (Russ 2009), implying that Poplar and its related developments' aim had been to promote gentrification.

In fact, OHCD had originally intended Poplar to be something quite the opposite. *Home* argued in 1993 that new subsidized housing should "offset development pressure" and "protect the area as an affordable housing resource" (1993, 5). In any event, the ability of OHCD's subsidized housing to improve surrounding neighborhood conditions was dubious. A 2002 study found no impact on these conditions by Poplar in its first few years, concluding that "real estate activity and trends in real estate prices in the Nehemiah tracts resemble those in other poor tracts in the city." Nor did the researchers find that Yorktown had any impact either, even though it had been there much longer. Examining sales data from 1986 to 1997, the researchers found "no impact of proximity to Yorktown on real estate prices in neighboring areas" (Cummings et al. 2002, 351–52).

Notwithstanding Kromer's claim, one could draw quite the opposite conclusion from the construction of Poplar, Yorktown, and other social housing developments, namely that their primary benefit was the high-quality housing they provided their low-income inhabitants, not their leveraging of private market action. The evidence that Yorktown and Poplar did not change neighborhood conditions is only an effective argument against social housing from a neoliberal perspective on revitalization, where increasing private values is the paramount aim. From a social perspective, however, the fact that Yorktown provided stable and desirable housing for 435 moderate-income African American households over a thirty-year period in which the surrounding neighborhood got worse, not better, was a

tremendous achievement in and of itself. In Detroit, Lafayette and Elmwood Park provided similarly stable housing with markedly more suburban
designs. But social housing's role as an endogenous benefit to its inhabitants rather than a exogenous benefit to its (hopefully gentrifying) surroundings had substantially diminished by 2010, when the future of social
housing in neighborhoods across the United States was its cross-subsidizing
by the market, either as "inclusionary" units (e.g., Lerman 2006; Morgan
1995) or in mixed-income, market-subsidized developments such as
HOPE VI.

With the coming of contemporary "sustainable" design to North Philadelphia, which APM's development director described as "going from the
dark ages somewhat into the enlightened ages of real sustainable development" (Kerkstra 2010), one could see another battle line being drawn in
North Philadelphia, between abstract design associated with higher densities, high-income housing, and "green" technology, and vernacular design
associated with low densities, low-income housing, and public subsidy.
APM, as we observed previously, was strategic in laying claim to the prestige
associated with contemporary design, but doing so may have been somewhat misguided. Abstract, modern design is not always good, nor is it
always bad; by the same token, vernacular suburban design was unsophisticated urbanism whose real benefits to homeowners risked being lost in
highly abstract design. Low-income Philadelphians preferred vernacular design, whether at Yorktown or Poplar, because they were looking for "what
all folks are looking for," as another CDC official noted. At its best, vernacular design provided benefits like relatively familiar image, personalizabil-
ity, a relationship to the rest of the city, and a recognizable distinctiveness
that provided neither prestige nor stigma. All of these features are aspects
that Rowe (1993) recognized as elements of admirable modern housing,
and these aspects were just as critical in North Philadelphia as they were in
low-income environments anywhere in the world.

To end the story here would ignore the precedent that North Philadelphia's postdecline suburban design seemed to set for future rebuilding in
other depressed areas of the city. In building out large areas of Lower North
Philadelphia at very low densities, OHCD achieved the aims that it set out
in *Home*: relatively large numbers of new social housing occupying as much
low-value land as possible. *Home*'s strategy had been so successful, in fact,
that Lower North Philadelphia in 2010 did not have large amounts of low-
value land anymore; as in Jefferson-Chalmers, the easily available sites were
gone, and the market was no doubt eyeing many of the remainders.

But North Philadelphia had many more parcels of vacant land. In November 2010 the University of Pennsylvania calculated that Philadelphia had 39,896 parcels of vacant land, of which only slightly more than 9,000 were in public ownership (PIUR 2010). Using a slightly different vacant land inventory, The University of Pennsylvania's Cartographic Modeling Laboratory (2007) showed 15,991 vacant parcels in the part of North Philadelphia bounded by Lehigh Avenue, the Delaware River, and Vine Street. About three-fourths of this area could not support market activity (PIUR 2010, 6) because values were so low that new construction would be worth less than its construction cost.

Philadelphia's vacancy problem far exceeded Lower North Philadelphia, and because market-based solutions would not soon be arriving in those areas, subsidy would be the only answer for these still-shrinking areas of Philadelphia, just as it was across almost all of Detroit. If Philadelphia's vacant parcels were going to be redeveloped, then policymakers would have to fund substantial numbers of new housing, and the proven model for very low-income neighborhoods after 1990 was suburban-style housing. If Upper North Philadelphia was to be rebuilt, its future would likely be more suburban, not less, unless policymakers could apply a different redevelopment model than the one OHCD first proposed in *Home in North Philadelphia*.

Chapter 5

Toward Social Urbanism for Shrinking Cities

> [People] would say that if [slum-dwellers] are poor,
> whatever you give them, they are winning, because they
> have nothing. But I had a statement, and it turned out to
> be very popular: "The most beautiful things, for the
> humblest people in this city."
> —Sergio Fajardo, Curry Stone Design Prize interview, 2010

Medellín's Revolution

Far away from the shrinking cities of the United States, the rapidly growing city of Medellín, Colombia, experienced a revolution between 2003 and 2010. This was a political revolution, but not the kind that one might expect given Latin America's twentieth-century history. Medellín's revolution was one of architecture, political economy, and social justice—in short, a revolution of *social urbanism*. This was the term coined by Alejandro Echevarri, director of Empresa de Desarrollo Urbano (urban works) in Mayor Sergio Fajardo's administration (2003–7). Medellín was a very different city from both Detroit and Philadelphia—its population increased by 620 percent during the same period (1950 to 2000) that Detroit's dropped by 50 percent—but it shared these shrinking cities' concentrations of poor people, just as it shared the dilapidated neighborhoods where its impoverished citizens lived. And Medellín also differed in that its political administration tackled the problem of "slum upgrading" with an energy and innovation that the shrinking cities of the United States seemed to lack.

In a city of just over three million people, Medellín's urban revolution was either staggeringly ambitious or surprisingly modest. In a period of just three years, Fajardo's administration constructed five *parques bibliotecas*, or modern libraries; built ten *colegios de calidad* (quality schools); renovated 141 existing schools; constructed more than twenty new police stations or substations; and built a series of new *centros de desarrollo empresarial zonal* (enterprise centers) and a *metrocable*, or gondola, linking a low-income neighborhood to the city's metro line (Samper 2010, 113–50). While each initiative was individually beneficial, the Fajardo administration coordinated many of them in what they called a *Proyecto Urbano Integral* (PUI), or integrated urban project, to benefit poor neighborhoods comprehensively. Medellín's PUIs involved not only new projects but community participation and social outreach as part of their social urbanist vision (Samper 2010).

Design and planning were the centerpieces of Fajardo's social urbanism. While Medellín's new projects had undoubted practical utility for the city's numerous poor, their visual splendor, particularly Plan B Arquitectos' *Orquideorama* (orchid garden) and Giancarlo Mazzanti's *Biblioteca Parque España* (library), also provided them extremely high visibility in the international press (e.g., Romero 2007; Martignoni 2009; Rochon 2009; Hawthorne 2010). Mayor Fajardo seems to have had various reasons for making design the centerpiece of his administration: he claims to have been inspired by Barcelona's Olympics-era urban improvements (Hawthorne 2010) as well as by the *Favela-Bairro* (slum neighborhood) plan instituted in Rio de Janeiro in the early 1990s (Werthmann 2008 in *Harvard Design Magazine*, 46–49; Blanco and Kobayashi 2009). Fajardo is also the son of an architect, and this no doubt exposed him early to design's transformative potential. And Fajardo was also operating within a larger tradition of Latin American "statist" urbanism where strong leaders, such as Brazilian president Juscelino Kubitschek (1956–60), have sometimes used design to both improve social well-being and build political power (Evenson 1973, 105–16). The tradition of statism in Latin America is strong, and while at its best it can produce the splendid urbanism of Fajardo's Medellín or Kubitschek's Brasilia, statism also has its negative side, for it is not always associated with democracy.

Like Mayor Rendell in Philadelphia a decade and a half earlier, Fajardo was creative, charismatic, and ambitious. In 2010, retired from the mayor's office by term limits, he ran for president of Colombia, just as Rendell successfully ran for governor of Pennsylvania. And like Rendell, Fajardo's timing was excellent; the extreme violence that characterized Medellín in the late 1980s and early 1990s had substantially diminished by the time he was elected, and previous administrations had initiated key infrastructure projects, in particular the Medellín Metro, in the 1990s. Even the *metrocable* was a policy initiative from a previous administration that was realized during Fajardo's term (Samper 2010, 138). Yet just as Rendell unarguably revolutionized Philadelphia in the 1990s, Fajardo's accomplishments were substantial, particularly in a city whose problems were far worse than Philadelphia's. Mayor Fajardo was able to succeed in part because of a supportive political culture that permitted his administration's innovations to operate, but one must also acknowledge that Medellín's innovative social urbanism would never have existed in the absence of his administration.

The tremendous good press given Fajardo's social urbanism indicated that the mayor's initiatives were a stroke of genius as well as plain common sense. From the commonsense perspective, one would have expected Latin American cities to have initiated many such urban improvement efforts long ago, for the region is plagued by social inequality and has a resulting history of political instability. The need for social urbanism in Latin America's cities should be obvious to all, not least to the millions of poor in every city's informal or semiformal settlements. Yet achievements on the order of Fajardo's are rare. Medellín's commonsense and badly needed social program and its innovative design captured the world's attention while it addressed pressing urban needs. Social urbanism not only gave Colombian designers a new sense of social purpose—"the most beautiful buildings in the poorest parts of the city," as Fajardo said—but also reconnected Colombian social planning to the visual culture of architecture and high design. Whatever the lasting benefits of Medellín's *urbanismo social*, its existence is a reminder of the generally unfulfilled potential of urban design and social planning to jointly improve severely distressed cities and urban populations—a potential as badly needed in the U.S. as it is in cities around the world.

The Wake of Urban Renewal

The post-1970 experience of America's shrinking cities showed the lack of an equivalent program of social urbanism just as it demonstrated that postrenewal urban redevelopment was mostly ineffective in reversing, or even alleviating, population and housing losses. This is unsurprising given the diminution of resources dedicated to redevelopment after the end of urban renewal. Just as Douglas Rae concluded that even New Haven's

set[ting it]self against history" (2003, 360) in the 1950s and 1960s was ineffective, Philadelphia and Detroit's redevelopment of the 1980s, 1990s, and
2000s showed that decentralized, small-scale urban design could not con-
vert a shrinking city into a growing one.

Detroit was clearly a worst-case scenario: against a landscape of severe
diminution in the city's population, economy, and building stock, the city
pursued a sporadic policy agenda driven solely by political or developer
imperatives. Detroit's political capacity was variably spirited (Young),
sometimes marginally competent (Archer), and sometimes woefully incom-
petent (Kilpatrick), but it mattered little. Losses occurred irrespective of
heavily subsidized interventions like the Renaissance Center and the two
new stadia of the late 1990s, or costly middle-class subdivisions like Victoria
Park and Jefferson Village. At the local level, neighborhood interventions
were expensive but effective; there is little doubt that Victoria Park improved market perceptions of Jefferson-Chalmers. But amid the much
larger landscape of decline, Detroit's focus on a few heavily subsidized projects in market-friendly areas left most of the city adrift. It was almost as if
both the market and the city government had colluded to retain only a few
neighborhoods intact, letting the rest go to waste. A conspiracy-minded
resident might easily see this as purposeful neglect; this was unlikely, but
Detroit's attempts to confront decline did reflect the unfortunate combination of political myopia, standard growth-machine politics, and a lack of
productive participation from the planning and design disciplines.

The policy landscape of Philadelphia was much healthier than Detroit's.
Not only was the city's decline far less severe, with many stable neighborhoods including Center City, but as early as the 1950s the city showed a
particular capacity for policy innovation and restraint in its redevelopment
in the person of Edmund Bacon. This capacity made Philadelphia's redevelopment famous, though it did not arrest the city's overall downward trend.
After two decades of ineffective leadership coinciding with the first decade
and a half of decentralized redevelopment policy, the city's policy capacity
rose to the fore again in the 1990s during the Rendell administration. John
Kromer's centralized redevelopment policy for North Philadelphia occurred in near-perfect cadence with the nationwide "return to downtown"
and a regional economic boom, from Washington, D.C., to Boston, which
activated Philadelphia with new residents and activities. Both endogenous
and exogenous factors helped Philadelphia just as their lack hurt Detroit,
and they generated considerable benefits even in North Philadelphia, the

worst-off area of the city. Yet North Philadelphia remained poor and disinvested, even after the city's real estate boom of the early 2000s reactivated
the market in parts of the neighborhood.

The urban design outcomes in both cities were disappointing—as architecture, as neighborhood design, and, in Detroit, at the scale of the city.
None of the new housing constructed in either city's distressed neighborhoods exhibited much architectural innovation; low construction costs
were a factor, but so was the fact that innovative design never entered into
the thinking of the agencies, developers, and public officials involved in
housing development. At the neighborhood scale, even the most ambitious
projects, particularly Poplar Nehemiah in Philadelphia and Victoria Park
in Detroit, did little beyond construct versions of the suburban subdivision
in an inner-city setting. Even the creative reinterpretation of row houses
found at Yorktown was absent: 1990s and early 2000s urban design negated
the urban context more than it interpreted or even imitated it. Nor was
HOPE VI public housing an exception: the rebuilt Cambridge Plaza and
Richard Allen Homes were as suburban as Poplar Nehemiah. Needless to
say, commercial uses were absent from all of these residential developments: subsidies did not permit them, and weak markets made retail an
even more difficult proposition. Their wholly residential nature only emphasized their suburban inspiration and lack of relationship to the existing
city. Finally, the lack of rebuilding policy in Detroit resulted either in the
scattered, small-scale nonprofit development argued against by Kromer in
Home in North Philadelphia or in low-density, market-rate development
concentrated in desirable areas. Subsidizing development in active market
areas strengthened parts of the city that already had advantages but did
very little for those located far away from healthy areas. *Home in North
Philadelphia* represented a productive alternative siting policy, concentrat-
ing redevelopment in one of the weakest areas of the city, far enough from
active areas that sites could be acquired but close enough that market-rate
development could grow outward to subsidized redevelopment, as began
to happen in Northern Liberties in the early 2000s.

Even as urban decline made the need for policy intervention in shrinking cities ever stronger, the rebuilding efforts of the postrenewal era made
it painfully clear that municipal policy apparatuses were only intermittently
up to the task. Certainly the end of urban renewal did not encourage experimentation or ambition on the part of urban designers and planners; instead, it seemed to push planning and design into ever more reductive

strategies that either handed initiative entirely to the market or relied on the architecturally modest interventions of the postmodern era. The intrusive and offensive monuments of urban renewal were gone, but so was the mix of innovation, ambition, and sensitivity that had characterized the best redevelopments of the late Modern era. In the postrenewal era, Philadelphia and Detroit struggled for the most part simply to make do; social urbanism like that of Medellín was out of the question.

Toward the Future

After the 2008 election of a Democrat as president, it seemed possible that the federal government might begin a reinvestment process in the nation's cities. Not only had this not come to pass as of early 2011, but no federal policy innovation appeared to be on the horizon. HUD remains committed to a market-driven model where private capital can lead development and public money can support it. "I'm in government because of the role of government in setting rules and working in partnership with the private sector," said Shaun Donovan, current secretary of HUD, when he was New York City's housing commissioner in 2006. And President Obama has proposed to deemphasize cities, arguing against an " 'outdated' urban agenda that focuses exclusively on our cities, and ignores our growing metro areas" (Staley 2010). President Obama's metropolitan agenda may (or may not) palliate skeptical suburban voters, and HUD secretary Donovan's interest in public-private partnerships may bring salutary results in places like New York City with prosperous economies, but neither of these federal policy approaches, even if they become firm policy, will have much of an effect on the blighted landscapes of shrinking cities. Help, if it arrives at all, will have to come from local initiatives.

Ironically, though redevelopment of shrinking cities' distressed areas never attracted enough political attention to become the subject of citywide policy, demolition did. In fact, demolition was a favored policy in shrinking cities, particularly after 2000 as the reality of persistently high numbers of abandoned buildings became clear. Even after three decades of housing loss and demolitions Philadelphia had more than 27,000 vacant structures in 1999 (Saidel et al. 1999), and Detroit had 40,000 empty lots (Gavrilovich and McGraw 2000, 295). Given Philadelphia's high level of political capacity, it was not surprising that it was one of the first shrinking cities to tackle

Figure 5.1. Philadelphia's Neighborhood Transformation Initiative (NTI) removed almost six thousand abandoned buildings between 2001 and 2007, but, without a redevelopment strategy for the cleared lots, most NTI-generated parcels stayed vacant. Photograph by Daniel Campo.

vacancy head-on. Immediately upon his election as Rendell's successor in 2001, former city council president John F. Street instituted the grandly titled Neighborhood Transformation Initiative (NTI) to address the city's persistent housing vacancy problem. Between 2001 and 2007, Philadelphia spent $306.7 million under NTI, mostly generated through bond sales (Kromer 2010, 115), to demolish 5,657 vacant buildings (Gelbart 2008), clean and replant empty lots, and remove an amazing total of 289,000 abandoned cars (by administration count) from city streets. NTI was the largest and most expensive such demolition effort during this period, but its success could only be called mixed. John Kromer was cautiously optimistic, saying that NTI could be labeled "a hodgepodge . . . that had relatively little impact" or more hopefully a policy that "removed . . . the worst of the vacant-structure inventory and . . . enhanced . . . development activity" (2010, 115).

In North Philadelphia, NTI did have some relationship to redevelopment, paying for site assembly at phase III of the Moore Homes as well as for APM's nonprofit housing developments in eastern North Philadelphia. But NTI responded to rather than initiated these projects: as with the city's tax abatement policy, the money simply followed the development. Mayor Street failed to associate a spatial strategy with NTI, except for distributing NTI dollars to all City Council districts irrespective of their vacancy problems (Kromer 2010, 126). In this sense, Street's Philadelphia was little better than Detroit, where redevelopment and the disbursement of public dollars served as a means of political redistribution or currying the favor of private interests.

Ultimately, NTI generated more vacant lots all over the city, particularly in North Philadelphia, where vacant structures were concentrated (Figure 5.1). While abandoned buildings were clearly a cause of blight, vacant lots seemed to generate conflicting fiscal results. A 2010 Penn Institute for Urban Research study indicated that vacant parcels, particularly in north Philadelphia, depressed land values by up to 20 percent (PIUR 2010), but an earlier Penn study (Wachter 2005) found in contrast that improved vacant lots such as those generated through NTI could improve property values, though not enough to restore the market in depressed neighborhoods. Ultimately, NTI demolished a lot of houses, but it did not end Philadelphia's vacancy problem: in mid-2010, the *Philadelphia Daily News* reported that there were 40,000 vacant properties in the city, at least 9,000 of which were vacant structures—and likely many more, since NTI had demolished fewer than 6,000. "We're largely dealing with the same problems we were dealing with before NTI," said a former Street administration official (Lucey 2010).

Not dissuaded by the travails of NTI, other shrinking cities also pursued demolition-based initiatives with great vigor. In Buffalo, a city whose population dropped from 580,000 to 293,000 between 1950 and 2000, Mayor Byron Brown established in 2007 a "5 in 5 Initiative" (City of Buffalo 2007), with the goal of demolishing 5,000 vacant and abandoned homes over a five-year period. By mid-2010 the city had demolished more than 3,100 houses, but funding cuts derailed further demolitions (Wooten 2010). Flint, Michigan, another city whose population dropped by 50 percent in the second half of the twentieth century, attracted much interest for a county-based land bank that used funds derived from sales of tax-foreclosed suburban land to demolish vacant buildings and improve vacant parcels within the shrinking city of Flint itself (Gallagher 2010, 135–42). "Decline is like gravity, a fact of life," said County Treasurer Daniel Kildee in 2009, referring to Flint's inexorable abandonment. "We need to control it instead of letting it control us" (Streitfeld 2009). But vacant land alone could accomplish little in Flint, even in city ownership, unless there was a viable strategy for its future. Detroit, with perhaps the largest vacant-land inventory of any city in the country, also embarked upon a demolition policy in 2010 with the election of its new mayor Dave Bing, a former basketball star. In April 2010 Bing announced that he wanted to demolish 10,000 vacant, abandoned houses by the end of 2013, and by early 2011 the city had already demolished 1,850 houses (Associated Press 2011). Yet this additional demolition only added to Detroit's already vast stretches of vacant land.

Apart from being very costly for their impoverished sponsors, the demolition strategies carried out in shrinking cities after 2000 suffered from a basic flaw: they were driven by a simple imperative to demolish vacant buildings, with little idea about what the vacant lots would be used for. This lack of vision was doubly costly. First, without a physical vision of the future city in mind, cities like Philadelphia and Buffalo simply demolished buildings where it was politically expedient or where life safety issues drove demolition crews to act quickly. This parcel-by-parcel removal strategy effectively led to random vacant lots scattered among remaining properties, a result that differed little from the scattershot demolitions of previous decades that had failed to generate the contiguous areas of vacant land that developers preferred, as the infill travails of Detroit's Jefferson Village and Philadelphia's Cecil B. Moore Houses demonstrated. A second problem was that, once demolished, vacant parcels were more or less unmarketable, both because they were scattered and because they were in depressed neighborhoods where there was little market demand for land either before or after demolition. Demolition removed abandoned structures, but it did not generate spatial strategies for depressed neighborhoods, and it did not create development markets where there had been none before.

The lack of a spatial strategy behind Philadelphia's NTI was recognized somewhat belatedly by Terry Gillen, director of the city's Redevelopment Authority, in 2010. "I think we've got to talk about what land-use priorities are," she said. "Is it a priority to give land to people who operate homeless shelters? Is it a priority to give land to people who develop jobs?" (Lucey 2010). Coming from the head of a major city agency, in what was still the sixth-largest city in the country in 2009, Gillen's puzzlement was dismaying, and it was far from atypical. Across the United States, whether in Flint, Detroit, Buffalo, Cleveland, Youngstown, Philadelphia, or Baltimore, shrinking cities simply did not know what to do with their proliferating vacant land or how to treat the communities of low-income residents that still lived in partially abandoned areas of the city. This policy paralysis was perhaps the most damaging legacy of the rise of neoliberal postrenewal urbanism: in the absence of market demand or interest from the growth machine, public policy makers and urban planners could say little, and do less, about the future of deteriorating neighborhoods.

The Challenge of Nonreformist Reform

The prospects for a social urbanism equivalent to that of Medellín may seem an elusive prospect in today's shrinking cities. Certainly the postrenewal era, with its relative freedom from federal initiatives, did not offer a very promising precedent. Decentralization promised a grand opportunity for cities like Detroit or Philadelphia to address urban problems on their own, but the evidence indicates that the vacuum left by urban renewal was at best incompletely filled. The sad reality is that American mayors, even in severely troubled cities like Detroit, had much less to gain from social urbanism than did Sergio Fajardo, mayor of a city where the population is growing due to rural-urban migration and where 64 percent of residents live below the United Nations Development Program's poverty line (UNDP 2010). In a developing nation like Colombia, populist mayors can obtain political support by providing for the poor, but the same is hardly true in the United States. Even a city like Philadelphia, with 25 percent of its residents below the poverty line in 2000, is still mostly middle class, and this constituency has very different demands.

But these political realities should not preclude the reconsideration of urban design policy in shrinking cities, no matter how discouraging the evidence. In her recent book *The Just City* (2010, 17), planning theorist Susan Fainstein explains the dilemma for those who wish to "propos(e) strategies for reform of urban programs." As Fainstein explains it, the first of two challenges for reformers is that cities are not autonomous. Not only are they subject to political forces beyond their control, such as skeptical red-state legislators or federal budget crises, but they face a myriad of even larger-scale issues such as population movement, globalizing economies, and even climate change. Of course, all cities face these problems, but one might still argue pessimistically that the deck against cities like Detroit, Cleveland, or Buffalo is so stacked that reform is impossible. Political capacity is at best spotty; suburban municipalities may be uninterested or even hostile; state legislators have other problems; the federal government is consumed with issues like national defense. One might easily conclude that urban design issues in shrinking cities are not only relatively trivial but unlikely to affect these larger issues, and also that cities are the helpless victims of forces beyond their control.

Fainstein refutes this skeptical perspective by arguing (2010, 17–18) that cities vary considerably from each other—Boston is not San Francisco, New York is not London, and, as we saw, Philadelphia is not Detroit. Historical, geographical, cultural, economic, and political factors differ from place to place, and these differences offer opportunities for policy makers, politicians, and planners to generate different strategies in turn. At a more local level, the appreciation of difference is known as "asset-based" planning; even the most disinvested neighborhood has some good qualities. Fainstein also notes that cities have substantial autonomy. Accentuating the positive potential of such autonomy was certainly President Nixon's aim when he decentralized urban policy in the 1970s, and the resulting disappointing outcomes can therefore be seen as a failure of individual urban initiative as much as a failure of federal concern. While it is true that when left to their own devices cities such as Detroit simply answered the wishes of the loudest and most powerful private voices, the potential nevertheless remains in each city to generate innovative, new policy ideas with each new administration. Good ideas therefore have a ready market with each election, as Philadelphia demonstrated during the Rendell-Kromer years.

A second problem for reformers is more existential, and one that urban policy makers rarely concern themselves with, for obvious reasons. As Fainstein bluntly puts it, this is the possibility that "redistribution (is not) possible under capitalism" (2010, 18)—in other words, that the existing economic system of the United States does not permit a true reform of current practice. Given existing realities, this is a defeatist road for policy makers to explore, and Fainstein refutes it by arguing that improvement can occur through an approach that she calls "nonreformist reform" (Fraser and Honneth 2003, 79; Gorz 1967), which argues for change even as it accepts realities of the existing political and economic system. Fainstein adds that this approach is a refutation of Marxism, a concern in academia, perhaps, but hardly so in the professional world where the word is rarely uttered.

Applied to shrinking cities, an approach of nonreformist reform would neither reject capitalism nor deny political, social, or economic realities such as suburbanization, weak federal policy, or social desires. Instead, a nonreformist reformer would see these realities as preconditions within which a politically aware architect or clever social planner might work to achieve innovation within the existing system. Philadelphia had both in different eras, in the persons of Edmund Bacon and John Kromer; neither was able to reverse the larger course of events (clearance-based urban renewal and poorly funded decentralized planning), but both made notable progress within these constraints. It is in this spirit that this chapter's suggestions for urban design in the shrinking city are offered.

Urban Design Ideals: Everyday Urbanism

The demolition-based strategies promulgated in the first decade of the 2000s did correctly grasp the signal problems of shrinking cities: that large numbers of buildings were abandoned, that the market had no immediate need for them, and that their continued existence represented a problem. But these strategies ignored another critical aspect of the shrinking city that was arguably more important. However many people had departed from shrinking cities, a significant number still remained, and many of those remaining were isolated, underemployed, and living in poverty. Demolition may have removed superfluous, blighted housing that was no longer needed, but apart from eliminating possible neighborhood hazards, demolition did little to improve the quality of life for remaining inhabitants. Whether demolition occurred or not, housing in distressed neighborhoods was still old, the inhabitants were still poor, and the neighborhood was arguably just as blighted as it had been before. Demolition of unnecessary structures may not have been irrational, but it also did not constitute a vision of what shrinking neighborhoods could be in the future, unless that vision was one of the same unstructured shrinkage that had been occurring since the 1970s. Demolition of unnecessary structures did not in and of itself deliver prosperity: cities like Buffalo and Detroit were as poor in 2000 as they had been in 1970, just with far fewer people. Jane Jacobs had noted the same phenomenon in *The Economy of Cities* when she observed that "in the United States, the poorest counties experience prolonged out-migration and absolute population drops, but the economic conditions of the people who remain is not improved as a result" (1969, 119). Piecemeal demolition did nothing to improve the lot of the people who remained in shrinking neighborhoods, nor did it provide development sites large enough to provide space for transformative clusters of new buildings. Demolition guaranteed that more and more of the shrinking city would consist of open space, but it could not ensure this space would be useful. Detroit's cityscape offered a forecast of how piecemeal demolition could play out over a number of decades. It was not a promising one.

Some theorists argued that the open space that occurred through piecemeal demolition provided additional opportunities for remaining residents to acquire adjacent open space to expand their personal properties. In Detroit, where the phenomenon labeled "blotting" was documented by Interboro Partners (Interboro 2008), residents formally or informally used adjacent, annexed lots for a variety of purposes, including new side porches, gardens, and garages. Most residents interviewed by Interboro saw "blotting" as a means of empowerment and improvement: vacancy increased rather than decreased their quality of life and neighborhood.

As an individually generated change of the urban landscape, blotting comprised part of a larger ideology of pragmatic urban planning and design that arose among planners and urban designers in the 1990s and early 2000s. For advocates of everyday urbanism (Chase et al. 2008), the existing urban environment, together with the small-scale changes that individual citizens made to them (either legally or illegally), were virtues rather than flaws. Everyday urbanism had a lineage at least as old as Jane Jacobs's 1961 argument that city lovers should "look closely, and with as little previous expectation as possible, at the most ordinary scenes and events, and attempt to see what they mean and whether any threads of principle emerge from them" (Jacobs 1961, 13) and her later plea that "we must pay close attention to reality or we shall be lost in fogs of our own making" (Jacobs 1984, 35).

Jacobs, of course, famously first described the everyday course of city life on her native Hudson Street, and then subsequently valorized it. Her recommendations for an ideal city differed little from the one that she already saw. In this sense, everyday urbanism merely reflected a form of passivism, in which the best way to "do something" about urban design was to do nothing at all. In a healthy city, this approach could make a certain amount of sense: certainly there was a beauty and order to older urban settlements that was easily disrupted by modernity, whether that settlement was Boston's North End or a casbah in a city in the developing world. The observation, by Interboro and others (Park 2005; Walters 2001), that valid and interesting human ecologies existed even in shrinking cities' severely deteriorated neighborhoods, was an important reminder that these places were more than just deteriorated buildings, vacant lots, and memories; they were *home* for thousands of people, many of whom remained deeply committed to their place of residence. But in shrinking cities everyday urbanism could also be a form of apologism for existing deteriorated conditions. Certainly the fact that many Detroit residents valued the vacant lot next door to their house did not reduce the problems caused by the large-scale abandonment of the city, nor did it suggest a strategy for alleviating those problems.

Small-scale strategies were not irrelevant, but they did not constitute a solution. Blotting "might not be a bad thing" (Interboro, "Improve Your Lot!" in *Cities Growing Smaller* 2008, 64), claimed Interboro, and doubtless it was not, just as Jacobs had argued that the way cities *were* was the way they should be. But both Jacobs and everyday urbanism dodged a critical fact: change could and did occur in cities, for the worse as well as for the better. Hudson Street may have been an "intricate sidewalk ballet" in the late 1950s, but by 2010 it was an intensely gentrified neighborhood where middle-class family life like Jacobs's was a near impossibility. Appreciating the former intricacy of the street could do nothing to prevent this change from occurring. Similarly, the shrinking-city everyday urbanism of annexing vacant lots or painting vacant houses (Figure 5.2) could intervene only at small intervals in a much larger landscape of desolation and poverty. Everyday urbanism, in other words, could aptly describe urban complexity, but it could not prescribe an urban future beyond more of what it already was. The movement was "not really even bottom-up," argued architect Michael Speaks, because "it is almost, or entirely, bottom. It never develops any kind of comprehensive proposals that might be activated by small-scale interventions . . . but is instead content to fetishize and tinker with the everyday things that it finds ready made. It is anti-design and begs the question: How do you design with the banal and to what end?" (Speaks 2005, 36).

On a professional level, everyday urbanism also reflected the impotence of urban planning and state-sponsored urban design in the postrenewal

Figure 5.2. Artist Tyree Guyton's Heidelberg Project in Detroit reimagined a devastated neighborhood through the transformative power of art. For over a decade, Guyton has been ornamenting houses, yards, even the street with whimsical commentaries on abandonment and optimism. Photograph by Daniel Campo, 2003.

era, suggesting that if positive change was impossible, then perhaps it was also undesirable. It therefore constituted an acceptance of state (and market) passivity, and even an antistate, antimarket approach that bordered on libertarianism. Even if the everyday urbanist perspective argued somewhat correctly that the role of the state and market in shrinking cities was not only negligible but unproductive, the ideology provided little counsel for larger-scale intervention in shrinking neighborhoods and shrinking cities, denying design a role in shaping the future of the city at a scale greater than the individual property owner.

Landscape Urbanism

If everyday urbanism's valorization of what was—an interspersed, deteriorating landscape of remaining homes and vacant properties—was not an optimal physical state for the shrinking city, what was? The widespread demolition of urban fabric suggested another urban design alternative: that large areas of the shrinking city might ultimately become a new form of landscape, with natural areas, suburban lawns, and even urban farms. Unlike everyday urbanism, which emphasized reality over ideals, the urban design movement known as *landscape urbanism* (Waldheim 2006) reflected a highly developed formal ideal as well as much greater opportunities for design. Large areas of shrinking cities, such as Philadelphia's Delaware River piers, Detroit's secondary rail lines, or Buffalo's long-obsolete grain elevators, had by the early 2000s been abandoned for decades and nature was quick to adopt these areas as her own. In the 1980s, intrepid explorers like Reyner Banham could see in Buffalo's ruins "work comparable to that surviving from ancient Egypt [or] Roman ruins . . . a monument to a different civilization . . ." (Banham 1986, 136, 166). Certainly no viable reuse strategies were likely to appear for structures like Detroit's Packard plant, where decades of economic development efforts had produced only frustration. With deer, pheasants, and even beavers ("Good Detroit News" 2009) flourishing in Detroit by the end of the first decade of the 2000s, nature was returning to the shrinking city whether anyone wanted it or not.

Given that shrinking cities were rapidly de-densifying—Chapter 2 states that St. Louis's population density of 5,625 people per square mile in 2000 was only 40 percent of its 1950 population density—the application of landscape ideals to shrinking cities made a certain amount of sense. Landscape was a particularly productive approach for designing the future of deindustrializing areas with abandoned facilities such as steel mills or automobile factories occupying large parcels of land, often with extensive natural areas and substantial environmental contamination. Perhaps the most compelling early demonstration of a landscape design strategy for a deindustrialized area was in the Nordrhein-Westfalen state in Germany, in what was known variously as the Emscher Landschaft-Park or the Duisberg-Nord Park. Here, on the site of abandoned steel mills, ironworks, and coal mines, a 10-year, DM5 billion effort (two-thirds of it public money) generated a 300-square-kilometer "landscape park" in a mixed landscape of deindustrialized and still-active sites, a cleaned-up Emscher River, 15 new technology centers, 2,500 new and 3,000 refurbished dwellings, reused industrial buildings and mine structures, social initiatives, and job training (Shaw 2002). Though the settings could not be more different, Emscher's comprehensive, state-financed approach to economic and social improvement through high-quality design bore many similarities to Medellín's social urbanism and *proyectos urbanos integrales.*

In the United States, landscape urbanism also signaled a long-delayed professional acceptance of the fact that America was a decentralized, suburban nation as much (or even more) than it was an urban one. With only a few well-known exceptions such as Boston's Back Bay neighborhood, America did not have the dense and well-maintained cities of Europe, nor did it have the distinct boundaries between city and landscape that characterized that continent. American cities were diffuse, green, and low density; in a very real sense they were already landscapes. Landscape architects, of course, had long advocated suburbanization: landscape pioneer Frederick Law Olmsted not only designed many early suburbs but designed distinctly antiurban park systems in Buffalo, Boston, Louisville, and elsewhere, and landscape architect Charles W. Eliot had played a formative role in the development of the urban planning profession. Landscape architecture and urban planning had even briefly merged at the Harvard Graduate School of Design in the 1950s before again separating.

But landscape urbanism's conceptual realignment of landscape design away from advocating parks within the city or the region toward the city itself as a sort of park or landscape was momentous, as it not only repositioned landscape as one of the primary professions shaping the built environment but also relegated traditional urban design, focused on density and, above all, buildings, to a lesser position. Landscape urbanism's claim on urban design was bolstered by its relationship to the environment and to environmentalism broadly considered. From works like Anne Spirn's *The Granite Garden* (1984), which reminded urbanists of nature's place within all urban ecosystems, to the claim of landscape urbanist Charles Waldheim that landscape "has become a lens through which the contemporary city is represented and a medium through which it is constructed" (2006, 15) as only a small step conceptually, though the professional leap was large indeed.

All of America may have been a landscape, but in the 1990s and early 2000s the finest landscape urbanism projects developed in places with healthy economies, vibrant cities, and strong state support for urbanism, including New York City (the High Line, by Diller and Scofidio, 2008), the Netherlands (Eastern Scheldt Storm Surge Barrier, by West 8, 1992), and Germany (Duisburg-Nord Park, Ruhr Valley, 1989–99). Shrinking cities participated in landscape urbanism to a lesser extent. Detroit constructed conventional open space projects such as the Dequindre Cut rail-to-trail and a pedestrian path along the Detroit River during the early 2000s, and urban farming (a mix of landscape and everyday urbanism) proliferated in the city's neighborhoods, with more than eight hundred community gardens and urban farms by 2010 (Gallagher 2010, 61).

The door seemed open for a landscape-based future for shrinking cities. But landscape urbanism was riddled with contradictions that made it a difficult design proposition for these places. First of all, landscape urbanism was very expensive. New York City's Freshkills Park, admittedly a giant at 2,200 acres in size, was slated to cost at least $192 million for phase I alone (NYC Department of Parks 2011), with an additional $410 million in landfill closure costs (NYC Department of City Planning 2006) associated with the park over its life span. Final costs were unknown but would doubtless be much larger: the park build-out was projected to last thirty years, but in 2010 construction had not yet begun, though the department hoped to have "a small part open within the next few years" (Barron 2010). The High Line, also in New York City, was a stellar success: a derelict elevated rail line became an elevated park path, at a cost of $152 million for one and a half miles (Pogrebin 2009), or approximately $100 million per mile. At a much smaller scale, Philadelphia's Pier 11 Park, a one-acre fragment of the city's mostly abandoned Delaware River waterfront, cost a modest $3.5 million (Saffron 2009) (Figure 5.3). Construction began in late 2010 (Pew 2010), but Pier 11 was merely a small park on a very big waterfront; it was hardly landscape urbanism.

Landscape urbanism also contrasted a promise of flexibility with a high degree of formal specificity. Rem Koolhaas argued, for example, that his 1991 competition proposal for the Parc de la Villette in Paris would "undergo constant change and adjustment. The more the park works, the more it will be in a perpetual state of revision . . . shift, modification, and replacement, or substitution (can) occur without damaging the initial hypothesis" (Koolhaas 1995, 921).

This was a tempting proposition. Certainly cities were "environment[s] in a perpetual state of revision," as was nature itself. Yet landscape urbanism's promise of flexibility clashed directly with its reliance on formally precise schemes with direct authorship in the form of a designer or team of designers. "Shift, modification, and replacement" were indeed routine in large-scale urban projects, but they rarely had salutary effects. Lafayette Park was an excellent example: less than one-third of the original Mies/

Figure 5.3. The landscape urbanism movement projected that deindustrialized areas like the Philadelphia Delaware River waterfront could become new arenas for design. The significant expense of these transformations, however, has thus far limited the realization of such schemes in shrinking cities to fragments, such as Field Operations' Philadelphia's Pier 11. Photograph by Daniel Campo, 2011.

Hilbersheimer plan was ever constructed, and the successor projects were far less interesting and were much lower quality than the original design. Landscape urbanism was comprised mostly of natural fabric, but it too was a form of design and as such could be adversely affected by abandonment of the original scheme. This happened in another Koolhaas project, this one a competition-winning scheme for Downsview Park in Toronto. The project was heavily lauded (e.g., Czerniak 2001), but the park itself was never constructed. After ten years of delays due to funding problems, Downsview was slated to become half redevelopment site, with 7,300 residential units, and half recreational space (Grewal 2010). This constituted an abandonment of the original scheme, not its modification, and it pointed out a signal paradox; if design A were adapted or modified too much, it ceased to be design A and became design B.[1] Whether or not landscape urbanism could truly evolve over time yet retain its original character, as did city fabrics such as Barcelona or Paris, remained to be seen.

Landscape urbanism attracted interest because the design approach accommodated abandonment, promised environmental remediation, and meshed well with both avant-garde design ideals and the modern reality of the decentralized city. But when implemented, landscape urbanism behaved similarly to traditional parks: the projects were expensive, they took a long time to build, and they required highly precise formal arrangements to achieve their impact. Like all elaborate designs, landscape urbanism also required high levels of maintenance to retain its impact. Even the venerable *AIA Guide to New York* wondered how long the High Line's "rather delicate details will endure trampling by millions of human feet" (White, Willensky, and Leadon 2010, 219).

All in all landscape urbanism was a provocative but challenging design approach to implement in the shrinking city. Nothing better described the vast postindustrial wildernesses of Buffalo or South Chicago, or the windswept, empty city blocks of Detroit or St. Louis, than the term "landscape." Landscape urbanism converted regret for the city that was gone into appreciation for the city that could be; it was both pragmatic and utopian, and it captured many contemporary concerns—from environmentalism to sustainability to the traditional American pastoral ideal—as well as the interest of sophisticated designers.

But shrinking cities were very difficult environments in which to implement landscape urbanist projects. First and foremost, they were poor; New York City might be able to afford $192 million to convert its landfill into a park, but it was highly doubtful that cities like Buffalo or Cleveland, never mind Flint or Youngstown, would be able to afford to convert their swathes of postindustrial landscape accordingly at anywhere near the level of quality required to accord them status in the canon of landscape urbanism. And the openness of shrinking cities was also somewhat illusory: open land was often divided into small parcels with dispersed ownership. As Jefferson Village's developers learned to their chagrin, this land, even if empty and city owned, could not be easily aggregated to single ownership without condemnation proceedings, and even then it could be challenging. The depopulated residential landscapes of shrinking cities may have looked like promising sites for large-scale landscape interventions; but they were not. The hidden fragmentation of this landscape was something that everyday urbanists like Interboro Partners correctly identified; this was a landscape that was amenable to decentralized, even informal action, but highly resistant to large-scale schemes, particularly those with little immediate economic rationale, such as a large park. Unlike the High Line, the open lands of shrinking cities were far away from prosperous areas; they were often the least valuable parts of the city, not the most. High-Line-type scenarios were simply not a reality in these places—not even in dense cities like Philadelphia or Baltimore.

Everyday urbanism "succeeded" in shrinking cities like Detroit precisely because it meshed with the reality of decentralized, scattered habitation in the postindustrial environment; inhabitants were left to their own devices; the state was weak, distracted, and often indifferent; and public development action, when it happened, was sporadic and usually far away from depopulated areas. Jefferson Village was an exception to this reality, not the rule. Landscape urbanism, on the other hand, required conditions that were generally the opposite of those that obtained in shrinking cities: large sites, single ownership, a strong state, and extensive capital. This did not mean that facilities like Philadelphia's Pier 11, the Detroit Packard plant, or the Buffalo River could not be reconceived as landscapes. But it did mean that conventional landscape urbanism would not apply to these areas without some relaxation of authorship and design precision. To adapt to the shrinking city, landscape urbanism needed more of the everyday.

New Urbanism

Urban design as public policy had only a weak influence in Detroit and Philadelphia in the postrenewal era. With low levels of privately financed development almost everywhere in the city, zoning per se had little influence on shaping city form except downtown where the urban design of tall buildings was sometimes an issue, particularly during the mid-1980s' office boom. In distressed neighborhoods, however, development was subsidized, and controlling density was hardly the problem. This is not to say, however, that urban design was not of great interest to decision makers. On the contrary, the form, image, and density of Detroit and North Philadelphia's largest housing developments were of intense importance to both developers and policy makers. Both cities saw design as a key variable that might attract middle-class audiences back to poor neighborhoods or, conversely, provide middle-class amenities, including the intangibles of neighborhood pride and stability, to working-class homeowners. But Victoria Park, Poplar, the Cecil B. Moore Homes, and the many other housing developments in Philadelphia's and Detroit's poor neighborhoods were guided less by an abstract, ideal view of neighborhood form than by a pragmatic appeal to market expectations. Urban design mattered only insofar as it could generate housing and neighborhoods consistent with those constructed for the middle class—an urbanism of conformity, not novelty.

This pragmatic design approach marked a substantial conceptual shift from urban renewal, in which formal innovation rather than conformity marked urban redevelopment. Innovation was promoted in part because Modernism was predicated on it, and in part because the problems of American cities in the 1950s and 1960s were seen as so desperate that only dramatic measures, constructed by top professionals, would do. In New Haven, for example, Maurice Rotival, a French urbanist and Yale faculty member, consulted on downtown's redesign (Rae 2003, 319). In Chicago, Skidmore, Owings, and Merrill, the leading architecture firm of the postwar era, designed much of the redeveloped South Side (Whiting 2001, 676). Even conservative Boston held a national design competition for its new government center (Freeman 1969, 50). Cities matched this outside expertise with planning directors such as Philadelphia's Bacon or Detroit's Blessing hired from elite educational institutions (Cornell and MIT, respectively). None of this expertise, of course, corrected for the signal conceptual problems of High Modernism, and some cities, notably Boston and New Haven, later wished they had had less rather than more expertise. But in other cities such as Philadelphia, professional expertise, backed by the activist federal policies of the postwar era, generated redevelopment that was more humane, attractive, and restrained than it might otherwise have been.

Reliance on expertise changed dramatically in the postrenewal era. While architects such as I. M. Pei and Mies van der Rohe designed urban renewal projects in Philadelphia and Detroit in the early 1960s, national practitioners were completely absent from 1990s and early 2000s redevelopment efforts. The design firms for Poplar, Ludlow, Cecil B. Moore, Victoria Park, Clairpointe, and Jefferson Village were all local, although the developer of Jefferson Village operated on a national basis. This localization of expertise reflected the reduced expectation and funding of the postrenewal era, but it also reflected the lack of visibility for postrenewal urban reconstruction efforts. Certainly policy makers such as John Kromer, whatever their level of accomplishment, were not about to land on the cover of *Time* magazine, as Edmund Bacon had in the 1960s. On every level, postrenewal urban redevelopment was smaller, less visible, more modest in scale, and of less design interest and quality. Experimentation was certainly out: modesty and even vernacular design culture was in.

Provincial design accentuated postrenewal redevelopment's position as a "policy backwater" (Altshuler and Luberoff 2003, 26), a position accentuated after the mid-1970s by the lack of an urban design ideal to shape redevelopment, except the ideal of the historic fabric itself. Detroit's Jefferson-Chalmers was a typical example: unassuming, humane, leafy, automobile accommodating, but pedestrian friendly as well. Built environments like Jefferson-Chalmers were familiar to almost every American, whether or not they lived in such neighborhoods. Even if residents had left cities for suburbia, the pleasant, friendly, attractive, residential neighborhood, with Victorian single-family homes and a Main Street shopping district within walking distance, remained a cultural ideal.

It was not so surprising that Postmodernism, with its appreciation for the past and witty reinterpretation of the past for the present, would extend its appreciation to historic urban patterns as well. Postmodernist appreciation of historic urbanism gained particular momentum through the design efforts of Andres Duany and Elizabeth Plater-Zyberk, a pair of architects who graduated from Yale in 1974, began designing buildings in Miami in the late 1970s, and received the commission for a small resort community called Seaside in 1979 (LaFrank 1997). Seaside was truly a mouse that roared: a tiny place with only 350 houses on 80 acres (Krieger 1991, 9), its neohistorical urbanism and architecture received tremendous acclaim, reigniting a professional interest in historic urban form that took further shape as the design movement called "New Urbanism" in the early 1990s. The movement's information and advocacy organization, the Congress for New Urbanism, enrolled more than 3,000 paid members by 2011 (Neyfakh 2011).

As a neotraditional movement, New Urbanism rejected both suburban sprawl and the High Modernism of urban renewal in favor of development that looked a lot like 1920s city neighborhoods, with the addition of ornamental features such as boulevards, neighborhood parks, and commercial and civic "town centers." New Urbanism's similarity to early twentieth-century developments such as Mariemont, Ohio; Yorkship Village, Camden, New Jersey; and British garden cities such as Letchworth was close and

completely intentional: its formal vision was unabashedly nostalgic, recall-
ing the "best (of) the traditional American city and town" (Calthorpe 2009,
51, in Cisneros and Engdahl 2009). This formal relationship was further
developed in publications (e.g., Duany, Plater-Zyberk, and Alminana 2003)
that compared New Urbanism to prewar urban developments from North
America and Europe.

New Urbanism's largest impact and greatest meaning was in postwar
North American suburbs with as few formal amenities as older city neighborhoods but with lower densities. Postwar suburbia was clearly attractive
to millions of Americans; otherwise they would never have settled there.
But New Urbanism also gained support from suburbanites who disliked
driving to buy a gallon of milk or dodging traffic to walk the dog, from
developers who wished to differentiate their product from their competi-
tors', and from designers and planners who longed to shape places that
looked a little bit more like a real city. New Urbanism answered all of these
longings. From the end of the 1980s onward, New Urbanism flourished as
a development option, particularly in the Sun Belt where sprawl was extensive, regulations light, and developer competition stiff. In the 1990s the
Disney Corporation joined the New Urbanist movement, constructing a
"blueprint for the pursuit of happiness" (Ross 1999, 4) called Celebration
near Disney World. Neotraditionalism could not alter Americans' prefer-
ence for single-family homes, big cars, or pastoral living, but it could and
did discipline these preferences into some well-designed new communities
on the fringes of urban North America.

What New Urbanism ironically could not influence much was the
form of existing cities, which were mostly fixed except in areas where
plots were large enough to provide space for self-contained new communities. And just as suburbanization flourished in Jefferson-Chalmers,
where the largest available redevelopment parcels were those left by
urban renewal, New Urbanism took root on sites created by urban renewal for public housing. Even as Seaside was being constructed in the
early 1980s, the widespread reevaluation of modernist public housing design was beginning as cities like Boston began rehabilitating and rede-
signing their public housing to incorporate lower-scaled buildings and
privatized outdoor spaces (Vale 2000, 2002). Public housing redevelopment reached the national scale in 1992 when a federally appointed commission recommended that the nation's most distressed housing projects
be reconstructed and redesigned. The "Housing Opportunities for People

Everywhere VI Urban Demonstration Program," or HOPE VI, began implementation in 1993. By 2007 HOPE VI had spent $6.3 billion to demolish 134,752 units and rebuild approximately 100,000 public housing units in 193 different distressed housing projects (U.S. Congress 2008, 14 and 44).

HOPE VI projects certainly looked more historic than Modernist public housing, with gables, symmetrical entrances, front stoops, and historic ornament. But the redevelopment of public housing was subject to the same political constraints that the original construction had been, and New Urbanist design ideals were often diluted or ignored by political processes or the demands of the market. In New Orleans, a developer constructed a Wal-Mart adjacent to a HOPE VI development over the protests of preservationists and planners (Elliott, Gotham, and Milligan 2004), and Philadelphia's Richard Allen Homes, reconstructed between 2001 and 2005, resembled neighboring Poplar Nehemiah's version of suburbia more than they did a Philadelphia row house. John Kromer observed that the HOPE VI project's "large lots with yards, driveways, and porch and gable features . . . resembled those that could be found on many suburban tracts" (2010, 93). The Richard Allen Homes were hardly by-the-book New Urbanism, but then again, Chicago's grim Robert Taylor Homes had not been by-the-book Modernism either. The truth was that New Urbanism, whatever its proponents' claims, was not a revolution in urban design, just a better-designed, slightly more urbane version of vernacular suburbia. In some cases, like the Allen Homes, New Urbanism was not even that.

Besides public housing sites, New Urbanism had comparatively little impact in either Detroit or Philadelphia. The latter city, of course, was extremely dense, so infill development like the Northern Liberties' Hancock Square apartments, constructed as urban infill, could be said to have New Urbanist characteristics. With its much higher levels of vacancy, Detroit had more urban fabric to reestablish by default, and projects such as Woodward Place, close to downtown, did provide an idealized version of a midwestern-scale urban neighborhood (Figure 5.4). Woodward Place recreated the Brush Park neighborhood's historic street grid, with alleys and vaguely historicist homes, but even so, this housing had little of the typological or land use diversity of historic Brush Park at midcentury, though it did recapture its unit density (Ryan 2002, 361–62).

Given that the housing design and density level of New Urbanist developments like Woodward Place differed little from those in historic Detroit

Figure 5.4. In a few areas close to downtown Detroit, developers in the 1990s and the first decade of the 2000s constructed New Urbanist housing developments such as Woodward Place at Brush Park. Photograph by Karen Gage.

(both were about twelve to fifteen units per acre), New Urbanism in this city often resembled infill development. The East Side Plan for north Jefferson-Chalmers started off as an ambitious New Urbanist scheme complete with new alleyways, retail, neighborhood parks, and historicist homes (Figure 3.10). If constructed, the East Side Plan would have represented an innovative form of New Urbanism accommodating scattered older homes of Jefferson-Chalmers. But with more than one thousand new homes projected, the East Side Plan was far too ambitious for Detroit's weak market, and only part of a single block of houses was constructed before the 2007 market crash. Detroit's innovative infill version of New Urbanism never came to pass.

In suburbia, New Urbanism was an important alternative to monotonous subdivisions. But in existing city neighborhoods, all that New Urbanism really represented was contextualism. Its urban design argued that historic city form was more or less also an optimal city form and that rebuilding the city more or less as it already was represented an end state for the future city. Given the grim reality of shrinking cities' deteriorated neighborhoods, this restorative perspective seemed to make sense. Wasn't *anything* better than these cities' deteriorated fabric?

New Urbanism did many things for shrinking cities that landscape urbanism or everyday urbanism did not. Most important, New Urbanism's components encompassed the full range of actual city components: housing, shops, streets, and small public spaces. Unlike everyday urbanism, New Urbanism also projected a vision of the future that was different from what already existed, though this future was derived from the past. New Urbanism's greatest advantage, however, was that it was immediately comprehensible to residents, developers, and policy makers as a design strategy for rebuilding deteriorated cities. Its ideals meshed not only with concerns for preservation and context, but with nostalgia for the departed city. Against new urbanism's vision of the future as past, everyday urbanism looked merely cynical or even apologist, while landscape urbanism seemed more like a strategy for uninhabited areas than one for an inhabited city. New Urbanism was not formally innovative, but it was conceptually ambitious, and its vision of the future could be appealing.

But existing conditions in shrinking cities were so extreme that they made a mockery of New Urbanism's restorative vision. Detroit's ultimately unbuildable East Side Plan projected more than 1,000 new houses in one small part of a city that had lost more than 150,000 housing units in the fifty years previous. New Urbanism's vision was derived from the past, but the past in cities like Detroit and Philadelphia was forever gone. Detroit's 150,000 departed houses would never be rebuilt, nor would the more than 300,000 people who left North Philadelphia between 1950 and 2000 ever return. Against these statistics, New Urbanism was unmasked as a fantasy: shrinking cities could never be rebuilt as they were during the industrial age. Nor could New Urbanism effectively answer the questions that stemmed from that admission: How much of Detroit *should* be rebuilt? As much as possible? Which fabric should be restored? What about the rest? Dependent on an idealized vision of a continuous, historicist urban fabric, New Urbanism had little to say about future city form in an age of shrinkage. New Urbanist developments like Woodward Place might whistle against the wind of shrinkage, but they could not go far to reverse it.

As the vacancy-based strategies of cities like Youngstown and Detroit gained visibility at the end of the first decade of the 2000s, New Urbanists began to acknowledge that the neotraditional approach to city design lacked relevance in shrinking cities. Longtime New Urbanist advocate Philip Langdon admitted in early 2011 that "a case can be made that industrial cities, after suffering decades of decline, are better off recognizing their reduced condition than denying it" (Langdon 2011, 1). But Langdon had little to offer as an alternative beyond glumly noting the obvious fact that "development (has) 'been very slow'" in shrinking cities. Indeed. And as Andres Duany nervously noted landscape urbanism's increasing claims on hot-button issues like environment and sustainability against New Urbanism's weaker claims to the same (Duany 2010), even the Congress of the New Urbanism had to admit that "as some cities shrink in the post-recession economy, a call has arisen for new ways for thinking about human settlement. Can or should parts of Detroit revert to farm land? Is urban agriculture a serious solution for distressed cities?" (New Urban Network 2010). Trapped by their commitment to density, historic city form, and neotraditional architecture, New Urbanists could raise important questions for shrinking cities, but they could not begin to answer them.

The Era of Non-experimentation

The neohistorical architecture and city form of New Urbanism marked the fear of experimentation that characterized urban design in the era after urban renewal. The mistakes of urban renewal showed all too painfully that cities were difficult things on which to experiment. Not only was construction too costly and land too scarce, but people's lives were too important. Perhaps the most reprehensible aspect of High Modernism was the sense it provided that cities and their inhabitants were simply a grand experiment, a canvas for designers, planners, and social policy makers to lay out schemes for the improvement of human well-being. Jane Jacobs directly targeted Modernism's confusion between experimental art and experimental urbanism when she argued that "a city cannot be a work of art" (1961, 372). Jacobs was dreadfully clear about Modernism's mistakes: "To approach a city, or even a city neighborhood, as if it were a larger architectural problem, capable of being given order by converting it into a disciplined work of art, is to make the mistake of substituting art for life. The results of such profound confusion between art and life are neither life nor art. They are taxidermy. . . . [Modernism] is a life-killing (and art-killing) misuse of art. The results impoverish life instead of enriching it" (1961, 373). Jacobs was unfortunately right, not only about the life-killing aspect of Modernism but about its art-killing aspect as well. The grand experiment of High Modernist city design resulted not only in the failure of urbanistic experiments like Cedar-Riverside, but in the failure of the ability to experiment with city design at all.

The provincial urbanism of the post–urban renewal era, beginning with Charlotte Gardens and extending right up to the completion of phase III of Philadelphia's Cecil B. Moore Homes in 2010, was the most telling indication that experimentation and innovation in city design ended after 1975, at least insofar as innovation impacted the life of the average city dweller (some innovative high-income housing continued to be constructed, and it probably always will). But one could also view post-1975 design after decline as another, different era of experimentation or innovation in city design, one in which the purpose was to experiment only as much as private developers, city residents, and municipal administrations were willing to do. The results were clear: experimentation was undesired by all actors involved. The postrenewal redevelopment of Detroit and Philadelphia represents the story of only two cities, but both reveal the same thing about why, and how, shrinking-city urban design ceased to be innovative. Developers constructed what they already knew and knew would sell; residents wanted what they already knew and knew others wanted as well; and policy makers wanted what both developers and residents wanted and knew would make their city look like everywhere else. Each actor seemed to desire the same thing: conservatism.

In retrospect, the end of innovation—what Jacobs called the killing of art—was perhaps High Modernism's most damaging legacy, even more than the direct damage—the killing of life—that it caused in its heyday. In declining American cities, Modernism's failures (of which urban renewal was only one) not only enraged urban citizens but provided grist for the ascendance of neoconservative policies that have still not run their course and that have made it difficult to project any return of a substantive urban policy to the federal agenda. None of these trends have benefited shrinking cities, where needs are arguably the most acute and where policy innovations are demonstrably most needed.

Conservatism serves a purpose when the present has a function that is deemed desirable. But if the dramatic economic decline, population losses, and physical deterioration of shrinking cities indicate anything, it is that the present is not desirable. What is perhaps most ironic about the postrenewal experience of shrinking cities is that innovation in city design perished in a physical setting that needed it the most. It is easy to imagine a myriad of ways in which housing, neighborhoods, and even cities might be redesigned, replanned, or redeveloped to make the quality of life better for their residents. That this has not happened, in large part due to the triad of developer, resident, and municipal policy maker conservatism, is an indictment of the decentralized urban redevelopment of the postrenewal era. Jane Jacobs, despite her dislike of Modernist experimentation, was a fervent advocate of innovation: her later works (1969, 1984) are paeans to economic innovation and to the benefits that they bring. What she failed to observe was that foreclosing upon urban design innovation precluded the possibility that such innovation can deliver benefits as often as it makes mistakes. Conservatism, on the other hand, may deliver tried-and-true benefits, but its transformative potential is nil.

Post-renewal urban design's conservatism may have been an appropriate reaction to the excesses of Modernism. But urban renewal's absence did not save shrinking cities, and neither did postrenewal's nonexperimentation. If the future of shrinking cities is to be in any way better than the present, urban design innovation will have to play a role. Yet if the future of shrinking cities does not resemble either the problematic past of High Modernism or the nostalgic conservatism of New Urbanism, what *will* it look like?

Toward Social Urbanism: Five Principles
for Shrinking-City Urban Design

In the spirit of a renewal of urban design innovation and social urbanism in shrinking cities, I propose five principles for future urban design in the following pages. These principles are keyed to the particular conditions of the American shrinking city but are applicable everywhere population and housing loss occurs. These five principles are (1) palliative planning, (2) interventionist policy, (3) democratic decision making, (4) projective design, and (5) patchwork urbanism. Each is discussed in turn.

Palliative Planning

Any redevelopment effort in shrinking cities must recognize that they are declining for reasons that are beyond the immediate means of developers, designers, or policy makers to remedy. In analyzing New Haven's unremitting decline, Douglas Rae said that the city's "manufacturing loss stemmed from convergence of two potent historical trends" (2003, 361–62), which he labeled "relative regional decline" and "suburbanization." He might also have added other forces like the technological shifts that permitted these changes to happen, the global shifts that altered the United States' economic competitiveness, and many others. None of these trends were within the control of urban renewal policy makers; none were under their control during the postrenewal age of shrinkage; and none will be under their control in the future, whatever that future may bring. This reality is sobering, but it does not call for passivity, acquiescence, or surrender to the inevitable. Rather, it calls for what Fainstein called "nonreformist reform," or for what in this context may be called *palliative planning*.

Palliative planning recognizes that intervention can alleviate, though not reverse, the negative changes of shrinking cities. The analogy to a person in hospice is direct and purposeful. Whatever economists would like to believe, not every person in a shrinking city can relocate to a place with a better economy; people also remain in cities because they want to or because they have to. Whether or not people should logically remain in shrinking cities, many will, for people's lives do not operate according to wholly rational standards, and decisions whether to stay or leave are personal ones in which the state cannot interfere. Municipal policy makers should recognize their responsibility to carry out palliative planning that makes the lives of their constituents better, even if those constituents are slowly diminishing in number.

Palliative planning argues that shrinking-city policy makers should alleviate suffering for practical reasons alone. Politicians have nothing to lose and everything to gain by losing as few additional city residents as possible. Buffalo, New York, may never return to its 1950 population of 580,000 people, but it still had 290,000 residents in 2000, and it is still losing people today. Palliative planning should seek to arrest future losses as much as possible by improving the quality of life in areas where residents are likely to leave, where population loss and housing abandonment is steepest. Given that distressed neighborhoods are clearly vulnerable to additional population loss, these places should be primary targets for palliative planning. Neighborhoods with an improved quality of life are places that people will be less likely to leave. Because severely distressed neighborhoods have the worst quality of life in the city, their improvement should be a policy priority.

Palliative planning calls for city policy makers to improve existing deteriorated neighborhoods by providing additional reasons for remaining residents to stay instead of leaving. Given that housing that gets abandoned is often in poor condition, offers a poor standard of living, provides few contemporary amenities, and is often located in unstable, deteriorated neighborhoods, a logical palliative planning strategy would be to create new city neighborhoods that could retain residents who might otherwise leave and even attract new residents that might diversify and stabilize the neighborhood. This was exactly OHCD's strategy in Lower North Philadelphia, and it succeeded in attracting and retaining working-class residents who valued the neighborhood, though as palliative planning it did not alter North Philadelphia's larger shrinkage trajectory or the city's larger trajectory of deindustrialization. The palliative planning of Poplar Nehemiah was only partially implemented—only housing was constructed, not other elements of neighborhood life such as schools or retail—but it indicated the promising potential of future palliative planning.

Interventionist Policy

Urban renewal was predicated on interventionism: city problems were extensive enough to require substantial federal capital and policy attention. Of course, Modernist interventionism failed: perhaps the problem was too great, or perhaps the remedy was too brutal. In either case, the Nixon administration tired of imposing policies that angered constituents and that did not seem to be bringing about positive results. A similar counterreaction seems to be happening today with the Obama administration's health care legislation, as conservative policy makers work overtime to reverse it. Many Americans are anti-interventionist: they wish to be left to their own devices, and they resent government policy impacting their lives, even if those lives could conceivably be improved by government policy.

Similar skepticism exists in shrinking cities, where memories of urban renewal are surprisingly fresh and where clumsily executed redevelopment efforts like Jefferson Village have done little to reassure residents of public officials' competence or commitment to improving their lives. But on a larger scale, the call for policy intervention in shrinking cities has never been stronger. Demolition of abandoned housing was a campaign issue for both Mayor Street of Philadelphia and Mayor Bing of Detroit, and demolition is also a mayoral-level initiative in Buffalo and Baltimore. The recent institution of expensive, city-level demolition policies indicates that city policy makers are not averse to intervening in shrinkage or to executing the fiscal machinations like bond issuance (Philadelphia) or state grants (Detroit) necessary to make policy intervention possible. This friendliness toward interventionism is good news for planners and designers, but at the same time, the repetition of demolition strategies indicates that simple interventionism alone is not enough to solve the problem of housing abandonment. Policy makers must engage in positive interventionism, not just negative; demolition must be balanced with construction that indicates that policy makers have the ability to construct a new city in addition to destroying the old one.

Interventionist policy, of course, is risky in that the more interventionist it is, the more intrusive it will be, and the greater will be the risk that if the policy fails, it will backfire on those who initiated and promoted it. Interventionism expends political capital, and policy makers therefore need to achieve positive results or risk losing support. This is precisely what happened with urban renewal; Nixon's withdrawal and cancellation of the policy can be seen as ideologically motivated by conservatism, but also by a politically pragmatic desire to renounce policies declared by a predecessor (President Lyndon B. Johnson) that seemed to be failing. Urban planning's commitment to urban renewal interventionism was equally costly for the profession when that policy was abandoned, as Chapter 1 discussed. But the same visibility and impact that makes interventionist urban development risky also can make it rewarding when it succeeds. For this reason, large-scale development has always been politically popular, for construction of a substantial project makes it look like an administration is doing something, even if it is just another professional sports stadium. This was as true when Coleman Young "achieved" the construction of the Renaissance Center and two new automobile plants as it was when John Street "achieved" the demolition of more than five thousand abandoned houses in Philadelphia's NTI.

The small scale of most postrenewal development demonstrated the flip side of noninterventionism: small projects were lower cost, but they also had little public visibility and therefore little political effect. The scattered housing developments constructed under Mayor Wilson Goode and inventoried in the *North Philadelphia Plan* had little effect on public perceptions that North Philadelphia was deeply troubled, nor did the scattered, small-scale, low- and moderate-income housing constructed in Detroit during the Young and Archer administrations reverse perceptions. Interventionism is thus in a sense its own reward; the larger the scale of the intervention, the larger the public visibility of the effort and the larger the political benefits. Detroit mayors Young and Archer both grasped this when they supported Victoria Park and Jefferson Village, as did Kromer when he channeled CDBG funding toward the construction of Poplar Nehemiah.

Political considerations are not the sole reason for supporting interventionism. In a deteriorated neighborhood, larger-scale interventions can enlarge the area that is transformed, creating a sense of distinct community, strengthening community ties, and therefore promoting social stability. The community identity provided by a large, distinctive development was seen in developments as diverse as Odhams Walk, Charlotte Gardens, and Yorktown, all of whose residents noted their allegiance to the development even more than to the neighborhood. Only interventionism—development that is scaled and designed to achieve an impact—can achieve these salutary results of mutually reinforcing physical impact, social cohesion, and political support.

Democratic Decision Making

The lot of impoverished people in shrinking cities is a very poor one. In a place with a declining economy, poor people have the least choices of any

resident, whether for employment, place of living, or choice of neighborhood. Shrinking cities, quite simply, are terrible places to be poor, and they
unfortunately are places with a lot of poor people. Improving the quality
of life of these residents in whatever way possible should be a priority by
any standard of justice or democracy.

Redevelopment in the postrenewal era generally did little to improve
the lives of the very poor. Instead, homeownership policies benefited middle-
class and working-class households who were perceived to stabilize neighborhoods with their presence. Municipal policy makers often had little
choice in this matter. The Nehemiah program that funded Poplar Nehemiah was a homeownership program, as was the Homeownership Zone
that funded the Cecil B. Moore housing. Victoria Park and Jefferson Village
were constructed for middle-class homebuyers. Given that funding guidelines often promoted homeownership, policy makers who wished to take
advantage of these programs had to comply with guidelines that did not
permit the very poor to buy houses. Even HOPE VI was intended less to
rehouse public housing residents than to diversify the income range of people living in former all–public housing developments.

Given the concentration of the poor in shrinking cities, redevelopment
or rebuilding should keep the interests of the poor in mind even if new
construction cannot always benefit the poor directly. Indirect benefits can
occur in multiple ways. Yorktown, for example, physically communicated
with its surroundings through its housing and block design. This conveyed
an interest and relationship to its surroundings, even though Yorktown
residents were better off than residents of the surrounds. Victoria Park,
conversely, conveyed the opposite approach with its boundary fence and
single entrance. Jefferson Village did something similarly negative by condemning and relocating former residents of the area instead of allowing
them to remain adjacent to the new development or rehousing them in the
new development. The costs of constructing and maintaining new housing
make it unlikely that such housing will ever house the poorest of the poor.
But new housing that is physically connected to its surroundings can lend
stability to those surroundings. Additional benefits to surrounding areas
can come from new neighborhood institutions or commercial space constructed together with new housing. The commercial facilities constructed
adjacent to Victoria Park on Jefferson Avenue, for instance, benefited consumers in the whole neighborhood.

By the same token, dispersing new development within different disinvested areas of a shrinking city can widen the exposure of residents in different parts of the city to the benefits conferred by new neighborhoods, even if they do not live in them. Neither Detroit nor Philadelphia achieved this dispersion; large developments were concentrated in only a few areas, as much by policy decisions as by funding limitations. Upper North Philadelphia, for instance, received very little of the policy attention devoted to Lower North Philadelphia, even though it had a similar need for new housing.

Dispersing new development in distressed neighborhoods will achieve greater equity for residents of those areas, but it will also require the abandonment of ideas that public investment should always leverage additional private investment. It is unlikely, for example, that large new subsidized housing developments in many parts of Detroit will incentivize additional housing, because these neighborhoods are too far from areas where the market is healthy. Yet the need in these neighborhoods is equally as great as it is in neighborhoods closer to healthy areas of the city. Policy makers motivated by a concept of democratic decision making will wish to distribute the benefits of new development as much as they can. Distributing new development also conveys a message to residents in "remote" disinvested neighborhoods that they have not been written off, that their neighborhood matters as much as those where the market is active or close to being active. Of course, funding limits will restrict the provision and construction of new development everywhere it is needed, but the same democratic instinct that motivated Medellín mayor Fajardo to construct "the most beautiful buildings for the humblest people" should be a paramount concern in shrinking cities, where many have much less than many others.

Another area of democratic concern should be in the planning and design of new developments. New housing should meet residents' needs and aspirations, and the development process should not grossly violate the rights of existing residents who have remained in disinvested neighborhoods. These residents need to be assured that they will not be displaced; or that if some displacement is necessary, that they will be provided new homes or that their homes will be moved; and that the new neighborhood will be a substantial improvement over the old. The construction of new neighborhoods subsidized by the public sector is a fundamentally democratic action, and the design and planning of this development need convey the commitment of public agencies to the fundamentally democratic intent of new urban design in shrinking cities.

Projective Design

Perhaps the most appealing aspect of High Modernism was the sense it conveyed that the city was moving toward a positive future, one that would be better than the present. The failure of this vision—Modernism's optimistic future converted into a nightmare—occurred in only a few High Modern developments, but it happened often enough—in events such as the collapse of Ronan Point in London and the rampant crime and disorder of Cabrini-Green in Chicago—to breed a mistrust and even a contempt for any design that dared to project a future radically different from that of the present. The conservatism of New Urbanism was in this sense an appropriate reaction to Modernism's overreach: the future had failed, so perhaps it was better to retreat to the past.

But this neohistorical design was an overreaction. As we saw in Odhams Walk and Yorktown, Modernism could provide design that was both projective—future oriented and clearly of its day—and socially sensitive. Peter Rowe's *Modernity and Housing* (1993) is a detailed exploration of reformed Modernism that concludes with six authoritative standards for the design of modern housing in the contemporary city: "being and becoming," "open-endedness and predetermination," "redundancy and precision," "normalcy and distinction," "appreciable abstraction," and "projects in the city" (Rowe 1993, 271–330). Together, Rowe's standards provide a wealth of detail on the ways in which modern housing can simultaneously meet social needs and exist as contemporary, meaningful design. Achieving both of these aims is a challenge: we are far more familiar with design that achieves either too much abstraction (High Modernism) or too much imitation (Postmodernism) than with design that succeeds in being both projective and responsive.

While a certain projective quality is arguably important for all architecture, projective design is particularly important for places like shrinking cities where most of the existing environment is filled with negatives. Projective design is rare but not unknown in shrinking cities. One of the best-known cases is in New Orleans, where the Make It Right Foundation has constructed thirty-three new homes in the Lower Ninth Ward, a neighborhood where Hurricane Katrina flooding was particularly severe (Make It

Right 2011). The Make It Right homes are certainly projective; the designs are modern and abstract, and each home has environmentally efficient features such as energy-efficient design and stormproof materials. Certainly the Make It Right homes, on an individual architectural level, convey a more forward-looking approach than do, say, the perfectly ordinary houses of Cecil B. Moore phase III in Philadelphia.

Yet the Make It Right homes fail as projective design in two other respects. First, they fail to project an image of a cohesive, coherent urban community; the homes are all different from each other, and the overall visual image that they present is disparate and even competitive (unsurprising, since each was designed by a different architect). The Make It Right homes do not convey the pleasing cohesion of the best urban environments but rather a sort of petty architectural competition akin to that found in mansion neighborhoods of the nouveau riche. At the same time, the Make It Right homes have not attempted to extend their projective quality to the Ninth Ward neighborhood itself: each home simply reoccupies a vacant site in the existing street grid, leaving the larger neighborhood structure intact and unquestioned. Given that the Ninth Ward's neighborhood design stems from a nineteenth-century speculative survey with little public open space, street hierarchy, protection from through traffic, or exposure to (or protection from) environmental amenities, it is clear that Make It Right has overemphasized projective architectural design but underemphasized projective urban design. A fully developed projective approach to shrinking cities should consider both dimensions.

Rowe's standards of "appreciable abstraction" and "normalcy and distinction" are especially important for projective design that complements democratic decision making. Yorktown succeeds as both neighborhood and modern architecture because its design provides residents with a sense of achieved aspiration and conformance with social ideals. At the same time, it communicates cohesion with the Modern movement that existed at the time of its construction. Yorktown's abstraction, in other words, was appreciable by its residents. The development's sense of normalcy, of being part of a larger body of Philadelphia working-class housing, was also balanced by its distinctive improvement over the quality of older Lower North Philadelphia housing. No such sense of balance was present in Detroit's or Philadelphia's postrenewal housing. Certainly the sense of normalcy was there, as was the housing's conformance with social expectations, but any architectural abstraction or distinction was absent or suppressed rather than accentuated. The resulting housing was understandable as being desirable by its residents, but its design failed to be projective.

Balancing design's projective aspect and its democratic capacity is critical in disinvested neighborhoods. High Modernism's legacy of social and formal experimentation is a heavy one; certainly policy makers and designers cannot oblige society's more vulnerable members to live in design experiments whose very distinction can too quickly slide into stigmatization. This was made painfully clear in the massive failure of high-rise, high-poverty public housing. But by the same token, reactivating shrinking cities with new neighborhoods is too important—and too expensive—a task to be achieved with meaningless architecture. One wonders whether the invisibility of urban redevelopment on the national scale has any relationship to the comparative invisibility of the architecture constructed in developments like Victoria Park or Poplar Nehemiah. If policy makers are going to commit large amounts of public funds to interventionist development, the design of the development should be accordingly interventionist and meaningful. The fact that the most recent ten years of demolition policies, such as Philadelphia's NTI, have not generated even one new development whose design could be considered to be projective, is distressing. Many opportunities have been missed, but many yet remain.

Patchwork Urbanism

If the dead hand of the past is felt anywhere in the city, it is felt in the urban pattern itself. Once established, the arrangement of streets and building lots in a city is protected by the high levels of public and private investment embedded in the structures constructed on those lots. At high levels of density and value, the arrangement of the urban pattern becomes ever more rigid; this makes the block network of a place like Manhattan extremely difficult to alter. Even the mighty urban renewal efforts of Robert Moses could only alter this island's grid pattern around the edges; the center remained inviolate. Altering the urban fabric can be a difficult and costly enterprise.

As cities decline, however, and property becomes worth less and less, the urban pattern consequently assumes greater flexibility. Less capital is required to obtain the properties lying thereon, and the need for change and reconfiguration is felt to be greater. In the 1950s Philadelphia had to resort to condemnation to assemble the blocks required for Bacon's Society

Hill redevelopment, but it could afford to do so because the area had declined so much that property values were relatively low. Even in the more fiscally straitened 1990s, Philadelphia's Office of Housing could condemn parcels and reshape blocks and streets for the Poplar Nehemiah housing. But depressed Lower North Philadelphia's large numbers of remaining row houses made this street reconfiguration challenging. Reconfiguration can go even further in Detroit, where the extreme level of shrinkage means that home values in many neighborhoods are near zero, and housing abandonment is so great that many blocks stand near empty. The city's inner-city suburban developments of the 1990s demonstrated that this looser street pattern could be substantially reshaped, even if it was just to create convincing simulacra of suburban culs-de-sac.

The nineteenth-century street grids of Detroit and Philadelphia illustrate both the benefits of grids—regularity and predictability—and their disadvantages—monotony, confusion, lack of hierarchy, and overexposure to traffic. In a healthy city, urban designers can do little with the existing urban pattern, whatever its deficiencies, unless tremendous investments such as new sports arenas or convention centers make reconfiguration possible. But in a shrinking city, the urban fabric erodes differentially as some neighborhoods decline and lose housing while others remain healthy or even grow. In an eroded fabric, the city street grid can be reimagined, with streets closed, blocks aggregated, or new streets added. The nature of changes will depend upon the specific design of new neighborhoods, but certainly the reconfiguration of the nineteenth-century network should be open to question.

On a larger scale, as housing loss proceeds in shrinking cities, as it now has for forty to fifty years, a new urban pattern begins to emerge composed of different patches of urban fabric: areas that are more or less intact, areas that are being abandoned and losing housing and areas that have nearly completed the process of abandonment and may have very few inhabited houses. As shrinkage continues these patches of emptiness often spread in a pattern of "constant outward diffusion, sort of like an expanding solar system," as a Baltimore housing commissioner put it (Janes 2011, personal communication).

The irregular levels of density, habitation, building stock, and open space in the shrinking city are the precise opposite of the level, homogenous urbanism of the historical industrial city that can still be seen in intact areas of older cities. The new urban pattern resulting from shrinkage may be

called *patchwork urbanism*. The patchwork is dynamic, shifting and changing over time as abandonment, demolition, and new development each
make their mark. If left alone, patchwork urbanism is messy, inexact, and
somewhat unpredictable. But the patchwork can be influenced, for new
development can also form part of it. Where redevelopment occurs, the
patchwork pattern of the shrinking city can be reconfigured, slowed down,
or even frozen due to the stabilizing effect of new development, as it was
in those parts of Jefferson-Chalmers and Lower North Philadelphia where
new development occurred in the 1990s and early 2000s.

Patchwork urbanism implies that urban design, rather than acting ho-
mogenously across urban space in the same manner as zoning, acts in a
strongly differential mode, influencing certain areas of the city much more
than others. This mode of urban design is not unique to the shrinking city;
market development is generally far more concentrated in some parts than
in others, so parts of cities have historically changed at a great rate while
others changed slowly or not at all. These differential rates of change were
identified by Kevin Lynch early in his career (Lynch 1947). Patchwork urbanism acknowledges that the power of urban designers and policy makers
is not infinite; new development, particularly when subsidized by public
money, can only intervene in the urban fabric at intervals, in a form of
urban acupuncture.

Given that new neighborhoods take years to construct, the patchwork
fabric of shrinking cities will continue to shift even with new construction.
As parts of the city are rebuilt, others will continue to be abandoned. If
shrinkage continues, the city pattern may eventually stabilize, with surviving intact areas of the city that are maintained by market activity, new
patches of urban fabric constructed through public policy, and empty or
near-empty areas of the city where few houses remain. The ultimate form
and distribution of this patchwork will differ in each city and will be dependent not only on the market, as it is currently, but also on the urban design
policy interventions made over time. The progression of patchwork urbanism may be seen in a series of drawings of change over time in a typical
shrinking city (Figures 5.5–5.8).

Patchwork urbanism is not unique to the shrinking city. If one thinks of
carefully designed areas of cities as patches within larger areas of vernacular
construction, one can perceive the fabric of most cities as a type of patchwork. In Los Angeles, Reyner Banham, describing what he called the city's
"art of the enclave," emphasized that the city's spatial organization as

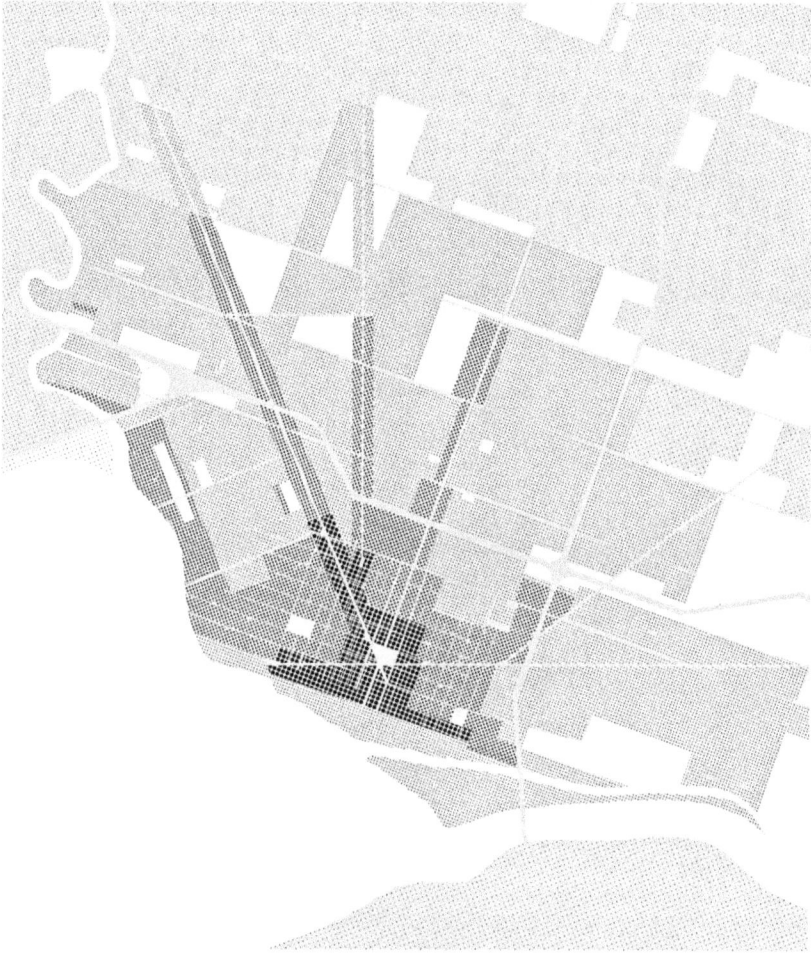

Figure 5.5. The historic industrial American city was composed of a mostly homogenous urban fabric, with higher densities toward downtown and along major avenues. This illustration projects the form of one such typical city around 1950. Illustration by author and Allison Hu.

"clusters of towers in a sea of single-family dwellings" was "not as desperate as some professional planners might feel" (1971, 137). Banham argued that "systematic planning," for example urban design, was only to be found in "privileged enclaves" and "pedestrian precincts" such as the Santa Monica Pier, Venice Beach, and old Los Angeles's Olvera Street Plaza. What

Figure 5.6. After 1950, the typical city shrinks as buildings and even entire neighborhoods are abandoned. As the urban fabric evaporates, the city assumes a patchwork appearance. Illustration by author and Allison Hu.

Banham was saying, in other words, was that Los Angeles was a city that was carefully designed only at intervals and that the rest of the city was more or less endless suburbia linked by infrastructure.

Shrinkage and decline have long been thought of as sad things, not only for the social and economic problems that they bring, but because shrinkage has caused the destruction of much of the historic city. Yet the historic

Figure 5.7. Conventional postrenewal redevelopment scenarios in typical shrinking cities focus on subsidizing private development in and around downtown and on small nonprofit developments elsewhere in the city. The result is a scattershot development pattern motivated by individual actions. Illustration by author and Allison Hu.

fabric of most American cities is little more distinctive than Los Angeles's "sea of single-family dwellings." Accepting the decline and destruction of much of the urban fabric in shrinking cities permits urban designers the opportunity to reconsider ideas about housing, neighborhoods, and urban patterns, and for policy makers to consider new opportunities for placing

Figure 5.8. An alternative redevelopment strategy would cluster housing in larger developments strategically placed in different shrinking neighborhoods along major roads or highways where there was much vacant land. Illustration by author and Allison Hu.

public development interventions strategically and comprehensively, as Kromer did in Lower North Philadelphia, rather than simply following the lead of developers, as occurred in Detroit. In the hands of proactive, interventionist policy makers and innovative urban designers, shrinking cities could be the harbinger of an entirely new form of city composed of

Figure 5.9. Before decline, typical shrinking-city neighborhoods were moderate-density environments with one- and two-family apartments, with commercial buildings on major streets. Illustration by author and Allison Hu.

interspersed areas of fabric and open space, with varying levels of density and types of fabric to meet the needs of a diverse populace (see Figures 5.9–5.11). This was precisely the dream of Kevin Lynch, who imagined that the urban fringe might serve as a site for this ideal (Lynch 1981, 293–317). But American suburbia has in reality proved to be a poor place for the realization of ideal urban form, both because suburbanites fanatically resist density and because market pressures and fragmented municipal structures have effectively prohibited large-scale urban design from acting there except in the reductive form of low-density zoning.

Shrinking cities are different. Whether by choice or by accident the market is mostly absent, leaving public and nonprofit agencies with the default responsibility of carrying out development. By the same token, the large geographical areas governed by cities provide policy makers with high levels of control over much larger areas of space than suburban municipalities have. The poverty and high levels of need in shrinking cities make

Figure 5.10. During decline, this typical neighborhood assumes a familiar appearance of vacant lots, abandoned houses, and scattered, still-inhabited buildings. Illustration by author and Allison Hu.

intervention a necessity rather than a matter of choice, and the scale and quality of development interventions is limited as much by bureaucratic capacity and designer imagination as it is by funding limitations or economic problems. From this perspective, the urban design opportunities available in shrinking cities are as great as those in any built environment in the United States, and greater than many.

Conclusion: A Semi-topia, 2061

In the first half of the twentieth century, the city grew tremendously. In 1950 it led the nation in several areas of industrial production, leading an association of corporate executives to commission a master plan that projected a 50 percent population gain by 1980. But instead the city started

Figure 5.11. Progressive urban design could reconstruct such neighborhoods with new housing that improved upon the old, with new public and semipublic open spaces, and with new street patterns. Urban designers could shift still-inhabited houses elsewhere on the site and offer relocation opportunities in new housing to existing residents. This "new neighborhood" can be imagined as one of those shown in Figure 5.8. Illustration by author and Allison Hu.

losing population. Throughout the 1950s and 1960s it constructed highways and cleared slums with great vigor, but nothing seemed to work. Population loss continued, and many neighborhoods that had not been cleared by urban renewal started to empty out as well. Abandoned houses soon became a common sight, and housing values plummeted. The last urban renewal project occurred in the early 1970s for a new factory that soon went bankrupt. Hundreds of homes had been cleared, but the site remained vacant for the next thirty years. In the mid-1970s the city nearly went into default, crime accelerated, and residents elected a mayor on a law-and-order platform. For two decades municipal policy focused on crime prevention, fiscal stability, and major downtown developments such as a convention center. But neighborhoods continued to lose population; the city in 1990 had 40 percent fewer residents than it did twenty years previous, and some neighborhoods had lost 70 percent of their housing stock. Scattered subsidized housing constructed by nonprofits did not seem to arrest shrinkage, nor did heavily subsidized market-rate developments constructed at the edge of downtown in the late 1990s. In 2005, with population loss continuing, a new mayor declared a citywide demolition program to remove ten thousand more abandoned houses. The projected cost was $600 million, but funding was lacking and progress slow.

In 2012, the city's last major industrial firm departed; the transition to the service economy was now complete. With a new mayor in office, the city's housing, planning, and redevelopment agencies decided to take a new tack, focusing redevelopment dollars on only a few large-scale projects instead of distributing them across the entire city. Using a plan prepared by a national consultant, the city elected to build in three different areas of the city with high levels of vacancy (Figure 5.8). The cost was high, and public money previously dedicated to demolition and nonprofit efforts was reduced. Nonprofit organizations protested at first, but the new neighborhood developments provided many new opportunities for community and nonprofit partnerships, alleviating concerns that the city was ignoring its residents and community capacity.

The policy agenda behind the new neighborhoods was straightforward; new housing was primarily homeownership, intended for low- to moderate-income buyers, with some adjacent rental housing for lower-income residents. Almost all funding came from federal and state sources, as the city was still repaying bonds from its earlier demolition policies. The sites of the new neighborhoods had some inhabited houses, but residents could have their house moved or receive a new one in the new neighborhood. Less than 5 percent of residents refused both options; the other residents were satisfied with their new living situation. Each new neighborhood was designed by a team of nationally known architects and city planners, and each contained a mix of moderate-density housing, multifamily dwellings, open space, and multifunction community/retail space on major streets (Figure 5.11). With three to four hundred new homes in each new neighborhood, retail recruitment was successful in attracting convenience stores to space in each of the new neighborhoods. Most of the commercial space remained occupied.

The city's dramatic new strategy attracted substantial national attention in the popular press as well as in the professional literature, which gave the city badly needed new and positive visibility. Costs were lower than expected; the large numbers of houses and novel construction methods introduced by designers brought costs down. Critics were particularly pleased with the homes' sustainable design features and sensitivity to the needs of families with children and senior citizens. The groundbreaking of one of the neighborhoods featured the secretary of HUD, and the mayor obtained a private commitment for additional funding. Next year, the city's CDBG allocation increased.

The new neighborhoods took eight years to construct and added 1,500 new units to the city's housing stock. During the same period an additional 3,000 older houses were abandoned, but the net loss was lower than it would otherwise have been, and many lower-income residents who might have left the city moved into the new houses instead. The new neighborhoods did not interfere with private-sector development; the city's stable neighborhoods remained stable, and market-rate development continued in other parts of the city as it always had. Modest subsidies continued to incentivize private development, but the city established a firm policy to prohibit deep subsidies to the private sector unless the housing was for moderate or low-income households.

In 2023, with its first three new neighborhoods complete, the city decided to construct two more, each slightly larger than the first two. One was in an area of the city with high vacancy levels where no new construction had occurred for decades. The other new neighborhood was constructed on land between two of the first-generation neighborhoods along a major street. The now-amalgamated planning, redevelopment, and housing department elected to construct this new neighborhood at higher densities along the major street, leaving some of the blocks behind for adventure playgrounds and community gardens surrounded by low- to moderate-density housing.

Together, the first and second generation new neighborhoods formed a patch of new city fabric surrounded by different varieties of open space, including many city blocks whose houses continued to be abandoned. The city's economic decline could not be arrested, nor could policy makers act everywhere in the city at the same time. In 2025, the city finally elected to deed streets on which only one house to the house's owner. Maintenance would thereafter be the owner's responsibility. Many isolated homeowners elected to abandon their houses after this decision, but others adopted the former public infrastructure as their own. The former city grid started to evolve into a differentiated pattern of smaller and larger blocks, with higher and lower concentrations of density.

Over the next four decades, the city continued to lose population and housing even as it continued to construct new neighborhoods. Many areas of the city assumed an abandoned appearance, and nonprofit organizations assumed management of most vacant areas, planting native vegetation or using the land for shifting patterns of urban agriculture. A few blocks were "adopted" by their new owners and became wild gardens, mysterious art projects, or what might kindly be called junkyards. But no one was offended; the city was big after all, the owners were often proud of their creations, and there were few neighbors. A few projects even became moderate tourist attractions.

The city had abandoned areas, but it was far from abandoned. A few areas continued to gentrify in the old way as professionals rehabilitated and restored older homes. But by 2061, fifty years after the change in redevelopment policy had begun, about 15 percent of the city's housing stock, more than ten thousand units, were found in the new neighborhoods constructed through the dedicated efforts of the two generations of policy makers, designers, and planners. The city was nationally recognized as a laboratory for humane, sustainable, and innovative design; several of its new neighborhoods had won design awards, and many were the site of regular visits by architecture schools. As early as the 2020s, the city's new neighborhoods strategy had attracted national attention, and other cities had adopted this approach to reconstruction.

In places the old city was almost unrecognizable; occasionally a historic landmark such as a fire station or public school could be found as a stabilized ruin in the natural areas of the city, and in new neighborhoods many historic homes were incorporated into the reconfigured fabric. The city was certainly poorer and less populated than it had been at its economic peak a century earlier, but its population and housing loss had slowed almost to nothing. The city was not what anyone would have predicted in 1950 or even in 2000, but most of its residents felt that it was a good place to live and felt confident that the future would be better than the past. In 2011, the city had been labeled shrinking, but in 2061 few could call it that, and many residents would have been surprised to hear that their city was once thought of as troubled. By 2061 the future had arrived, and the age of shrinkage was over.

Notes

Chapter 1

1. The disowning of urban renewal was peripheral to the larger phenomenon of urban sprawl that would increasingly occupy planners' attention. Outside the city, the project of developing, regulating, and attempting to stop low-density settlement proceeded almost unimpeded through the urban policy revolution of the 1970s (Bruegmann 2005, 121–36). The struggle against sprawl would eventually contribute to renewing the place of design within planning, as discussed in Chapter 5's section on new urbanism.

2. 1960 total population = 554,958; white population = 433,796 (78%). 1980 total population (100% count) = 284,392; white = 57,977; black = 135,403; other = 2,390; Hispanic = 80,338; not Hispanic = 8,175; therefore Black and Latino = 215,741 (76%).

3. http://www.zillow.com/homedetails/1545-Charlotte-St-Bronx-NY-10460/297 83367_zpid/ (accessed January 20, 2011).

Chapter 2

1. The 1950 US Census recorded a Detroit city population of 1,849,568 and a "sum population of adjacent areas" of only 824,211, indicating that approximately 69 percent of the metropolitan region lived in the city. By 2000 this figure had more than inverted, with only 21.4 percent of the Detroit Primary Metropolitan Statistical Area living in the city (4,441,551 PMSA residents, 951,270 Detroit residents).

2. Tract-level analysis is complicated in Detroit because many of the city's census tracts were "re-tracted" between 1970 and 1990 as a result of the city's severe population decline. The total number of tracts in the city shrank 30 percent from 460 to 319, resulting in substantial changes to tract boundaries between 1970 and 1990. In most cases 1970 tracts were combined, then redivided, to make larger 1990 tracts. For example, five 1970 tracts could be combined into three 1990 tracts sharing the outer boundaries of the 1970 tracts, but redrawn inside that common boundary. This made it impossible to compare tract-level data in re-tracted areas except by combining the data from re-tracted tracts. To compare 1970 and 1990 data in re-tracted areas I combined all 1970 tract data within the common boundaries of the tracts and averaged it

out across the number of 1990 tracts. The results for each of these tracts were thus common to the group of tracts from which their figure was derived. The averaging process may have led to erroneous gain or loss data for individual tracts within tract groups, but it accurately reflects change at the somewhat larger scale of the tract group.

Chapter 3

1. Logan and Molotch (1987) created the term "growth machine" to describe the public-private consortiums, often ad hoc, that rallied around development as a means of promoting political aims and furthering private profit in the neoliberal, post–urban renewal era. Urban renewal, however, was not immune from growth machine politics, as Anderson (1964) detailed.

2. The probability of urban renewal's beneficial effect on homeowners escaping devaluing properties does not, of course, imply that all homeowners were pleased with condemnation or that rental tenants necessarily benefited from condemnation. Homeowners' and renters' objections to condemnation would be made clear in the late 1990s Jefferson Village project.

Chapter 4

1. The phrase "deserving poor" originated in Elizabethan England to describe those poor who were willing to work. The deserving poor were considered by authorities to be more deserving of aid than those poor who were unwilling to work.

2. This relationship holds true even in deteriorated North Philadelphia neighborhoods today. The irregular intersection of Ridge Avenue and 16th Street, a few blocks west of Poplar, is typical.

3. For sale link, see www.ablerealestate.net/listnow/listings.html?p = 005c7e5b bc38-47c1-a114-6552f9a10b10 (accessed January 3, 2011). For rent link, see www.my favoritehomesearch.com/homes/11222061/PA/Philadelphia/1314-Poplar-Street-191 23/ (accessed February 1, 2011).

Chapter 5

1. The damaging effect of unplanned alterations on older park landscapes, diminishing their design impact, was well documented by August Heckscher in *Open Space: The Life of American Cities* (HarperCollins, 1978).

Works Cited

68 Stat. 590 (1954). Public Law 83-560/Chapter 649, 83rd Congress, Session 2. An Act: To Aid in the Provision and Improvement of Housing, the Elimination and Prevention of Slums, and the Conservation and Development of Urban Communities.

Academy for Sustainable Communities. "Odhams Walk: A Thriving Community in the Heart of the City." 2010. http://asc2.futura.com/CaseStudies/Odhams/Impact/Default.aspx. Accessed November 11, 2010.

Adams, Carolyn, David Bartelt, David Elesh, Ira Goldstein, Nancy Kleiniewski, and William Yancey. *Philadelphia: Neighborhoods, Division, and Conflict in a Postindustrial City.* Philadelphia: Temple University Press, 1991.

Altshuler, Alan, and David Luberoff. *Mega-projects: The Changing Politics of Public Investment.* Washington, D.C.: Brookings Institution Press; Cambridge, Mass.: Lincoln Institute of Land Policy, 2003.

Anderson, Martin. *The Federal Bulldozer: A Critical Analysis of Urban Renewal.* Cambridge: MIT Press, 1964.

Ankeny, Robert. "Title Problems Beset Jefferson Village Plans." *Crain's Detroit Business,* July 31, 2000, 40.

———. "Work Begins on Phase II of Woodward Place." *Crain's Detroit Business,* June 4, 2001, 47.

Anson, Brian. *I'll Fight You for It!: Behind the Struggle for Covent Garden.* London: Cape, 1981.

Associated Press. "Detroit's 3,000 Demolished Home Goal Within Reach." January 7, 2011. http://www.mlive.com/news/detroit/index.ssf/2011/01/detroits_3000_demolished_home.html.

Bacon, Edmund. *Design of Cities.* New York: Viking Press, 1967.

Bailey, James. "An In-city New Town Stalled by Environmentalists." *AIA Journal* (December 1974): 33–34.

Ball, Don. "Foreclosures Costing FHA Millions." *Washington Post,* December 12, 1971.

Ballon, Hilary, and Jackson, Kenneth, eds. *Robert Moses and the Modern City: The Transformation of New York.* New York: W. W. Norton & Co., 2007.

Banham, Reyner. *Los Angeles: The Architecture of Four Ecologies.* London: Allen Lane, 1971.

———. *Megastructure: Urban Futures of the Recent Past.* London: Thames and Hudson, 1976.

———. *A Concrete Atlantis: U.S Industrial Building and European Modern Architecture, 1900–1925.* Cambridge: MIT Press, 1986.

Barkholz, David. "Developers Plan Subdivision on Detroit's East Side." *Crain's Detroit Business,* December 10, 1990, 3.

Barron, James. "Turning Trash Piles into a Bird-Watcher's Paradise." *New York Times,* January 26, 2010.

Bauman, John F. *Public Housing, Race, and Renewal: Urban Planning in Philadelphia, 1920–1974.* Philadelphia: Temple University Press, 1987.

Beardsley, John, and Christian Werthmann. "Improving Informal Settlements: Ideas from Latin America." *Harvard Design Magazine* (28) 2008.

Belanger, Duane E. "Building the City's Future." *Detroit News,* November 26, 1991.

Birch, Eugenie Ladner. "Downtown Living: A Deeper Look." *Land Lines* 14:3 (July 2002): 12–15

———. "Edith Elmer Wood and the Genesis of Liberal Housing Thought." Thesis, Columbia University, 1976.

———. "Who Lives Downtown?" In *Redefining Urban and Suburban: Evidence from Census 2000,* edited by Berube et al. Washington, D.C.: Brookings Institution Press, 2006: 44–61.

Blanco, Carolina, and Hidetsugu Kobayashi. "Urban Transformation in Slum Districts Through Public Space Generation and Cable Transportation at Northeastern Area: Medellín, Columbia." *Journal of International Social Research* 2:8 (Summer 2009): 78–90.

Bloom, Nicholas Dagen. *Public Housing That Worked: New York in the Twentieth Century.* Philadelphia: University of Pennsylvania Press, 2008.

Bluestone, Barry, and Bennett Harrison. *The Deindustrialization of America: Plant Closings, Community Abandonment, and the Dismantling of Basic Industry.* New York: Basic Books, 1982.

Bolger, Rory Michael. "Recession in Detroit: Strategies of a Plantside Community and the Corporate Elite." Diss., Wayne State University, 1979.

Bolton, Charles Knowles. *Brookline: The History of a Favored Town.* Brookline, Mass.: C. A. W. Spencer, 1897.

Bradbury, Katherine L., et al. *Urban Decline and the Future of American Cities.* Washington, D.C.: Brookings Institution, 1982.

"Bronx Housing Slated." *New York Times,* November 24, 1960, 34.

Bruegmann, Robert. *Sprawl: A Compact History.* Chicago: Chicago University Press, 2005.

Bryan, Jack. "New Town/Out of Town, New Town/In Town: Twin Cities of Minneapolis, St. Paul Have New Sets of Twins." *Journal of Housing* (April 1972): 119–31.

Calthorpe, Peter. "HOPE VI and New Urbanism." In *From Despair to Hope: HOPE VI and the New Promise of Public Housing in America's Cities.* Washington, D.C.: Brookings Institution, 2009: 49–63.

Caulfield, John. "Changing Direction: A Developer's Detours to Address Philadelphia's Affordable Housing Shortage." *Builder*, January 2009. www.builderonline.com/affordable-housing/. Accessed January 3, 2011.

Campo, Daniel. "In the Footsteps of the Federal Writers' Project: Revisiting the Workshop of the World." *Landscape Journal* 29 (2010): 2–10.

Caro, Robert A. *The Power Broker: Robert Moses and the Fall of New York.* New York: Vintage, 1974.

Carter, Edward. *The Future of London.* Harmondsworth, Middlesex, UK: Penguin Books, 1962.

Cedar-Riverside Adult Education Collaborative. "Who Are We? A Short History of Cedar-Riverside." www.cr.themlc.org. Accessed December 26, 2010.

Cedar-Riverside Associates. *Cedar-Riverside New Community: Narrative Description.* Minneapolis: Cedar-Riverside Associates, 1971.

CensusCD Neighborhood Change Database (NCDB): Selected Variables for US Census Tracts for 1970, 1980, 1990, 2000 and Mapping Too! East Brunswick, N.J.: Geolytics, 2001.

CensusCD 1960. East Brunswick, N.J., 2001.

CensusCD 1970. East Brunswick, N.J. : Geolytics, 2001.

CensusCD 1980. East Brunswick, N.J.: Geolytics, 2001.

Center City District. *Center City: Planning for Growth, 2007–2012.* Philadelphia: Center City District, 2007.

———. *Center City Reports: Residential Development 2010: Diversification Pays Dividends.* Philadelphia: Center City District, 2010.

Chafets, Ze'ev. *Devil's Night: And Other True Tales of Detroit.* New York: Vintage Books, 1991.

Chargot, Patricia. "A Nice Neighborhood Gone Wrong." *Detroit Free Press*, February 3, 1980, 1A.

———. "Optimism Amidst Urban Blight." *Detroit Free Press*, February 4, 1980, 3A.

Chase, John, Margaret Crawford, and John Kaliski, eds. *Everyday Urbanism.* 2nd ed. New York: Monacelli Press, 2008.

Christensen, Jean. "Planned Towns as Big Business." *New York Times*, August 5, 1973, 137.

Cisneros, Henry G., and Lora Engdahl. *From Despair to Hope: HOPE VI and the New Promise of Public Housing in America's Cities.* Washington, D.C.: Brookings Institution Press, 2009.

City of Buffalo Department of Administration, Finance, Policy and Urban Affairs. "Mayor Brown's '5 in 5' Demolition Plan." *Moving Buffalo Forward: Policy Briefs from the Brown Administration* 1:1 (August 2007): 1–4.

City of Detroit City Council. *Notice of Public Hearing: Modified Development Plan for the Jefferson-Chalmers Neighborhood Development Program Area, Mich. A-4-1.* January 22, 1973.

———. *Notice of Public Hearing: Modified Development Plan for the Jefferson-Chalmers Neighborhood Development Program Area, Mich. A-4-1.* September 28, 1976.

Clark, Vernon. "New Temple Student Housing Stirs Renaissance West of Broad Street." *Philadelphia Inquirer,* October 15, 2010.

Cleveland City Planning Commission. *Cleveland Policy Planning Report.* Cleveland: Cleveland City Planning Commission, 1975.

Cohen, James R. "Population Thinning Strategies for Baltimore: Implications for Historic Preservation, Citizen Participation, and 'Smart Growth.'" Thinning Cities Conference, Cornell University. Ithaca, N.Y., September 8–9, 2000.

Colborn, Marge. "Couple Builds Urban Dream House: Detroit's Victoria Park is a City Neighborhood with a Suburban Feel." *Detroit News,* January 10, 1998, D20.

Covent Garden Planning Team. *Covent Garden's Moving: Covent Garden Area Draft Plan: Consortium of Greater London, City of Westminster and London Borough of Camden.* London: Greater London Council, 1968.

Crosswinds. "Jefferson Village." www.crosswindsus.com/michigan/detroit_jefferson_village/models.html. Accessed December 19, 2010.

Cummings, Jean L., Denise DiPasquale, and Matthew E. Kahn. "Measuring the Consequences of Promoting Inner City Homeownership." *Journal of Housing Economics* 11 (2002): 330–59.

Curry Stone Design Prize. "Sergio Fajardo + Alejandro Echeverri: Transformative Public Works Initiative." Interview. 2010. http://currystonedesignprize.com/2009/finalists/fajardo_and_echeverri. Accessed January 15, 2011.

Czerniak, Julia, ed. *CASE: Downsview Park, Toronto.* Cambridge, Mass.: Harvard University Graduate School of Design, 2001.

Daughen, Joseph R., and Peter Binzen. *The Cop Who Would Be King: Mayor Frank Rizzo.* Boston: Little Brown, 1977.

Davidoff, Paul. "Advocacy and Pluralism in Planning." *Journal of the American Institute of Planners* (November 1965): 331–38.

Dembart, Lee. "Carter Takes 'Sobering' Trip to South Bronx." *New York Times,* October 6, 1977, 66.

"Detroit Developers Set to Break Ground on One of the Largest Eastside Housing Developments in Years." *PR Newswire,* March 24, 2003.

"Detroit to Host Builders Association of Southeastern Michigan Homearama, Mayor Young Announces." *PR Newswire,* April 19, 1991.

"Detroit Subdivision on Track Despite Mayor's Warning." *Detroit News,* July 2, 1991.

Dobrin, Peter. "Kimmel Weighs Renovations: Low Public Use of the Arts Center and an Inferior Acoustic Are the Top Targets for Planners." *Philadelphia Inquirer,* November 19, 2008.

Dreussi, Amy Shriver, and Peter Leahy. "Urban Development Action Grants Revisited." *Review of Policy Research* 17:2–3 (June 2000): 120–37.

Duany, Andres, Elizabeth Plater-Zybrek, and Robert Alminana. *The New Civic Art: Elements of Town Planning.* New York: Rizzoli, 2003.

———. "A General Theory of Sustainable Urbanism." In *Ecological Urbanism,* edited by Mohsen Mostafavi with Gareth Doherty. Baden, Switzerland: Lars Muller Publishers, 2010: 245–50.

Edmonds, Patricia. "Young's Grand Vision: New Towns, Industry." *Detroit Free Press,* September 24, 1986, 1A, 15A.

Elliott, James R., Kevin Fox Gotham, and Melinda J. Milligan. "Framing the Urban: Struggles Over HOPE VI and New Urbanism in a Historic City." *City & Community* 3:4 (December 2004): 373–94.

Elrich, M.L. "New Homes Bring Hope for Detroit Neighborhood's Revival." *Detroit Free Press,* March 27, 2003.

Evenson, Norma. *Two Brazilian Capitals: Architecture and Urbanism in Rio de Janeiro and Brasilia.* New Haven, Conn.: Yale University Press, 1973.

Fainstein, Susan. *The Just City.* Ithaca, N.Y.: Cornell University Press, 2010.

Featherman, Sandra. "Early Abandonment: A Profile of Residential Abandonment in the Early Stages of Development." In *Papers in Urban Problems 1.* Philadelphia: University of Pennsylvania Department of City and Regional Planning, 1976.

Fogelson, Robert M. *Downtown: Its Rise and Fall, 1880–1950.* New Haven, Conn.: Yale University Press, 2001.

Fraser, Nancy, and Axel Honneth. *Redistribution or Recognition? A Political-Philosophical Exchange.* New York: Verso, 2003.

Freeman, Donald, ed. *Boston/Architecture: The Boston Society of Architects.* Cambridge: MIT Press, 1969.

Frej, William, and Harry Specht. "The Housing and Community Development Act of 1974: Implications for Policy and Planning." *Social Service Review* 50:2 (1976): 275–92.

Frieden, Bernard J., and Lynne Sagalyn. *Downtown Inc.: How America Rebuilds Cities.* Cambridge, Mass.: MIT Press, 1989.

Gallagher, John. *Reimagining Detroit: Opportunities for Redefining an American City.* Detroit, Mich.: Wayne State University Press, 2010.

Garvin, Alexander. *The American City: What Works and What Doesn't.* New York: McGraw-Hill, 1996.

Gavrilovich, Peter, and Bill McGraw. *The Detroit Almanac: 300 Years of Life in the Motor City.* Detroit: Detroit Free Press, 2000.

Gelbart, Marcia. "The Street Legacy: Agenda for Renewal, Overshadowed." *Philadelphia Inquirer,* January 6, 2008, A1.

Gillette, Howard. *Camden After the Fall: Decline and Renewal in a Post-industrial City.* Philadelphia: University of Pennsylvania Press, 2005.

Glaeser, Edward L., and Joseph Gyourko. "Urban Decline and Durable Housing." *National Bureau of Economic Research Working Paper Series* 2001: 1–72.

Goldberger, Paul. "Design: The National A.I.A Awards." *New York Times,* May 18, 1975, 69–70.

———. "Ruling Against Model High-Rise Disputes Federal Housing Ideas." *New York Times,* October 8, 1976, 1.

"Good Detroit News: Beaver Signals Cleaner River; Cleanup of Detroit River Is Starting to Pay Off, Officials Note." MSNBC, February 16, 2009. www.msnbc.msn .com/id/29222122/ns/us_news-environment/. Accessed December 13, 2010.

Goode, W. Wilson, with Joann Stevens. *In Goode Faith*. Valley Forge, Pa.: Judson Press, 1992.

Goodin, Michael. "Sold!: Victoria Park Has Buyers for Most Homes." *Crain's Detroit Business*, March 9, 1992, 1.

———. "Rehab Would Cover Entire Neighborhood." *Crain's Detroit Business*, August 30, 1993, 1.

———. "Land Along Riverfront May Become Battleground." *Crain's Detroit Business*, January 1, 1996, 3.

"Graimark Realty Advisors, Inc.: Detroit City Homes Affordable; Single Family Housing Development." *PR Newswire*, October 24, 1997.

Gray, Madison. "Podcast: Will Light Rail Lay Tracks in Motown?" *Time: The Detroit Blog*. detroit.blogs.time.com/2010/08/06. Accessed December 29, 2010.

Greater London Council, Department of Architecture and Civic Design. *Covent Garden's Moving: Covent Garden Draft Plan*. London: Greater London Council, ca. 1969.

———. *GLC Architecture 1965/70: The Work of the GLC's Department of Architecture and Civic Design*. London: Greater London Council, 1970.

———. *GLC Architects Review 2*. London: Academy Editions, 1976.

———. *The Greater London Council (Covent Garden) GLC Action Area Plan: Resolution of Adoption, Written Statement, Proposals Map*. London: Greater London Council, 1978.

———. *New Directions in Housing: GLC Architects Review 3*. London: Academy Editions, 1977.

———. *Review, 1974/Greater London Council Architects Department*. London: Greater London Council, 1974.

Grewal, San. "What's Going On with 10 Major Projects Around the GTA." *The Star*, May 25, 2010. www.thestar.com/813841. Accessed January 24, 2011.

Grutzner, Charles. "Issue of 'Fair Trade' Still Very Much Alive." *New York Times*, June 3, 1951, 149.

Grzech, Ellen. "Jefferson-Chalmers Agency Plants 200 Townhouses." *Detroit Free Press*, June 26, 1976, 6-A.

Hall, Peter. *Cities of Tomorrow: An Intellectual History of Urban Planning and Design in the 20th Century*. 3rd ed. Oxford: Blackwell, 2002.

Hauser, Michael, and Marianne Weldon. *Hudson's: Detroit's Legendary Department Store*. Charleston, S.C.: Arcadia, 2004.

Hawthorne, Christopher. "Medellín, Colombia's Architectural Renaissance." *Los Angeles Times*, May 8, 2010. http://articles.latimes.com/2010/may/08/entertainment/la-ca-medellin-20100509-1.

Heller, Gregory L. "Salesman of Ideas: The Life Experiences That Shaped Edmund Bacon." In *Imagining Philadelphia: Edmund Bacon and the Future of the City*, edited by Scott Gabriel Knowles. Philadelphia: University of Pennsylvania Press, 2009: 19–51.

Henderson, Tom, and Robert Ankeny. "Complex Deals Help Projects Pay Off: Creative Financing, Incentives Drive Detroit Development." *Crain's Detroit Business,* August 21, 2006, 14.

Henion, Andy. "People Mover Grows Up: Proposal Would Extend Route to New Center." *Detroit News,* December 23, 2006. www.detnews.com/article/20061223/ METRO/612230387. Accessed December 29, 2010.

Herbers, John. "House Passes Bill with Broad Provisions for New Communities." *New York Times,* December 20, 1970, 32.

Heron, W. Kim. "$50 Million Awarded for Chrysler Plant: Grant, Loan to Preserve Jefferson Ave. Jobs." *Detroit Free Press,* September 24, 1986, 1A.

Hinds, Michael deCourcy. "After Renaissance of the 70s and 80s, Philadelphia Is Struggling to Survive." *New York Times,* June 21, 1990, A16.

———. "Its Cash and Tempers Short, Philadelphia Seeks Solvency." *New York Times,* September 11, 1990, A1.

Home, Robert, and Sebastian Loew. *Covent Garden.* London: Surveyors, 1987.

"Honor Awards Go to Nine Buildings: The 25-Year Award to a Glass House." *American Institute of Architects Journal* (May 1975): 26–43.

Hoyt, Homer. United States Federal Housing Administration. *The Structure and Growth of Residential Neighborhoods in American Cities.* Washington, D.C.: U.S. Government Printing Office, 1939.

Huxtable, Ada Louise. "The Gospel According to Giedion and Gropius Is Under Attack." *New York Times,* June 27, 1976, 47.

Ilka, Douglas. "New Subdivision Will Mark Rebirth of Single-Family Housing in Detroit." *Detroit News,* November 22, 1991.

Interboro Partners. "Improve Your Lot!" In *VERB Crisis: Architecture Boogazine.* Barcelona: Actar, 2008: 240–69.

———. "Improve Your Lot!" In *Cities Growing Smaller.* Cleveland: Kent State University, Cleveland Urban Design Collaborative, 2008: 46–64.

Jackson, Kathy. "Ford Engineer's Island Dream Is Nearing Reality." *Crain's Detroit Business,* July 3, 1989, 11.

Jackson, Kenneth T. *Crabgrass Frontier: The Suburbanization of the United States.* New York: Oxford University Press, 1985.

Jackson, Samuel C. "New Communities." *HUD Challenge,* August 1972, 4–23.

Jacobs, Jane. *The Death and Life of Great American Cities.* New York: Vintage, 1961.

———. *The Economy of Cities.* New York: Random House, 1969.

———. *Cities and the Wealth of Nations.* New York: Random House, 1984.

Jencks, Charles. *The Language of Post-Modern Architecture.* New York: Rizzoli, 1981.

Johnson, Saunia. "Mellon PSFS Keeps North Philly Revitalization Going." *Philadelphia Tribune,* January 13, 1998, 3A.

Kerkstra, Patrick. "Special Report: A Surprising Mix of Bricks, Mortar, and Imagination." *PlanPhilly,* December 2, 2010. Planphilly.com/special-report-surprising-mix-bricks-mortar-and-im agination. Accessed January 3, 2011.

Kieran, Christopher. "One Hancock Square: A Kaleidoscope of Color and Light Graces the Façade of Erdy McHenry Architecture LLC's Mixed-use Project." *Architectural Record*, June 2008. Archrecord.construction.com. Accessed January 4, 2011.

Klatt, Bebbe, ed. *GLC/ILEA Architecture 1976–1986: An Illustrated Record of the Work of the GLC/ILEA Department of Architecture and Civic Design in the Decade 1976–1986.* London: Architectural Press, 1986.

Kleinman, Kent. "Detroit's Michigan." *Arkkitehti* (1997): 28–31.

Klemek, Christopher. "From Political Outsider to Power Broker in Two 'Great American Cities': Jane Jacobs and the Fall of the Urban Renewal Order in New York and Toronto." *Journal of Urban History* 34 (January 2008): 309–32.

———. "The Rise and Fall of the New Left Urbanism." *Daedalus* 138:2 (Spring 2009): 73–82, 144.

Knowles, Scott Gabriel, ed. *Imagining Philadelphia: Edmund Bacon and the City of the Future.* Philadelphia: University of Pennsylvania Press, 2009.

Koolhaas, Rem. *S M L XL.* New York: Monacelli Press, 1995.

———. "Miestakes." In *Mies in America*, edited by Phyllis Lambert. New York: Harry N. Abrams, 2001.

Kraemer, Kenneth L. *The Concept, Theory, and Objectives of Urban Renewal.* Los Angeles: University of South California, City and Regional Planning and School of Public Administration, 1965.

Krause, Charles. "HUD Blamed as Detroit Homes Rot." *Washington Post,* March 15, 1976, A1, A3.

Krieger, Alex. "Since (and Before) Seaside." In *Towns and Town-Making Principles.* Cambridge, Mass.: Harvard University Graduate School of Design, 1991.

Kromer, John. *Fixing Broken Cities: Implementation of Urban Development Strategies.* New York: Routledge, 2010.

———. *Neighborhood Recovery: Reinvestment Policy for the New Hometown.* New Brunswick, N.J.: Rutgers University Press, 2000.

Kromer, John, to Reverend Ralph Blanks. Memorandum. April 6, 1993.

Kromer, John, to Ronald Wilson. Memorandum, April 3, 1992.

LaFrank, Kathleen. "Seaside, Florida: 'The New Town—The Old Ways.'" *Perspectives in Vernacular Architecture* 6, Shaping Communities (1997): 111–21.

Langdon, Philip. "'Shrinking' the City Cannot Be the Whole Solution." *New Urban Network,* January 12, 2011. http://newurbannetwork.com/article/%E2%80%98shrinking%E2%80%99-city-cannot-be-whole-solution-13849. Accessed February 20, 2011.

Lee, Rebecca. "The Affordable Option: Charlotte Street Manufactured Housing." In *The Unsheltered Woman: Women and Housing in the 80s,* edited by Eugenie Ladner Birch. New Brunswick, N.J.: Center for Urban Policy Research, Rutgers University, 1985: 277–82.

Leonardo, Joseph, Chief, Community Planning Division, Philadelphia City Planning Commission, to Sharon Grinnel. Memorandum, September 21, 1994.

Lerman, Brian R. "Mandatory Inclusionary Zoning: The Answer to the Affordable Housing Problem." *Boston College Environmental Affairs Law Review* 33:2 (2006): 383–416.

Leven, Charles L., et al., eds. *Neighborhood Change: Lessons in the Dynamics of Urban Decay.* New York: Praeger, 1976.

Logan, John, and Harvey L. Molotch. *Urban Fortunes: The Political Economy of Place.* Berkeley: University of California Press, 1987.

Loos, Adolf. "Ornament und Verbrechen." In *Trotzdem, 1900–1930,* by Adolf Loos. Innsbruck: Brenner-Verlag, 1931.

Lucey, Catherine. "40,000 City Properties Abandoned: Now What?" *Philadelphia Inquirer.* July 28, 2010. articles.philly.com/2010–07–28/news/24969809_1_abandoned-property-tax-delinquent-properties-numerous-city-agencies. Accessed December 17, 2010.

Lueck, Thomas J. "Giuliani Plans Inducements to Revive Wall Street Area." *New York Times,* December 16, 1994.

Lynch, Kevin. "Controlling the Flow of Rebuilding and Replanning in Residential Areas." Bachelor's thesis, Massachusetts Institute of Technology, 1947.

———. *Good City Form.* Cambridge, Mass.: MIT Press, 1981.

Macdonald, Christine. "How Former HUD Chief's Detroit Housing Project Failed." *Detroit News,* April 14, 2011. www.detnews.com/article/20110414/METRO/10414 0394, Accessed April 22, 2011.

Mahler, Jonathan. *Ladies and Gentleman, the Bronx Is Burning: 1977 Baseball, Politics, and the Battle for the Soul of a City.* New York: Farrar, Straus and Giroux, 2005.

Make It Right. "Our Work and Progress: Track Our Progress." *Make It Right.* 2011. www.makeitrightnola.org/index.php/work_progress/track_progress/. Accessed February 20, 2011.

"Making Housing Affordable: The Newest Inner-City Houses Have Amenities That Match Many in the Suburbs; Keeping the Cost Down Is Hard Work." *Philadelphia Inquirer,* May 11, 1997.

Marchand, Yves, and Roland Meffre. *The Ruins of Detroit.* Göttingen, Germany: Steidl, 2010.

Markiewicz, David A. "Hometown Model." *Detroit News,* June 1, 1992, 3F.

Martignoni, Jimena. "How Medellín Got Its Groove Back." *Architectural Record* 197:3 (March 2009): 37.

Martin, Judith A. *Recycling the Central City: The Development of a New Town-in Town.* Minneapolis: Center for Urban and Regional Affairs, University of Minnesota, 1978.

McDonald, Maureen. "Success Spreads Around Development: Victoria Park Sparks Growth in City's Once Blighted Areas." *Detroit News,* December 24, 2002. http://www.crosswindsus.com/news_2002-dec-24.html. Accessed December 1, 2010.

McKee, Guian. "A Utopian, a Utopianist, or Whatever the Heck It Is: Edmund Bacon and the Complexity of the City." In *Imagining Philadelphia: Edmund Bacon and*

the Future of the City, edited by Scott Gabriel Knowles. Philadelphia: University of
   Pennsylvania Press, 2009: 52–77.

Midgette, Anne. "A Regional Center Is Set to Replace a Hall That Has Been Problematic for Nearly a Century." *New York Times,* March 28, 1999, AR37.

Miller, Nancy A. "Arrested Development: Can Ralph Rapson's Progressive Vision for
   America's First 'New Town-In Town' Be Recovered in the Beleaguered Cedar
   Square West?" *Architecture Minnesota,* January–February 2006, 38–43, 54, 56.

Minneapolis City Planning Commission. *Riverside: Challenge and Opportunity.* Analysis report, Winter 1965–66, Publication No. 168, Neighborhood Series No. 10.

Mishler, Tom, Pennsylvania Horticultural Society, to Anne Fadullon. Memorandum.
   September 22, 1994.

Montgomery, Paul. "New Towns Here Held Essential to Ease Pressures." *New York
   Times,* May 11, 1971, 35.

Morgan, Jennifer M. "Zoning for All: Using Inclusionary Zoning Techniques to Promote Affordable Housing." *Emory Law Journal* 44 (Winter 1995): 359–93.

"National Transportation Statistics 2002." *Bureau of Transportation Statistics.* December 2002. www.bts.gov/publications/national_transportation_statistics/2002/excel/
   table_highway_profile.xls. Accessed July 24, 2009.

Neubacher, Jim, and Ellen Grzech. "Charting the Tragedy of the Lower East Side—a
   Fifth of It Has Vanished." *Detroit Free Press,* December 11, 1977, 1B.

Newman, Oscar. *Defensible Space: Crime Prevention Through Urban Design.* New York:
   Macmillan, 1972.

New Urban Network. "Waldheim/Duany Dialogue CNU 19." *New Urban Network.*
   December 6, 2010. http://newurbannetwork.com/article/waldheimduany-dialogue-
   cnu-19-13669. Accessed February 20, 2011.

New York City Department of City Planning. *Fresh Kills Park: Draft Master Plan.*
   March 2006.

New York City Department of Parks. "Freshkills Park." www.nycgovparks.org/
   sub_your_park/fresh_kills_park/html/fresh_kills_park.html. Accessed January 24,
   2011.

The New York Yankees 1977 World Series. Directed by A&E Home Video. 1977, 2007.

Neyfakh, Leon. "Green Building." *Boston Globe,* January 30, 2011. www.boston.com/
   bostonglobe/ideas/articles/2011/01/30/green_building/. Accessed February 4, 2011.

Nixon, Richard. "Radio Address About the State of the Union Message on Community
   Development." Paper 68, March 4, 1973. In *Public Papers of the Presidents of the
   United States: Richard Nixon; Containing the Public Messages, Speeches, and Statements of the President, 1973.* Washington, D.C.: U.S. Government Printing Office,
   1975: 164–68.

———. "State of the Union Message to the Congress on Community Development."
   Paper 73, March 8, 1973. In *Public Papers of the Presidents of the United States:
   Richard Nixon; Containing the Public Messages, Speeches, and Statements of the
   President, 1973.* Washington, D.C.: U.S. Government Printing Office, 1975:
   171–80.

Northrup, Becki, to John Kromer. Memorandum, February 12, 1992.

OKKS Development. "Cecil B. Moore Homeownership." http://okksdevelopment .com/Current_Projects.html. Accessed January 3, 2011.

Okrent, Daniel. "Detroit: The Death- and Possible Life- of a Great City." *Time*, September 24, 2009. www.time.com/time/printout/0,8816,1925796,00.html. Accessed December 29, 2010.

Oser, Alan. "About Real Estate: US Re-evaluating 'New Towns Program.'" *New York Times*, July 23, 1976, 10.

———. "Owner-Occupied Houses: New Test in South Bronx." *New York Times*, April 1, 1983, A17.

Ostmann, Robert, Jr. "Jefferson-Chalmers Troubled: E. Side Renewal Miracle Falters." *Detroit Free Press*, December 13, 1976, 1A, 10A.

Oswalt, Philipp, ed. *Shrinking Cities*. Vol. 1, *International Research*. Ostfildern-Ruit, Germany: Hatje Cantz, 2005.

Palm, Kristin. "One Building's Struggle: Hudson's Department Store, Detroit." *Metropolis*, June 1998, 33, 39, 41.

Park, Kyong. *Urban Ecology: Detroit and Beyond*. Hong Kong: Map Book Publishers, 2005.

Pawlowski, Diane. "Development May Stop Demolition: Jefferson-Chalmers Pact Signals Area Rebirth." *Detroit News*, April 16, 1976.

Penn Institute for Urban Research, with Econsult Corporation and May 8 Consulting. *Vacant Land Management in Philadelphia: The Costs of the Current System and the Benefits of Reform*. Philadelphia: Penn Institute for Urban Research, 2010.

Pennsylvania Horticultural Society. *Urban Vacant Land: Issues and Recommendations: Executive Summary*. Philadelphia: Pennsylvania Horticultural Society, 1998.

Pepper, Jon. "Building Homes Inside Detroit Is a Strong Step Toward Rebuilding the City." *Detroit News*, November 17, 1991, 1D, 2C.

Pew Charitable Trusts. "Delaward Waterfront Corporation Breaks Ground for Race Street Pier." www.pewtrusts.org.

Philadelphia City Planning Commission. *North Philadelphia Databook*. Philadelphia: Philadelphia City Planning Commission, 1986.

———. *North Philadelphia Plan: A Guide to Revitalization*. Philadelphia: Philadelphia City Planning Commission, 1987.

———. "Meeting minutes." September 23, 1993.

Philadelphia Office of Housing and Community Development (OHCD). *Home in North Philadelphia*. Report, 1993.

———. Poplar Nehemiah Project Development Team. "Meeting minutes." April 28, 1994.

———. "Meeting minutes." September 29, 1994.

———. "Meeting minutes." October 6, 1994.

———. "Learning from Yorktown." Report, 1996.

———. "Proposal for the Cecil B. Moore Homeownership Zone." Application to the Department of Housing and Urban Development, 1996.

———. Cecil B. Moore Project Development Team. "Meeting minutes." November 19, 1997.

———. "Year 27 Consolidated Plan, Fiscal Year 2002." 2002.

———. "Neighborhoods Online: OHCD Lower North." Phillyneighborhoods.org/. Accessed January 3, 2011.

Philadelphia Housing Authority. "About Scattered Sites." 2010. www.pha.phila.gov/housing%5CTypes_of_Housing%5CAbout_Scattered_Sites.html. Accessed December 19, 2010.

Philadelphia Housing Development Corporation. "Cecil B. Moore Homeownership Zone." www.phdchousing.org/cbm.htm. Accessed January 4, 2011.

———. *Ludlow Village III: 16 New Twin Townhouses.* Brochure, 1998.

———. *Ludlow Village IV: $45,000 Can Buy You a New Home in Philadelphia!* Brochure, 2001.

Philadelphia Redevelopment Authority. *Neighborhood Housing Strategy for the Cecil B. Moore Development Area.* Philadelphia: Philadelphia Redevelopment Authority, February 1996.

Pierce, Neil. "Massive Urban Renewal: Detroit's 21st-Century Formula." Washington Post Writers' Group, May 30, 2004. http://www.stateline.org/live/ViewPage.action?siteNodeId=136&languageId=1&contentId=15660. Accessed August 17, 2011.

Plunz, Richard. *A History of Housing in New York City: Dwelling Type and Social Change in the American Metropolis.* New York: Columbia University Press, 1990.

Pogrebin, Robin. "First Phase of High Line Is Ready for Strolling." *New York Times,* June 8, 2009.

Polshek, James S. *James Stewart Polshek: Buildings and Projects, 1957–1987: Context and Responsibility.* New York: Rizzoli, 1988.

Pope, John, to Wayne King. Memorandum, December 29, 1997.

Poplar Enterprise Development Corporation, to Poplar Nehemiah Project Development Team. Memorandum, September 22, 1994.

Pristin, Terry. "Voters Back Limits on Eminent Domain." *New York Times,* November 15, 2006, 6.

Puls, Mark. "Detroit's Claim on Land Premature: Property Records Changed Before Deal." *Detroit News,* March 4, 2001, 1C.

Rae, Douglas W. *City: Urbanism and Its End.* New Haven, Conn.: Yale University Press, 2003.

Reardon, Kenneth M. "State and Local Revitalization Efforts in East St. Louis, Illinois." *Annals of the American Academy of Political and Social Science* (1997): 235–47.

Reeves, Richard. "HUD Fiasco Haunts Liberals." *Detroit Free Press,* June 13, 1979.

Rich, William, Kenneth Geiser, Rolf Goetz, and Robert Hollister. "Holding Together: Four Years of Evolution at MIT." *Journal of the American Planning Association* 36:4 (January 1970): 242–52.

Risselada, Max and Dirk van den Heuvel, eds. *Team 10: 1953–81, in Search of a Utopia of the Present.* Rotterdam, Netherlands: Nai Publishers, 2005.

Roberts, Sam. "Charlotte Street: Tortured Rebirth of a Wasteland." *New York Times*, March 9, 1987, B1.

Robertson, Nan. "Helping the Elderly to Flee from Fear." *New York Times*, June 13, 1977, 48.

Rochon, Lisa. "From Slumdog Barrio to Beacon on the Hill: Catalytic Architecture, Visionary Social Spending and Simple Local Pride Are Remaking One of Colombia's Poorest Neighbourhoods." *Globe and Mail,* February 7, 2009, R8.

Rodwin, Lloyd, and Bishwapriya Sanyal, eds. *The Profession of City Planning: Changes, Images, and Challenges, 1950–2000.* New Brunswick, N.J.: Center for Urban Policy Research, Rutgers University, 2000.

Romero, Simon. "Medellín's Nonconformist Mayor Turns Blight to Beauty." *New York Times*, July 15, 2007, 3.

Rooney, Jim. *Organizing the South Bronx.* Albany: State University of New York, 1995.

Ross, Andrew. *The Celebration Chronicles: Life, Liberty and the Pursuit of Property Value in Disney's New Town.* New York: Ballantine Books, 1999.

Rossi, Aldo. *The Architecture of the City.* Cambridge, Mass.: MIT Press, 1982.

Rowe, Peter. *Modernity and Housing.* Cambridge, Mass.: MIT Press, 1993.

Rusk, David. *Cities Without Suburbs.* Washington, D.C.: Woodrow Wilson Center Press, 1993.

Russ, Valerie. "North to the Future." *Philadelphia Daily News*, September 8, 2009, 6.

Ryan, Brent D. *Privately-Financed Housing in Distressed Urban Neighborhoods: Lessons from Detroit.* Unpublished research report, Fannie Mae Foundation, 2006.

———. "Reconsidering the Grid: The Evolution of Philadelphia's Block Form, 1683–1900." Unpublished paper, Massachusetts Institute of Technology, 1998.

———. "The Suburbanization of the Inner City: Urban Housing and the Pastoral Ideal." Diss., Massachusetts Institute of Technology, Cambridge, Mass., 2002.

Ryan, Brent D., and Daniel Campo. "Demolition of Detroit: A History of the Automotive Industry, Demolition, and Deurbanization." Paper presented at Urban History Association, 5th Biennial Conference, Las Vegas, Nev., October 2010.

Saffron, Inga. "Changing Skyline: Four Reasons for Creating a Green Gem on the Waterfront." *Philadelphia Inquirer*, June 26, 2009, E01.

———. "Changing Skyline: Hometown Modernists; At Once Edgy and Down-to-Earth, the Architecture of Erdy McHenry Is Redefining the City's Look." *Philadelphia Inquirer,* August 25, 2006.

Samper Escobar, Jose Jaime. "The Politics of Peace Process in Cities in Conflict: The Medellín Case as a Best Practice." Master's thesis, Massachusetts Institute of Technology, 2010.

Sanborn Map Company. *Sanborn Fire Insurance Maps [microform]: Pennsylvania.* Ann Arbor, Mich.: Bell and Howell Information and Learning, 1984: Philadelphia sheets 366 and 367.

Schade, Rachel Simmons, Bolender Architects, National Trust for Historic Preservation in the United States, Philadelphia Office of Housing and Community Development, and Philadelphia City Planning Commission. *Philadelphia Rowhouse*

Manual: A Practical Guide for Homeowners. Philadelphia: City of Philadelphia, 2008.

Schwartz, Alex F. *Housing Policy in the United States: An Introduction.* New York: Routledge, 2006.

Schwieterman, Joseph, and Dana M. Caspall. *The Politics of Place: A History of Zoning in Chicago.* Chicago: Lake Claremont Press, 2006.

Scism, Leslie. "Focus: North Philadelphia: A Neighborhood Struggles for a Revival." *New York Times,* November 18, 1990, R5.

Scott Brown, Denise. "Between Three Stools: A Personal View of Urban Design Pedagogy." In *Urban Concepts.* New York: St. Martin's Press, 1990: 8–20.

Scully, Vincent J. *American Architecture and Urbanism.* New York: H. Holt, 1988.

Segal, Gloria M. "Cedar-Riverside: The Architect as Teacher." *Northwest Architect,* July–August 1972: 162–63, 174.

Shaw, Robert. "The International Building Exhibition (IBA) Emscher Park, Germany: A Model for Sustainable Restructuring?" *European Planning Studies* 10:1 (2002): 77–97.

———. "Taste of Suburbia Arrives in the South Bronx." *New York Times,* March 19, 1983, 1.

Siegel, Ron. "Archer's Kinfolks on Graimark Payroll." *Michigan Citizen,* February 28, 1998, A1.

———. "Archer Hatched Graimark Plan: Documents Contradict Earlier Administration Statements." *Michigan Citizen,* March 14, 1998, A1.

———. "Council Members Declare Themselves on Graimark Plan." *Michigan Citizen,* March 28, 1998, A1.

———. "DunCombe, Graimark Directors Are Partners." *Michigan Citizen,* May 2, 1998.

Slobozdian, Joseph A. "Renaissance." *Philadelphia Inquirer,* December 27, 2005, A1.

Sohmer, Rebecca, and Robert E. Lang. "Life at the Center: The Rise of Downtown Housing." In *Housing Facts and Findings 1:1.* Washington, D.C.: Fannie Mae Foundation, 1999.

"South Bronx Debate: Dig It Now or Plan It Later." *New York Times,* February 25, 1979, E7.

Spatt, Beverly Moss. "Dissenting Report of Commissioner Spatt." In *Plan for New York City 1969: A Proposal.* Vol. 1, *Critical Issues,* 174–75. New York: New York City Planning Commission, 1969.

Speaks, Michael. "Every Day Is Not Enough." In *Everyday Urbanism: Margaret Crawford vs. Michael Speaks,* edited by Rahul Mehrotra. Ann Arbor: University of Michigan, 2005: 35–50.

Special to the *New York Times.* "A City Within a City Is Guaranteed Loan." *New York Times,* June 29, 1971, 29.

———. "Public Housing Curb Scored in Carolina." *New York Times,* January 28, 1973, 45.

Spirn, Anne Whiston. *The Granite Garden: Urban Nature and Human Design.* New York: Basic Books, 1984.

Staley, Willy. "Urban Nation." *Next American City* (Winter 2010). http://americancity .org/magazine/article/urban-nation/.

Steinberg, Harris M. "Philadelphia in the Year 2059." In *Imagining Philadelphia: Edmund Bacon and the Future of the City*, edited by Scott Gabriel Knowles. Philadelphia: University of Pennsylvania Press, 2009: 112–44.

Stern, Robert A. M. "Subway Suburb." In *The Anglo-American Suburb*, edited by John Montague Massengale. New York: St. Martin's Press, 1981.

Stevenson, Richard W. "Take a Ride on the Reading: Collect $25 Million." *New York Times,* September 22, 1985.

Stewart, Barbara. "Market's Nod to a Rebirth: Property Values Rise in a South Bronx Enclave." *New York Times*, November 2, 1997, 37.

Streitfeld, David. "An Effort to Save Flint, Mich., by Shrinking It." *New York Times,* April 21, 2009.

Sugrue, Thomas. *The Origins of the Urban Crisis: Race and Inequality in a Postwar Detroit.* Princeton, N.J.: Princeton University Press, 1996.

Talen, Emily. "Sprawl Repair." *Planning*, November 2010, 32–36.

Talley, Brett. "Restraining Eminent Domain Through Just Compensation: Kelo v. City of New London." *Harvard Journal of Law and Public Policy* 29:2 (2006): 759–69.

"The Little Firehouse That Couldn't Beat the Convention Racket." *Classical Values*, May 28, 2008. www.classicalvlues.com/archives/2008/05/the_little_fire.html. Accessed December 31, 2010.

Thomas, June Manning. *Redevelopment and Race: Planning a Finer City in Postwar Detroit.* Baltimore: Johns Hopkins University Press, 1997.

Thompson, Lawrence. *A History of HUD.* Washington, D.C.: Lawrence Thompson, 2006.

Toy, Vivian S. "Detroit Subdivision on Schedule Despite Mayor's Warning." *Detroit News*, July 2, 1991, 3B.

United Nations Development Programme. *Human Development Report 2010: 20th Anniversary Edition; The Real Wealth of Nations: Pathways to Human Development.* New York: United Nations Development Programme, 2010.

U.S. Congress. House. Committee on Financial Services. *HOPE VI Improvement and Reauthorization Act of 2007: Report, Together with Additional Views (to Accompany H.R. 3524) (Including Cost Estimate of the Congressional Budget Office).* Washington, D.C.: U.S. Government Printing Office, 2008.

U.S. Department of Housing and Urban Development. *FY 2002 Formula Allocations for Michigan.* Washington, D.C., November 28, 2001. www.hud.gov/offices/cpd/ communitydevelopment/budget/2002allocations/michigan.pdf. Accessed January 7, 2011.

———. *New American Neighborhoods: Building Homeownership Zones to Revitalize Our Nation's Communities.* Washington, D.C., 1996.

————. *Section 108 Loan Guarantee Program.* www.hud.gov/offices/cpd/community-development/programs/108/. Accessed January 23, 2011.

U.S. National Advisory Commission on Civil Disorders [Kerner Commission]. *Report of the National Advisory Commission on Civil Disorders.* New York: Praeger, 1968.

University of Minnesota News. "Ralph Rapson Dies at 93." *University of Minnesota.* April 3, 2008. www1.umn.edu/umnnews/Feature_Stories/Ralph_Rapson_dies_at_93.html. Accessed July 24, 2009.

University of Pennsylvania Cartographic Modeling Laboratory. *Philadelphia NIS NeighborhoodBase: Summary Statistics: Vacant Land Parcels, 7/1/2007.* http://cml.upenn.edu/nbase/nbStatsRequest2.asp. Accessed August 18, 2011.

Vale, Lawrence J. *From the Puritans to the Projects: Public Housing and Public Neighbors.* Cambridge, Mass.: Harvard University Press, 2000.

————. *Reclaiming Public Housing: A Half-Century of Struggles in Three Public Neighborhoods.* Cambridge, Mass.: Harvard University Press, 2002.

"Vast Shopping Center with 100 Retail Units Planned by Store in Suburbs of Detroit." *New York Times,* June 4, 1950, R1.

Venturi, Robert. *Complexity and Contradiction in Architecture.* New York: Museum of Modern Art, 1966.

Vergara, Camilo Jose. *The New American Ghetto.* New Brunswick, N.J.: Rutgers University Press, 1997.

Von Hoffman, Alexander. *House by House, Block by Block: The Rebirth of America's Urban Neighborhoods.* Oxford: Oxford University Press, 2003.

Wachter, Susan. *The Determinants of Neighborhood Transformations in Philadelphia Identification and Analysis: The New Kensington Pilot Study.* Philadelphia: Wharton School, University of Pennsylvania, 2005.

Waldheim, Charles, ed. *CASE: Hilberseimer/Mies van der Rohe, Lafayette Park, Detroit.* Cambridge, Mass.: Harvard University Graduate School of Design, 2004.

————. *The Landscape Urbanism Reader.* New York: Princeton Architectural Press, 2006.

Walter, Joan. "Hidden Soul: Old Area Bristles with Hope: Jefferson-Chalmers Works Hard to Shed 'Ghetto' Image." *Detroit News,* July 20, 1981: 1B.

Walters, Wendy S. "Turning the Neighborhood Inside Out: Imagining a New Detroit in Tyree Guyton's Heidelberg Project." *TDR: The Drama Review* 45:4 (Winter 2001): 64–93.

Warner, Sam Bass, Jr. *The Private City: Philadelphia in Three Periods of Growth.* Philadelphia: University of Pennsylvania Press, 1968.

White, Norval, Elliot Willensky, and Fran Leadon. *AIA Guide to New York City.* 5th ed. New York: Oxford University Press, 2010.

Whiting, Sarah. "Bas-Relief Urbanism: Chicago's Figured Field." In *Mies in America,* edited by Phyllis Lambert. Montreal: Canadian Center for Architecture, 2001: 642–91.

Whyte, William H. 1970. *The Last Landscape.* New York: Anchor Books.

Willis, Carol. *Form Follows Finance: Skyscrapers and Skylines in New York and Chicago.* New York: Princeton Architectural Press, 1995.

Wilson, William J. *The Truly Disadvantaged: The Inner City, the Underclass, and Public Policy.* Chicago: University of Chicago Press, 1987.

———. *When Work Disappears: The World of the New Urban Poor.* New York: Knopf, 1996.

Woodward, Christopher, and Kenneth Campbell. "Two Perspectives on Odhams: Odhams Walk, Covent Garden, London." *Architects' Journal* (February 3, 1982): 31–46.

Woolf, Virginia. "Mr. Bennett and Mrs. Brown." London: Hogarth Press, 1924.

Wooten, Michael. "Special Report: Abandoned Housing Crisis in Buffalo." *WGRZ,* May 11, 2010. www.wgrz.com/news/local/story.aspx?storyid = 76773&catid = 37. Accessed February 20, 2011.

Wowk, Mike. "Detroit Would Like to Build on the Success of Victoria Park." *Detroit News,* May 4, 1993, B1.

Yardley, Jim. "A Master Builder's Mixed Legacy: Forgotten by the Public, 'Mr. Urban Renewal' Looks Back." *New York Times,* December 29, 1997, B1.

Zillow.com. "1545 Charlotte Street, Bronx, NY 10460." www.zillow.com/homedetails/ 1545-Charlotte-St-Bronx-NY-10460/29783367_zpid/. Accessed November 11, 2010.

Index

Page numbers in italics indicate figures and tables.

5 in 5 Initiative, 181

8 Mile Road neighborhood (Detroit), 64

abandoned housing and sites: artistic additions to, 187, *188*; "blotting" phenomenon and, 186, 187, 194; of Charlotte Gardens, 40; hopes for, 224; and housing types, 50; in Jefferson-Chalmers area, 93–94, *95*, 116–17; landscape ideals applied to, 189–90; landscape urbanism and, 193–94; "missing" or "broken teeth" streets in, *60*, 61; in North Philadelphia, 81–83; origin and long-term effects of, 58, *60*, 60–61; Philadelphia map of, *62*; population losses and, 45–46; shrinking cities' current level of, 179–80; urban renewal mixed with, 84–85, 95–96, 113–15; vision absent for development of, 126–27, 179–83. *See also* urban renewal clearances

Adams, Anthony: on Jefferson Village, 117, 118; Victoria Park development of, 99, 101, 103, 105, 108; Victoria Woods proposal of, 116

advocacy planning, 19

African Americans: displacement of, 71, 72; emerging middles class of, 101, 107–8; high-quality housing for, 171–72; housing aspirations of, 140; migrations and opportunities for, 89, 91; mortgage foreclosures and, 92–94. *See also* racial transition

AIA Guide to New York, 29, 193

APM (Asociación de Puertorriqueños en Marcha), 133, 168–69, 172, 181

Archer, Dennis: housing condemnation of, 87, 88, 118; Jefferson Village fiasco of, 117–20; marginal political capacity of, 177; small-scale developments under, 207; use of subsidies for development under, 110, 112

architects: design revolution against Modernism, 11, *12*, 13–14, *15*, 16, 30–33; Modernism associated with, 17–19; Modernism critiqued by, 9; planners separated from, 19–20, 33; urban policy as backwater for, 8–9, 196. *See also* urban design

architecture. *See* housing types; Modernism and High Modernism; Postmodernism; urbanism

art in semi-abandoned sites, 187, *188*

Asociación de Puertorriqueños en Marcha (APM), 133, 168–69, 172, 181

asset-based planning concept, 184

automobile industry: decentralization of industry, 67; deindustrialization of, 91; plant construction in, 89, 207. *See also* Detroit

automobiles: decentralized retail developments and, 123, 124–25; abandoned, 180; row-house developments geared toward, *139*, *142*, 142–43, *143*, 146; twin, conjoined single family houses and, 148, *148*, *149*, 155, *155*, 157–58, 162, *163*, *164*; *zeilenbau* housing and, 138. *See also* suburban-style design

Avenue of the Arts (Philadelphia), 130

Bacon, Edmund: areas of Northeast Philadelphia designed by, 55–56; expertise of, 195; Society Hill project of, 80, 212–13; success of, 177, 185, 196; unusual redevelopment approach of, 78–79, 81–82, 129; "used house" program under, 81; Western Center City redevelopment under, 54

Ball, Donald, 14, 16

Baltimore: housing stock losses in, *46*, 47; housing types in, 50, *51*; market-based

Baltimore (*continued*)
  urban design and, 35–36; population
  losses of (moderate persistent loser), 41,
  42, 43, 44; row houses of, 77, 138; as
  shrinking city, x
Banham, Reyner, 189, 214–16
Barbican development (London), 1
Barcelona Olympics-era improvements
  (Spain), 175
Bauhaus design. *See zeilenbau* (rows of buildings) housing blocks
Better Neighborhoods Act (1974), 145
Bing, Dave, 109, 182, 206
BKP (Buell Kratzer Powell), 167
Blessing, Charles, 78, 87, 195
"blotting" phenomenon, 186, 187, 194
Bolger, Rory, 90–91
Boston: federal redevelopment funding in,
  25; household size change in, 49; housing
  condemnation in, 20–21, 114; housing
  stock increases in, *46,* 46–47; inelastic mu-
  nicipal boundaries of, 43–44; innovative
  design of Government Center in, 195;
  population density of, *44,* 45; population
  recovery of, 41, *42, 43*; postrenewal urban
  design approach in, x, xi, 35
Brazil: Brasilia, 175; Rio de Janeiro, *Favela-
  Bairro* plan, 175
Bronx. *See* Charlotte Gardens; South Bronx
Brown, Byron, 181
Buell Kratzer Powell (BKP, firm), 167
Buffalo: demolition-based initiative of, 181,
  182, 183; palliative planning for, 205; poverty level unchanged in, 185; as shrinking
  city, x

Cabrini-Green public housing (Chicago), 35,
  210
Cadillac Plant (Detroit), 124
Cambridge Plaza public housing (Lower
  North Philadelphia), *141,* 170, 178
Camden (N.J.), xi, 51
Canfield Lofts (Detroit), 123
Carley, Garry: on attached garages, 99, 123;
  persistence of, 109; Victoria Park develop-
  ment of, 98–99, 101, 103, 105–8; Victoria
  Woods proposal of, 116
Caro, Robert, 18, 21–22, 32, 35
Carter, Jimmy, 24–25
Cassway Albert (firm), 162–63

CCD (Center City District, Philadelphia),
  130–31
CDBGs (Community Development Block
  Grants), 6–7, 88, 106, 126, 150
Cecil B. Moore Avenue (Philadelphia), 77,
  129–30, 161
Cecil B. Moore Homeownership Zone
  (North Philadelphia): context of, 77, 129–
  30, 161; design of, 164–66, 195; design
  precedent for, 160–61, 162; development
  phases of, 161–63; experimentation absent
  in, 202; financial problems of, 163, 182;
  financing for, 161–62, 181; home ownership focus of, 208; homes of, *163, 164;* location of, *133;* pragmatic, market-oriented
  design of, 195, 211; Project Development
  Team (PDT) of, 164–65; success of,
  163–64
Cedar-Riverside neighborhood (Minneapolis), 2, 6
Cedar-Riverside New Town In-Town (Minneapolis): Charlotte Gardens compared
  with, 29; context of, 40; current condition
  of, 7–8; demise of later phases, 6–7, 32;
  designer of, 2–3; design of, 4, *5,* 6; as example of flawed Modernism, 34; failures
  of, xi, 6, 9, 202; funding for, 3–4; site
  clearance for, 3
Celebration (Fla.). *See* New Urbanism
census-tract-level mapping: balanced gains
  and concentrated losses in housing, *56, 57,
  59, 62*; challenges of, 225–26 n. 2; housing
  losses and clearance in, *64, 65, 66*; Jefferson-Chalmers neighborhood, 89–90, 94,
  96; localized population losses, *53, 54*;
  widespread population losses, *63*
Center City (Philadelphia): Avenue of the
  Arts in, 130; Detroit's downtown compared with, 66; geographic importance of,
  76; housing units developed in, 57, 131;
  Kimmell Center in, 130, 131; neighborhoods surrounding, 52–53; Pennsylvania
  Convention Center of, 79, 80, 130, 131;
  population growth and rebuilding of, 54;
  stability of, 177. *See also* Society Hill
Center City District (Philadelphia, CCD),
  130–31
Central Philadelphia Development Corporation, 130
Charlotte Gardens (South Bronx): current
  home values in, 30, 92; design innovation

absent in, 202; design of, 25, 27, 30–31; funding difficulties of, 28, 160; homes of, 27; legacy of, 29–30; location of, 23; modest design of, xi–xii; Odhams Walk compared with, 30–32; origins of, 24; political rhetoric about, 28–29; Poplar homes compared with, 148; popularity of, 85; site plan of, 26; suburban design of, 25, 27, 29, 134, 148; Victoria Park compared with, 107

Charlotte Street (South Bronx): abandonment of, 24, 25, 40, 47; redevelopment of, 25

Chestnut Hill neighborhood (Philadelphia), 144

Chicago: growth pattern of, 71; housing stock increased in, 46, 47; innovation in urban renewal of South Side, 195; Modernist public housing in, 17–18, 198, 210; population density of, 44, 45; population recovery of, 41, 42, 43. See also Gary (Ind.)

Chrysler-Chalmers plant (Detroit), 89, 91, 94, 96–97, 98

citizen participation: in Cecil B. Moore housing design, 164–66; in GLC's planning, 13–14, 16; in new left urbanism, 18–19; in Poplar front door dispute, 156–61; in Poplar housing design, 154–56, 155. See also community activism; democratic decision making

city form and geography: advantages of cities along Fall Line, 75; downtown location in, 76; industry and economy linked to, 67–68; low-density standalone houses in, 71–72, 78; New Urbanism and, 197–98; patchwork arrangement considered, 212–20; population losses in relation to inelasticity of, 42–44, 44

Civic Center (Detroit), 72

Clairpointe of Victoria Park development (Detroit): cost of, 112, 115–16; de-densification fostered by, 125; design of, 195; developer of, 114; homes of, 115

Cleveland: city master plan of (1975), 19; housing stock losses in, 46, 47; housing types in, 50, 51; market-based urban design and, 35–36; population losses of, 41, 42, 43, 44

Clinton administration, 133, 135, 161. See also HOPE VI

Colombia. See Medellín

community activism: artistic additions to semi-abandoned sites as, 187, 188; Covent Garden megastructure halted by, 13–14. See also citizen participation; democratic decision making

"community-based" rebuilding ideal, x. See also social planning and housing developments; social urbanism

Community Development Block Grants (CDBGs), 6–7, 88, 106, 126, 150

community development corporations. See Ludlow Development Corporation; National Temple Community Development Corporation; Poplar Community Development Corporation

condemnation of property. See housing condemnation

Congress for New Urbanism, 196, 201

Covent Garden (London): design relationship of Odhams Walk to, 31; gentrification of, 13, 16; plans for clearance of, 13–14. See also Odhams Walk

Cranbrook Academy, 2

Cross-Bronx Expressway (New York City), 21–22

Crosswinds Communities, 118–19. See also Jefferson Village (Detroit)

Crotona Park (South Bronx), 22, 23, 24

culs-de-sac: in Cedar-Riverside design, 4; midcentury row-house along, 78, 139, 140, 142–44; twin houses along, 152, 154, 155, 159. See also streets

Davenport, Robert, 108

Davidoff, Paul, 18–19, 21

decentralization: of automobile industry, 67; of federal funding and planning, xi, 7, 19, 20, 41, 82, 184; landscape urbanism and, 193–94; limits of, xiv, 177, 183–84, 203; of metropolis and nation, 99, 123, 124–25, 190, 193–94; rejected in Home (report), 145; of social planning policy, 29–32, 34, 35. See also suburban-style design; suburbs

defensible space theory, 157, 158

deindustrialization: concept of, 36, 67; effects of, 37–39, 42, 43, 90–91, 94, 205; landscape approach to, 189–90, 192; public policy and, 126–27. See also Detroit; Philadelphia; shrinking cities

Delaware River waterfront (Philadelphia), 189, 191

democratic decision making concept: as principle for shrinking-city urban design, xiv, 207–10; projective design balanced with, 211–12. *See also* citizen participation; community activism

demolition: current policy in shrinking cities, xiii, 179–83, 185; everyday life and, 185–86. *See also* abandoned housing and sites; urban renewal clearances

design. *See* urban design

design and planning principles for shrinking cities. *See* social urbanism; *and individual principles*

Detroit: abandoned sites and, 179, 189; arson in, 93; "blotting" phenomenon in, 186, 187, 194; as challenging environment for market-based urban design, 35; city form and growth of, 67–71, *69*, *70*; citywide population losses of, 32, 41, *42*, *43*, 44, 51, 96, 113, 174, 225 n. 1; Community Renewal Program of, 91; conditions in, xi, 37, 185; current challenges for, 126–27; dispersing development's benefits in, 209; downtown development success of, 110, 122, 123–24; East Side Plan of, 120, *121*, 200–201; geographical site of, 84; Heidelberg Project in, *188*; household size changes in, 49; housing stock losses in, *46*, *47*, *64*, 64–67, *65*, *66*, *74*, 112–13, 201; housing types in, 50, *51*; industrial base of, 67–68, 88–89; localized population losses in, 61, *63*, 64; New Urbanism in, 198, *199*, 200–201; as paradigm of urban blight, ix, 124–27, 177; park and landscape urbanism projects in, 190–91; Philadelphia compared with, xii–xiv, 64, 65, 66, 79, 131–32, 177–79, 184; policy reform in, 184; postrenewal rebuilding of, 98–99, 177–83, 194, 213; postrenewal redevelopment and politics in, 85, 87–88, 183, 226 n. 1; racial issues in, 71, 72, 74; rehabilitations in, 122–23; re-tracting in, 225–26 n. 2; tabula rasa urban renewal in, xiii, 72–75, 78, 81, 82, 91, 95–96, 112, 126, 182, 186; transportation and parking in, 123; urban design interests in, 194–95; vacancy and demolition of buildings in, 124, 179, 182, 213. *See also* Detroit, housing developments; *and specific developments*

Detroit, housing developments: architectural conservatism of, 122; East Side Plan of, 120, *121*, 200–201; gated developments in, 98–99, 114; Heritage Townhouses, 114; Jefferson Square, 96, *97*; list of, *104–5*; map of, *111*; market-based urban design hard to implement in, 35–36, 177; Neighborhood Enterprise Zone (tax abatement) program in, 110–11, 126; people per housing unit in, 49, *49*; postrenewal urban design in, 120, 122–27; post–Victoria Park, summarized, 109–10; Section 235 disaster in, 92–94, 114; subsidies for market-rate housing in, xii–xiii, 88, 107–8, 110–11, 115, 126, 177; waterfront areas, 70–71, 84, 98, 112, 116, 124, 191. *See also* Clairpointe of Victoria Park development; Highland Park; Jefferson-Chalmers neighborhood; Jefferson Village; Lafayette Park; Victoria Park

Detroit City Council, 106, 115, 119, 124

Detroit Economic Growth Corporation, 119

Detroit Free Press, 94, 97

Detroit Master Plan (1951), 91

Detroit News, 89, 108–9, 120

Detroit Works initiative, 109

displacements: democratic decision making and, 209–10; Detroit, xii, 72, 81, 88; London (U.K.), 13, 16; Minneapolis, 4; New Haven, 39–40; Philadelphia, 80; South Bronx, 24

Dorothy Brown Homes (Philadelphia), 83

Downsview Park (Toronto), 192

Duany, Andres, 196, 201

Duisberg-Nord Park. *See* Emscher Landschaft-Park

East Side Plan (Detroit), 120, *121*, 200–201

East St. Louis (Ill.), 51

East Tremont neighborhood (South Bronx), 21–22

Economic Development Initiative (EDI, HUD), 161

economy: diversity and dynamics of, 67–68; potential reform in capitalist, 184–85; unemployment and, 38. *See also* deindustrialization; subprime mortgage crisis and market crash

elasticity concept, 43

Elmwood area (Detroit), 81, 98, 114, 172

Emscher Landschaft-Park (Germany), 189–90
Enterprise Foundation, 150, 157
Enterprise Social Investment Corporation (ESIC), 154, 157
environment. *See* green housing; landscape urbanism; open spaces
environmental impact statements, 7
everyday urbanism: advocates of, 186–87; landscape urbanism compared with, 188–89, 193–94; limitations in shrinking cities, xiii–xiv, 187–88; New Urbanism compared with, 200; success of, 194
extreme population loss, 45

Fainstein, Susan, 183–85, 204
Fajardo, Sergio, 174–76, 183, 209
Fall Line, 75
Far East Side Plan (Detroit), 120, *121*, 200–201
federal government: decentralized funding mechanisms of, xi, 7, 19, 20, 41, 82, 184; end of centralized rebuilding funded by, 32; policy interest and innovation lacking in, 179; subsidized housing construction and, 6–7; weak urban policy of, 183–85. *See also* legislation; U.S. Department of Housing and Urban Development; *and specific administrations*
Federal Housing Acts: funds available, 39, 136, 140; requirements under, 17; Section 235, 92–94
Federal Housing Authority (FHA), 92–94
Federal Urban Development Grant, 28
Ferriss, Hugh, 138
Flies, Ron, 98, 99, 103, 106, 108
Flint (Mich.), 181–82, 183
fragmentation: of housing redevelopments, 118, 145; of municipal structures, 219; of neighborhoods, 61, 85, 117, 160, 193. *See also* abandoned housing and sites
Freshkills Park (New York City), 191
Frieden, Bernard J., xii, 73
front door dispute (Poplar Nehemiah project), 156–61

Gary (Ind.), 51
General Motors, Poletown plant area (Detroit), 73, 74, 87, 98

gentrification: of Covent Garden, 13, 16; of Lower North Philadelphia, 170–71; row house values in, 77–78; terms in debate about, 171, 187
geography. *See* city form and geography
Germany, landscape design for deindustrialized area in, 189–90
GLC. *See* Greater London Council Architecture Department
Golden Lane project. *See* Smithson, Alison and Peter
Goode, W. Wilson, 82, 128, 130, 150, 207
Graimark Associates, 117–18, 119. *See also* Jefferson Village
grain elevators (Buffalo), 189, 194
Gratiot area (Detroit). *See* Lafayette Park
Greater London Council Architecture Department: approach to, xii; demise of, 13; High Modernist projects of, 9, *10*, 11, 17–18; reformed Modernist projects of, 11, *12*, 13–14, *15*, 16, 30–32, 34. *See also* Odhams Walk; Queensferry Estate; Thamesmead New Town
green housing: aspirations for, 168; challenges for, 172–73; projective design and, 211
Greenwald, Herbert, 88
Greenwich Village neighborhood (New York City), 13
Greyhaven Island (Detroit), 98–99
Grosse Pointe (Detroit), 92–93, 98
growth machine concept, 17–18, 21, 112, 118, 119, 177
Guyton, Tyree, *188*

Hagood, Henry, 96
Hancock Square (North Philadelphia), 169–70, 198
Harvard Graduate School of Design, 190
Heritage Townhouses (Detroit), 114
Highland Park (Mich.), 51
High Line (New York City), 190, 191, 193, 194
highways. *See* streets and highways
Hilbersheimer, Ludwig, 72, 74, 191–92
historic preservation: as aspect of Postmodernism, 33; buildings demolished in Detroit, 124; rehabilitations, 81, 122–23, 161–62

home-a-ramas, 106, 107, 109. *See also* Victoria Park

Home in North Philadelphia (OHCD report): "affordable housing" intent of, 171; design ideals in, 147, 149, 153; low-density policy in, 145–46, 165, 172–73, 178

home ownership: Cecil B. Moore geared for, 161–66; condemnation and, 113, 226 n. 2; impoverished people excluded from, 208; Logue's ideal of, 25, 27–28; new owners' view of, 29; Poplar Nehemiah homes and, 149–50; Yorktown and, 140, 142–44. *See also* Cecil B. Moore Homeownership Zone; Jefferson Village; Ludlow Village; Poplar Nehemiah Homes; Victoria Park; Yorktown

Homeownership Zones (HUD), 161

HOPE VI (Housing Opportunities for People Everywhere VI Urban Demonstration Program): demolition and reconstruction under, 197–98; mixed-income, market-subsidized developments of, 172, 208; in North Philadelphia, 133, 135, 156, 170; suburban design in, 178

household size: population density and, 43, 44, 45; reduction of, in U.S. cities, 47, 49, 49–50

housing abandonment. *See* abandoned housing and sites

Housing Act (1949), 39, 136

Housing Act (1968), 94

Housing and Community Development Act (1975), 6–7

Housing and Urban Development Act (1970), 1–2

housing condemnation: in Jefferson Village (Detroit), xiii, 87, 118–20, 208; in North Philadelphia Plan, 129–30; in Poplar Nehemiah (Philadelphia), 153; property value decline and, 113, 226 n. 2. *See also* urban renewal clearances

housing density: abstract high-density green vs. vernacular low-density, 172; effect on de-densification of, 124–25, 189, 193; fragility of standalone houses in low-density areas, 71–72, 78; OHCD's low-density policy, 134–35, 144–47, 148, 149, 153, 156, 162, 164, 165, 171, 172–73, 178; in rowhouse designs, 77, 142. *See also specific housing developments*

housing stock: localized gains and losses of (Philadelphia), 56, 56–58, 57, 59, 60–61, 62; population losses in relation to losses of, 45–47, 46, 49, 49–51, 51; widespread losses of (Detroit), 64, 64–67, 65, 66, 74

housing types: developments in Detroit identified by, 104–5; durability and variety of, 50–51, 51; Le Corbusier's Unités d'Habitation, 4, 6; lofts, 123; low-density wooden standalone houses, 71–72, 78; Nehemiah funding and, 150–51; prefabricated tract single-family type, 25, 27, 29; public debate and selection of, 155–56; single family (Clairpointe of Victoria Park), 114, 115; single family (Jefferson Village), 117, 118; single family (Victoria Park), 98, 99, 100, 102, 108; twin houses (Cambridge Plaza/Richard Allen), 170; twin houses (Cecil B. Moore), 162, 163, 164; twin houses (Ludlow Village), 167, 168; twin houses (Poplar Nehemiah), 144, 148, 148, 149, 155, 155–60; as urban vs. suburban (front door dispute), 158–59. *See also* megastructures; row houses; suburban-style design; *zeilenbau* (rows of buildings) housing blocks

Houston: annexation and population growth in, 43, 44; housing stock increases in, 46, 46; population growth of, 41, 42, 43

Hoyt, Homer, 52

HUD. *See* U.S. Department of Housing and Urban Development

HUD scandal. *See* Detroit, housing developments

Hudson Motor Company (Detroit), 89, 91

Hudson's Department Store (Detroit), 37, 124

Hunts Point-Intervale neighborhood (South Bronx), 24

Hurricane Katrina, rebuilding after, 210–11

impoverished people: "deserving" segment of, 149, 226 n. 1; everyday lives of, 185–86, 207–8; everyday urbanism and, 186–88; housing geared for, 149–50; limited choices of, 207–8; as political constituency, 183. *See also* citizen participation; democratic decision making; neighborhoods

inclusionary zoning, 171

Independence National Historical Park, 80

inelasticity concept, 43–44
institutions: scattered clearance in areas near, 80; Western Center City redevelopment role of, 54. *See also* Temple University; University of Pennsylvania
Interboro Partners, 186, 187, 193
interventionist policy concept, xiv, 205–7

Jacobs, Jane: everyday urbanism and, 186–87; on experimental nature of Modernism, 202, 203; on planning and slum clearance, 20–21, 126; on poverty, 185–86; on urban renewal, x
Jefferson Avenue (Detroit), 71, 98, 109, 208
Jefferson-Chalmers neighborhood (Detroit): context in 1940s, 88–89; decline of, 84, 86, 90–94, 95, 96; fragmentation of sites in, 117–18, 126; housing developments, summarized, 114; large-scale infill development in, 120; location of, 84, 85, 114; Maheras Park in, 116; map of, 90; mortgage foreclosure scandal in, 90, 92–94; neighborhood interventions in, 177; neighborhood succession in, 89–90; New Urbanism in, 200–201; "Plantside" area of, 89, 91, 94, 96; political context of, 87–88; Poplar Nehemiah compared with, 159; postrenewal redevelopment strategies in, xii–xiii, 87, 88, 107–8; pros and cons of large- vs. small-scale sites and, 111–13, 116–17; provincial design of, 196; racial transition in, 89–91; rebuilding of, 98–108; scattered abandonment and contiguous clearance areas in, 84–85, 95–96, 113–15; stabilizing effect of, 214; urban renewal in, 87, 91, 92, 100, 113, 114. *See also* Clairpointe of Victoria Park development; Jefferson Village; Victoria Park
Jefferson Square (Detroit), 96, 97, 98
Jefferson Village (Detroit): Cecil B. Moore homes compared with, 165–66; current home values in, 119; de-densification fostered by, 125; design of, 119, 125, 195; development fiasco of, 118–20, 182, 193, 206; dissatisfaction with, 206; high cost of, 118, 177; homes of, 117; housing condemned for, xiii, 87, 118–20, 208; middle-class focus of, 208; and new housing, 98–99; origins of, 117–18; political support of, 118–19, 207

Jefferson Village North (Detroit), 120
Jencks, Charles, 9
Johnson administration, 85, 87, 206

Kelo v. City of New London (2005), 118, 120
Kerner Commission, 21
Kildee, Daniel, 182
Kilpatrick, Kwame, 87, 118–19, 177
Kimmell Center (Philadelphia), 130, 131
Kips Bay Plaza (New York City), 169
Kise, Franks, and Straw (KFS): Cecil B. Moore homes design of, 162, 163; Poplar Nehemiah homes design of, 151, 152, 153–54, 156, 157
Koch, Ed, 25, 28
Koolhaas, Rem, 191, 192
Kromer, John: on Cambridge Plaza, 170; centralized redevelopment approach of, 177–78; on HOPE VI, 198; on NTI, 180; as OHCD director, 132, 133–34, 144, 195; on Poplar Nehemiah development, 150, 153, 154, 160, 207; on Rendell, 130; on suburban-style developments, 171; success of, 184, 185, 218
KSK Architects Planners Historians, 151, 152

Lafayette Park (earlier, Gratiot area, Detroit): context of, 82, 91; design of, 72, 74, 88, 122; evoked by Young, 98; as for-profit development, 113; as harbinger of emptiness, 125; incomplete construction of, 191–92; as stable environment, 172; tabula rasa design approach in, xiii, 72, 74, 78, 85
landscape urbanism: contradictions and challenges in shrinking cities, xiii, 191–94, 201; design ideals of, 188–90; environmentalism and, 190; examples of projects, 189–91; presence of nature in, 189
land values: depressed by vacant lots, 113, 181; new construction and, 173, 212–13; post-bubble collapse of, 108, 119, 120; in prosperous vs. shrinking cities, 34–35; rationale for clearance and, 80, 114
LDC (Ludlow Development Corporation), 166, 167, 168
Learning from Yorktown (OHCD report), 146–47
Le Corbusier: Cedar-Riverside influenced by, 4, 6; Hancock Square influenced by, 169;

Le Corbusier (*continued*)
  Plan Voisin of, 72, 75, 138; *Ville Radieuse*
  (Radiant City) design of, 144
Lee, Richard, 21, 39, 40. *See also* New Haven
legislation (U.S.): Better Neighborhoods Act
  (1974), 145; Housing Act (1949), 39, 136;
  Housing Act (1968), 94; Housing and
  Community Development Act (1975),
  1–2; Housing and Urban Development
  Act (1970), 1–2; Urban Growth and New
  Community Development Act (1970),
  1–2, 7. *See also* Federal Housing Acts;
  HOPE VI
Lenox Waterfront Estates (Detroit), 114
Lescaze, William, 136
Levittown (N.Y.), 125, 139
Levy, Paul, 130, 131
Lewis, Marvin, 167
Logue, Edward, 25, 27, 28, 31
London: Barbican development in, 1; Golden
  Lane design for (unbuilt), 4, 6; New Town
  development in, 9, *10*, 11, *12*; overpriced
  property market in, 16; Ronan Point de-
  velopment in, 210. *See also* Greater Lon-
  don Council Architecture Department;
  Odhams Walk; Queensferry Estate;
  Thamesmead New Town
Los Angeles: household size changes in, 49;
  housing stock increases in, 46, *46*; inelastic
  boundaries of, 44, *44*; neoliberal urbanism
  in, 35; patchwork urbanism in, 214–18;
  people per housing unit in, 49, *49*; population density of, *44*, 45; steady population
  growth of, 41, *42*, *43*
Lower North Philadelphia: gentrification of,
  170–71; High Modernist redevelopment
  of, 135–47; low-value land absent in, 172;
  maps of, *133*, *141*; Modernism's post-2000
  return to, 168–73; palliative planning for,
  205; postrenewal redevelopment of, xiii;
  racial transition in, 135–36; Rendell's redevelopment policy in, 132–35; visual
  fragmentation of, 160–61. *See also* Cecil B.
  Moore Homeownership Zone; Ludlow
  Village; North Philadelphia; Poplar Nehemiah Homes; Yorktown
Ludlow Development Corporation (LDC),
  133, 166, 167, 168
Ludlow Village (North Philadelphia): design
  of, 166–67, 195; homes of, *167*, *168*; limited redevelopment in neighborhood, 129;

location of, *133*, *141*; Poplar's design precedent for, 160–61
Lynch, Kevin, 36, 214, 219

Maheras Park (Detroit), 116. *See also* Jeffer-
  son-Chalmers neighborhood
Make It Right Foundation, 210–11
Make It Right housing (New Orleans),
  210–11
Manhattan. *See* New York City
Marxism, 184–85
Massachusetts Institute of Technology
  (MIT), 2, 19
Medellín (Colombia): Emscher Landschaft-
  Park compared with, 190; social urbanist
  revolution in, 174–76, 179, 183
media coverage: abandoned homes and vacant properties, 94, 181; Bacon's success,
  80; Detroit's Far East Side Plan area, 120;
  federal funds for Chrysler-Chalmers plant,
  97; Hancock Square, 169–70; Jefferson-
  Chalmers area, 89; Jefferson Village fiasco,
  119; modernists' vision, 8; North Philadelphia, 128–29; Philadelphia's Renaissance,
  131; suburban-style developments, 171;
  Victoria Park, 108–9
megastructures: Cedar-Riverside buildings
  as, 4, *5*; community activists' success in
  stopping, 13–14; racial issues and, 82; single-family detached homes compared
  with, 29–30
metrocable (Medellín), 175
Miami, 196, 197
Michigan: anti-condemnation constitutional
  amendment in, 120; housing fairs in, 106,
  107; tax abatement program of, 110–11,
  126. *See also* Detroit; Flint; Highland Park
Michigan Citizen, 119
Mies van der Rohe, Ludwig: historic city
  structure rejected by, 138; Lafayette Park
  project of, 72, 74, 88, 125, 191–92; as leading urban renewal designer, 195
Minneapolis: neighborhood fabric in, 3, 6;
  Riverside West development in, xi, 2, *5*.
  See also Cedar-Riverside New Town In-
  Town
Minneapolis City Planning Commission, 3
MIT (Massachusetts Institute of Technol-
  ogy), 2, 19
model tenements, 17

Modernism and High Modernism: antiurban approach of, 138; conventional narratives about, 33–36; critiques of, 8–9, 11, 18–20; design revolution against, 11, *12*, 13–14, *15*, 16, 30–33; failures of, x–xii, 6, 7–8, 201–3, 210; innovation inherent in, 195; in London, 9, *10*, 11, 17–18; in Lower North Philadelphia after 2000, 168–73; and North Philadelphia's rebuilding, 135–47; projective design quality of, 210, 211; remnants of, ix–x; replacement of, 32–33. *See also* Reformed Modernism; urban renewal

Montgomery Townhouses (North Philadelphia), 83

Moore homes. *See* Cecil B. Moore Homeownership Zone (North Philadelphia)

Morrell Park (Northeast Philadelphia), 138–39, *139*

Moses, Robert, 18, 35, 40, 212. *See also* New York City

Mott Haven neighborhood (South Bronx), 22

Mount Airy (Philadelphia), 144, 156, 162

national survey grid (U.S.), 68

National Temple Community Development Corporation (National Temple CDC), 161

nature. *See* landscape urbanism

Nehemiah Housing Opportunity Grant (HUD), 149–50, 153, 161. *See also* Poplar Nehemiah Homes (Lower North Philadelphia)

Neighborhood Enterprise Zone (tax abatement) program, 110–11, 126

Neighborhood Housing Strategy for the Cecil B. Moore Area (report), 164

neighborhoods: artistic additions to, 187, *188*; "asset-based" planning and, 184; avoiding population loss in, 54–56; deindustrialization and, 67; fabric of local, 3, 6, 76, 79, 169–70; fragmentation of, 61, 85, 117, 160, 193; hip and developing areas of, 169–70; hopes for, 222–24; population and housing stock changes reflected in, 47, *48*, 58, 60; potential for new design of, 218–20, *219–21*; projective design and, 211–12; redevelopment approach to, xii; transitions in, 52, *55*. *See also* abandoned housing and sites; racial transition

neighborhood succession concept, 52

Neighborhood Transformation Initiative (NTI): Cecil B. Moore Homeownership Zone funds from, 162; demolitions under, 180, 207; example of lot, *180*; post-demolition strategy absent in, 181, 182–83, 212

neoliberalism: applied to North Philadelphia, 171; political philosophy of, 35–36; postrenewal urbanism and, 182–83

neotraditional movement. *See* New Urbanism

Netherlands, landscape urbanism project in, 190

New Communities program: demise of, 6–8; initiation of, 1–2; invocation by Coleman Young, 97–98. *See also* Housing and Urban Development Act; New Towns In-Town initiatives

New Haven (Conn.): decline of, 204; federal redevelopment funding per capita in, 25, 39, 40; Modern architecture remnants in, ix–x; redevelopment politics in, 21; urban renewal in, 39–40, 73, 176–77, 195

New Orleans: public housing redevelopment in, 198; unsuccessful projective design in, 210–11

New Towns In-Town initiatives: Charlotte Gardens approach compared with, 25; Coleman Young inspired by, 97; concept of, 1–2; demise of, 6–8; funding for, 2, 3–4, 6–7; in London, 9, *10*, 11, 17–18. *See also* Cedar-Riverside New Town In-Town (Minneapolis)

New Urbanism: Celebration as example of, 197; conservatism of, 203, 210; context of, 194–96; design ideals of, 196–97; infill version of, 198, *199*, 200; limits of, xiii, 197–98, 200–201; Seaside as built example of, 196, 197. *See also* Woodward Place at Brush Park

New York City: Battery Park City in, 29; federal redevelopment funding per capita in, 40; household size in, 49, *49*; housing stock increases in, 46, *46*–47; housing types in, 77; inelastic boundaries of, 44, *44*; landscape urbanism projects in, 190, 191, 193, 194; Master Plan of (1969), 18; Modernist public housing in, 17–18, 35, 136; Nehemiah program in, 150; New Town In-Town initiative in (Roosevelt Island), 2, 31; population density of, *44*, 45; recovering population of, 41, *42*, *43*; relationship

New York City (*continued*)
of economy and urban design in, 68; resistant city form of, 212; tax abatement program in, 131; urban crisis perceived in,
24–25. *See also* Charlotte Gardens; South
Bronx
New York City Planning Commission, 18
Nixon administration: Section 235 suspended by, 92; urban renewal "reforms"
under, 6–7, 8, 18, 19, 20, 82, 94, 184, 206
nonprofit corporations, xi, 116, 130. *See also*
public-nonprofit partnerships; *specific corporations*
nonreformist reform concept, 183–85, 204
Northeast Philadelphia neighborhood, 54–
55, 57, 138–39
Northern Liberties neighborhood (Philadelphia), 169–70, 178, 198
North Philadelphia: abandoned housing in,
58, *60*, 60–61; centralized OHCD redevelopment approach in, 132–35, 177–78, 218;
city plans for, 83, 128–30, 144, 207; development's benefits dispersed in, 209; high
housing density in (row houses), 77; housing losses and severely distressed areas in,
56, 57–58, *59*; limited urban renewal clearance in, 81; maps of, *133*, *141*; NTI-driven
demolition in, 179–81; OHCD's studies
of, 145–47; palliative planning for, 205;
population losses of, 201; post-2000 return
of Modernism and gentrification of,
168–73; problems in 1980s, 128–29; racial
transition in, 135–36; revived Modernist
design vs. suburban low-density design in,
172; stabilizing effect of development in,
214; urban design interests in, 194–95;
urban renewal–era construction in,
135–44; vacant land still existing in, 173.
See also Lower North Philadelphia; North
Philadelphia, housing developments
North Philadelphia, housing developments:
anticontextualism in, 159–60; Dorothy
Brown Homes in, 83; market-based urban
design hard to implement in, 35–36; scattered-site public housing in, 58; *zeilenbau*
(rows of buildings) public housing of, 136,
138–40. *See also* Cecil B. Moore Homeownership Zone; Lower North Philadelphia; Ludlow Village; Montgomery
Townhouses; North Philadelphia; Office of

Housing and Community Development;
Yorktown
North Philadelphia Plan: for Cecil B. Moore
Avenue, 129–30; housing developments
in, 83; limits of, 128–29, 144; recommen-
dations of, 207
NTI. *See* Neighborhood Transformation Ini-
tiative

Obama administration, 179, 206
Odhams Walk (Covent Garden): Charlotte
Gardens compared with, 30–32; contentious origin of, 13–14; current condition
of, 16; end of centralized planning marked
by, 30; exemplary design of, 14, *15*, 16, 210
Office of Housing and Community Development (OHCD, Philadelphia): Homeownership Zone project of, 161–62; Lower
North Philadelphia initiative of, 132–34,
213; Modernism's failure and, 135; palliative planning strategy of, 205; Poplar Nehemiah front door dispute and, 157, 158;
public planning process of, 154–56, *155*,
160; suburban-style, low-density approach
of, 134–35, 144–49, 153, 156, 162, 164,
165, 171–73, 178. *See also* Cecil B. Moore
Homeownership Zone; *Home in North
Philadelphia*; Ludlow Village; Poplar Nehemiah Homes; Yorktown
OKKS Development, 162, 163–64
Olmsted, Frederick Law, 190
open spaces: alterations of parks and, 226 n.
1; Bacon's admonition against, 129; of
downtowns and civic centers, 72, 124; of
Hancock Square, 169–70; of Jefferson
Square, 96, *97*; of Ludlow Village, 166; of
modernist structures, 1, 6, 11; as "movement system," 80; in Poplar Nehemiah development, 150, *151*, *152*, 153, 154; as
public good, 35; Yorktown's row-house
design and, 142–44; in *zeilenbau* blocks vs.
row houses, 139–40. *See also* abandoned
housing and sites; landscape urbanism;
suburban-style design; urban renewal
clearances
Oswalt, Philipp, 36

Packard Plant (Detroit), 189, 194
Packer Park neighborhood (South Philadelphia), 78, 138

palliative planning concept, xiv, 204–5
"Parade of Homes" (home-a-ramas), 106, 107, 109. *See also* Victoria Park
Paris, Parc de la Villette proposal (France), 191
patchwork urbanism: concept of, xiv, 214; existing city form relationship to, 212–13; new urban design approach as, *218*, 218–20, *221*; shrinking cities characterized by, 214–17, *215–17, 219–20*
PCPC. *See* Philadelphia City Planning Commission
PEDC (Poplar Enterprise Development Corporation), 148–50, 153, 154, 158
Pei, I. M., 80, 169, 195
Pennsylvania Convention Center (Philadelphia), 79, 80, 130, 131
Pennsylvania Horticultural Society (PHS), 154
People Mover (Detroit), 73, 123
persistent loser (population and housing) concept, 44, 45, 50
Philadelphia: 1980s problems of, 128–29; abandoned sites problem in, 179–80; bombing of MOVE cult (1985), 82, 128; city form and urban design policy in, 67–68, 75, 132, 213–14; conditions in, xi, 38, 135; decentralized redevelopment in, 183; democratic decision making as urban design strategy in, 209; Detroit compared with, xii–xiv, 64, 65, 66, 79, 131–32, 177–79, 184; downtown residential population in, 131; hip and developing neighborhoods in, 169–70; housing stock losses in, *46, 47, 52, 56,* 56–58, *57, 59,* 60–61, *62;* industrial base of, 67–68; landscape urbanism projects in, 191, *192,* 194; localized population losses in, 52–56, *53, 54, 55;* neighborhood fabric in, 76, 79; New Urbanism in, 198; original city plan of, 75–76; persistent population losses of, 32, 41, *42, 43,* 44, 51–52, 128; population density of, *44,* 45; post-1992 "renaissance" of, 131–32, 176; race and class issues in, 58, 80–82; street grid of, 143, 213; urban renewal approach in (Reformed Modernism), 78–81, 82–83, 177; vacant land parcels still existing in, 173. *See also* Camden (N.J.); Center City; Lower North Philadelphia; Neighborhood Transformation

Initiative; North Philadelphia; Office of Housing and Community Development; row houses
Philadelphia City Planning Commission (PCPC): design attempts in Northeast Philadelphia, 139; design guidance absent, 140; Poplar Nehemiah front door dispute and, 157–58; Poplar Nehemiah homes and, 153–54, 155; suburban standards accepted by, 142–43. *See also* Yorktown
Philadelphia Daily News, 171, 181
Philadelphia nonprofit and public agencies: Philadelphia Green (nonprofit agency), 154; Philadelphia Housing Authority, 81, 133–34, 136, 138–40, 162; Philadelphia Housing Development Corporation, 161–62, 166; Philadelphia Neighborhood Enterprise (PNE), 150, 153; Philadelphia Parks Department, 154; Philadelphia Police Department, 158
Philadelphia Inquirer, 131, 169–70
PHS (Pennsylvania Horticultural Society), 154
Pier 11 Park (Philadelphia), 191, *192,* 194
planning. *See* urban planning
Plantside neighborhood (Detroit). *See* Jefferson-Chalmers neighborhood
Plan Voisin (Le Corbusier), 72, 75, 138
Plater-Zyberk, Elizabeth, 196
Poletown (Detroit), 73, 74, 87, 98
policy backwater. *See* urban design policy
politics: Detroit's postrenewal redevelopment and, 85, 87–88, 226 n. 1; elections and, 184; impoverished people as constituency, 183; interventionist strategies and, 205–7; rhetoric about Charlotte Gardens and, 28–29
Poplar Community Development Corporation (Poplar CDC), 150, 161, 205
Poplar Enterprise Development Corporation (PEDC), 148–50, 153, 154, 158
Poplar Nehemiah Homes (Lower North Philadelphia): blight designation and clearance of, 153; Cecil B. Moore area compared with, 164–65; context of, 132–33, 147–48; current home values in, 160, 169; design precedent set by, 160–61, 162, 164, 178; design process of, 148, 153–56, *155,* 195; financing of, 149–50; front door dispute in, 156–59; home ownership and,

Poplar Nehemiah Homes (*continued*)
208; homes of, *148*, *149*; interventionist
scale of, 207; location of, *133*, *141*; low
public visibility of, 212; palliative planning
of, 205; pragmatic, market-oriented approach of, 195; Project Development
Team (PDT) of, 149, 154, 156–58; property condemnation and, 153; public planning process for, 154–56; site plans of, *151*,
152; street reconfiguration at, 148, 154,
213; as suburb in the city, 148, 158–61,
178; success of, 171–72

population: everyday needs of, in shrinking
cities, 185–86; New York City vs. Minneapolis, 2; shift from East and Midwest to
South and West, 41–43, *42*, *43*; steady
gainers, recovering cities, and persistent
losers categories of, 44–45. *See also* racial
transition; *and specific cities*

population losses: debate about, 38–39;
housing losses in relation to, 45–47, *46*, *49*,
49–51, *51*; inelastic boundaries and, 42–
44, *44*; population gains and, 41–45; post-
1950 trajectory of, xii, 32, 37–38, *42*, *43*;
real estate market destabilized by, 22, 24;
regional shift and, 41–43, *42*, *43*; shrinkage
localized, 52–56, *53*, *54*, *55*; shrinkage
widespread, 61, *63*, 64; urban renewal disconnected from, 40–41. *See also* shrinking
cities

postdecline city. *See* shrinking cities

Postmodernism: architects and planners separated by, 20; eclectic design of, 122; historic urbanism accepted in, 196; origins of,
9; problematic aspects of, 32–33; as urban
design philosophy, 36

postrenewal redevelopment: Detroit compared with Philadelphia, 176–79, 201–3;
everyday urbanism in, 185–88; in growing
cities, x; landscape urbanism in, 188–94;
New Urbanism in, 194–201; non-experi-
mentation era in, 201–3; as policy backwater, 8–9, 196; small scale of, xi–xii, 32, 207.
See also social urbanism

poverty. *See* impoverished people

PPPs. *See* public-private partnerships

projective design concept, xiv, 210–12

property condemnation. *See* housing condemnation

Proyecto Urbano Integral (PUI, integrated
urban project), 175

Pruitt-Igoe public housing (St. Louis), 34, *48*

public housing: Cedar-Riverside similarity
to, 7–8; Modernist examples of, 17–18, 35,
198, 210; New Urbanism and HOPE VI redesign of, 197–98, 208; in North Philadelphia, 136, 138–40, *141*; scattered-site type,
58, 81; *zeilenbau* (rows of buildings) principle in, 136, *137*, 138–40. *See also specific
developments*

public-nonprofit partnerships: homeowner-
ship zone project of, 161–62; in Lower
North Philadelphia, 132–35. *See also* Cecil
B. Moore Homeownership Zone

public-private partnerships (PPPs): current
emphasis on, 179; focus of, xi; housing
condemnation and, 119; People Mover
built by, 73, 123; Victoria Park as, 103,
105–8

Puerto Ricans, 136. *See also* Asociación de
Puertorriqueños en Marcha (APM)

Queensferry Estate (Tottenham, U.K.), *12*

racial segregation: neighborhoods, 89; public
housing, 7–8, 136

racial transition: concept of, 52, *55*; Detroit,
71, 72; Jefferson-Chalmers, 89–90; New
Haven, 39–40; North Philadelphia,
135–36; Philadelphia, 52, *55*, 58; South
Bronx, 22, 24, 225 n. 2

Rae, Douglas: on decline of New Haven, 204;
on "end" of urbanism, 38–39; on urban
policy, 21, 39–40, 176–77

railroad development: Detroit's plans for
light rail line, 123; elevated, redeveloped as
elevated park, 190, *191*, *193*, *194*; Philadelphia's Center City and, 79, 130

rail-to-trail paths, 124, 191. *See also* High
Line

Rapson, Ralph, 2–3, 4, 5, 6

Reagan administration, 28

real estate developers: center city redevelopment role of, 54; influence of, in Detroit,
125; public subsidies for market-rate
housing projects of, xii–xiii, 88, 107–8,
110–12, 115; suburban-style design focus
of, xii–xiii, 54–56, 98–99, *100*, 101; urban
renewal land clearance and, 113–15, 120,
122, 226 n. 1; Victoria Park lessons for,
108–13. *See also specific firms*

real estate market: current values of homes
in developments, 30, 92, 108, 119, 160,
169; "filtering" worst units to bottom, 58;
housing fairs and, 105–6; population
losses as destabilizing, 22, 24; pros and
cons of large vs. small-scale developments,
111–13, 116–17; row house values in,
77–78; tax abatement and boom in, 131;
Victoria Park's appeal to, 103, 105–7, 177.
See also subprime mortgage crisis and
market crash (2007)
Redevelopment Authority (RDA, Philadelphia), 153–54, 158, 182–83
Reformed Modernism: as GLC design approach, 11, *12*, 13–14; and High Modernism, 30–33, 210; as Odhams Walk, 14, *15*,
16; in Philadelphia, 78–81, 82–83, 177;
Yorktown as exemplar of, 142–44. *See also*
Modernism and High Modernism
Regional Planning Association of America,
17–18
rehabilitations, 81, 122–23, 161–62
relocations. *See* displacements
Renaissance Center (Detroit), 73, 122, 177
Rendell, Edward: Fajardo compared with,
175–76; Kromer appointed by, 144; Lower
North Philadelphia vision of, 132–35, 147,
149; success as mayor, 184; urban policy
approach of, 83, 130–31, 177
retail developments: absence of, 80, 146, 150;
automobile orientation of, 123, 124–25;
considerations in, 205, 222; demolition of,
37; lack of, at Poplar Nehemiah, 150, 178;
lack of, at Society Hill, 80; near Victoria
Park, 208; New Town ideal's inclusion of,
2; as new type of public space, 169, 200
"return to downtown" movement, 177–78
Richard Allen Homes (North Philadelphia),
136, *141*, 156, 158, 170, 178, 198
"rightsizing," 127
"Right to Buy" program (U.K.), 16
Rio de Janeiro, *Favela-Bairro* plan (Brazil),
175
Rizzo, Frank, 82, 83, 128
Robert Taylor Homes (Chicago), 198
Roche and Dinkeloo (firm), x
Ronan Point (London), 210
Roosevelt Island, 2, 31
Rowe, Peter, 31, 172, 210, 211
row houses (Philadelphia): aspirations for,
140, *142*, 146–47; British analogue to, 14,

15; historic units of, 50, *51*, *76*, 76–78;
maintained in Cecil B. Moore area,
164–65; midcentury models of, 138, *139*,
139–40, *142*, 142–44, *143*; modern analogue to, 80, 83; problems in historic units,
132, 144, 145; rehabilitations of, 81;
rooflines of, 156; *zeilenbau* housing blocks
compared with, 138–39
Rudolph, Paul, x
Rust Belt (U.S.), ix

San Francisco, xi, 35
SBDO (South Bronx Development Organization), 25, 27–30
Scollay Square neighborhood (Boston), 13
Seaside resort (Fla.), 196, 197. *See also* New
Urbanism
Section 235 "scandal." *See* U.S. Department
of Housing and Urban Development
Segal, Gloria, 3, 4
semi-topia concept, xiv, 220–24
severely distressed neighborhoods: in Detroit, 65–66; in Philadelphia, 58–59
shrinking cities: city form, industrial base,
and economy in, 67–68; as collective
urban policy failure, x–xi, xiii; current-day
policy paralysis in, 179–83; differences
among, 131–32; expanding city's problem
and, 174; experimentation absent in,
202–3; as harbingers of new form of city,
218–20, *219–21*; landscape ideals applied
to, 189–90; landscape urbanism projects
in, 190–94; mass transit and, 123–24; New
Urbanist vision and, 200–201; nonreformist reform challenges in, 183–85; overview
of redevelopment attempts, 176–77; people per housing unit in, *49*, 49–50; people's everyday needs in, 185–86;
postrenewal urban design revolution's implications for, 31–32; process of changes,
215–18; scattered housing abandonment
vs. contiguous clearance areas in, 95–96;
urban design reconsidered in context of,
35–36; urban fabric in, 213–14. *See also*
abandoned housing and sites; Baltimore;
Cleveland; deindustrialization; Detroit;
Philadelphia; population; social urbanism;
St. Louis; urban renewal; Washington,
D.C.

shrinking cities, recommended urban design
  principles for: approach to, xiv; context of,
  220–22; democratic decision making,
  207–10; hopes for, 222–24; interventionist
  policy, 205–7; Medellín as example, 174–
  76, 183; palliative planning, 204–5; patchwork urbanism, 212–20; projective design,
  210–12
single-family homes. *See* Charlotte Gardens;
  Clairpointe of Victoria Park development;
  housing types; Jefferson Village; Victoria
  Park; Woodward Place at Brush Park
site clearance. *See* urban renewal clearances
Skidmore, Owings, and Merrill (firm), 195
Smithson, Alison and Peter, 4, 6
social planning and housing developments:
  citizen participation in, 13–14, 16, 18–19;
  design innovation separated from, 17–20;
  GLC's High Modernist projects of, 9, *10*,
  11, 17–18; GLC's shift to humane, contextual, *12*, 13–14, *15*, 16; high-quality housing and, 171–72; narratives about,
  questioned, 34–36; suburban-style, low-
  density approach in, xiii; urban design
  and, 29–30; Yorktown's row-house design
  as, 142–44. *See also* Cecil B. Moore Homeownership Zone; Charlotte Gardens; Poplar Nehemiah Homes; social urbanism;
  Yorktown
social urbanism: challenges for, 183–85;
  democratic decision making principle of,
  207–10; hopes for, 222–24; interventionist
  policy principle of, 205–7; Latin American
  context of, 175; Medellín's revolution in,
  174–76, 183; palliative planning principle
  of, 204–5; patchwork urbanism principle
  of, 212–20; projective design principle of,
  210–12; recommended urban design principles of, xiii–xiv, 204
Society Hill (Philadelphia): assembling property for, 212–13; high-density residential
  development in, 54; lack of retail in, 80;
  low-income residents displaced from, 80;
  Modernist design of, 142; rehabilitations
  and, 81; sensitive design approach in, xii,
  82
Society Hill Towers, 80
South Bronx: "Fort Apache" area of, 24;
  highway construction's effects on, 21–22;
  map of, *23*; Melrose Court development

of, 31; North Philadelphia compared with,
  134; political rhetoric about, 28–29; population changes in, 22, 24, 225 n. 2; problems of, 22, 24; redevelopment ideas for,
  24–25. *See also* Charlotte Gardens
South Bronx Development Organization
  (SBDO), 25, 27–30
Southeast Michigan Builders' Association,
  106
South Philadelphia, 57–58, 76
Southwark Plaza public housing (Philadelphia), 80
Spain, Olympics-era improvements in Barcelona, 175
speculators, 77, 92–93, 106
sprawl, 33, 196–97, 225 n. 1
Spring Garden Homes (Philadelphia), 136
St. Louis: de-densification of, 189; housing
  stock losses in, *46*, *47*, *48*; housing types
  in, 50, *51*; housing values in, 92; population losses of, 41, *42*, *43*, 44; as shrinking
  city, x. *See also* East St. Louis (Ill.)
Street, John F., 147, 180–81, 206, 207
streets and highways: alleys removed in Poplar Nehemiah, 154–55; attempts to close
  for housing developments, 115; Detroit
  impacted by construction of, 71; "missing" or "broken teeth" in, *60*, 61; Philadelphia's Center City and, 79; safety issues,
  101; urban neighborhoods impacted by,
  21–22; *zeilenbau* (rows of buildings) principle and, 136, *137*, 138–40. *See also* culs-
  de-sac; walkways
streets in the sky concept. *See* Smithson, Alison and Peter
subprime mortgage crisis and market crash
  (2007): abandoned homes in, 93; Detroit
  at time of, xiii, 120; home and land values
  in, 108, 119, 120
subsidies: for building on cleared sites,
  114–15; commercial uses and, 178; for
  market-rate housing in Detroit, xii–xiii,
  88, 107–8, 110–11, 115, 126, 177; for Penn
  Center, 131; for Poplar Nehemiah homes,
  149–50
suburban-style design: of Charlotte Gardens,
  25, 27–30; city residents' aspirations for,
  29–30, 101, 140, 168, 172, 196; "community-based" rebuilding linked to, x; Detroit builders' focus on, xii–xiii, 98–99,

100, 101; Detroit's historic housing stock as, 69–71, *70*, 87–88, 124–25; experimentation absent in, 202–3; landscape urbanism linked to, 190–91; low-density population in, 43; midcentury row house incorporating aspects of, 139, 140, *142*, 142–44, *143*; New Urbanist similarity to, 196–97, 200–201; North Philadelphia's redevelopment as, 134–35, 146–47; peripheral areas as site for, 54–56; Philadelphia's Cecil B. Moore homes as, 162–66; Poplar Nehemiah front door dispute and, 156–61; problems on fragmented site, 117–18; rejected in *zeilenbau* (rows of buildings) housing, 138; superficial eclecticism of, 122; uninspired limitation of, 178; of Victoria Park, 99, *100*, 101–3, *102*. *See also* automobiles; *and specific developments*

suburbs: desirability of, 53; difficulty of redesign of, 219; housing prices in, 108; New Urbanism and, 197; parklike design of, 190; planned examples of, 138; similarity of Jefferson-Chalmers to, 84; similarity of Northeast Philadelphia to, 55; as site for relocated businesses and industries, 38; as site of large-scale architecture, x; white flight to, 38

subway suburbs concept, 27–28

superblock: at Cedar-Riverside, 4; at Victoria Park, 102; in *zeilenbau* concept, 136, 138

sustainable housing. *See* green housing

tax issues: residential tax abatement for conversions, 131; ten-year waiver for property taxes, 110–11, 126

Temple University, 54, 80, *133*, 170

Thamesmead New Town (U.K.), *10*, 11

Thatcher, Margaret, 13, 15

Time magazine, 80

Toronto, Downsview Park (Canada), 192

Town and Country Planning Act (U.K., 1947), 9

twin houses. *See* housing types

United Kingdom: New Town In-Town development in, 1; privatization measures in 1980s, 13; Reformed Modernism applied to social housing in, 13; "Right to Buy"

program in, 16; Town and Country Planning Act (1947) of, 9. *See also* Greater London Council Architecture Department; London

Unités d'Habitation (Le Corbusier), 4, 6

University of Pennsylvania: new left urbanism at, 18–19; population growth and land development near, 54; scattered clearance near, 80; studio abolished from planning curriculum at, 19; on vacant land parcels in Philadelphia, 173

urban decline: contrast with policy capacity, 178–79; suburban homes as solution to, 27–28; urban renewal elided with, 21–22. *See also* population; postrenewal redevelopment; shrinking cities; urbanism; urban renewal

urban design: abstract high-density vs. vernacular low-density, 172; architecture's absorption of, 33; dimensions of 1970s revolution in, 31–33; future shrinking-city role of, 214–20; modifications vs. replacement in, 192–93; paradoxical de-densification and concentration in, 124–25; Poplar Nehemiah front door dispute and, 156–61; redevelopment policy's lack of, 134–35; regulation vs. building in, xi; social planners' skepticism about, 36; *zeilenbau* (rows of buildings) principle in, 136, *137*, 138–40. *See also* Modernism and High Modernism; Reformed Modernism; social urbanism

urban design policy: absence of federal agenda, 32; everyday urbanist passivity in, 186–88; as federal policy backwater, 8–9, 196; included in rebuilding or not, 132; Logue's ideas about, 24–25, 28; middle-class-oriented approach of, 194–95; Modernism's decline and, 8–9; Modernist-era innovation and expertise in, 195–96; need to reconsider in shrinking cities context, 35–36; neoliberalist thinking applied to, 35–36, 182–83; nonreformist reform challenges in, 183–85; Philadelphia's policy debate over, 83; Philadelphia's responsive Modernism as, 78–81, 82–83, 177; in postrenewal Detroit, 120, 122–27; public housing as new idea in, 136; remaking neighborhoods with, 112; revolution against Modernism in, 11, *12*, 13–14, *15*,

urban design policy (*continued*)
16, 30–33; shortfalls of, 39–40, 101,
177–79; site control essential to, 120; slum
clearance focus of, 20–21; social planning
separated from, 17–20, 29–30; suburbanization as, 134–35. *See also* Modernism and
High Modernism; Reformed Modernism;
social urbanism
Urban Development Action Grants, 28
Urban Growth and New Community Development Act (1970). *See* Housing and
Urban Development Act (1970)
urbanism: "end" of, 38–39; patchwork concept of, 212–20. *See also* everyday urbanism; landscape urbanism; Modernism and
High Modernism; New Urbanism; Reformed Modernism; social urbanism;
urban design; urban design policy
urban patterns. *See* city form and geography
urban planning: architecture separated from,
19–20, 33; "asset-based" approach of, 184;
centralized form of, 14, 16; conventional
narratives about, 33–36; decentralization
of, 32, 145, 176–77; Modernism associated
with, 17–19; revolution against Modernism and, 11, *12*, 13–14, *15*, 16, 30–33; slum
clearance and, 20–21; urban decline elided
with, 21–22; urban renewal elided with,
20–21; urban renewal policy backwater
and, 8–9, 196. *See also* citizen participation; democratic decision making
urban renewal: blight criteria in, 153; Cedar-
Riverside as one of last projects, 2; conventional narratives about, questioned, 33–36;
demise of, ix–xii, 6–8, 17–20; Detroit's
tabula rasa approach of, xiii, 72–75, *74*, 78,
81, 82, 112, 182, 186; differences in neighborhood experiences, 113–14; formal innovation inherent in, 195; "growth
machine" and, 17–18; Philadelphia's approach to, xii, 54, 79–82; relief and disillusionment in wake of, xi–xii, 176–79;
shrinkage disconnected from, 40–41; turn
to, 39–40; as urban policy backwater, 8–9,
196; "used house" program in, 81. *See also*
Cedar-Riverside New Town In-Town;
housing condemnation; Modernism and
High Modernism; postrenewal redevelopment; urban renewal clearances
urban renewal clearances: benefits of, 113–
15, 120, 122, 226 n. 1; for Cedar-Riverside,

3; continuing paralysis in wake of, 182–83;
critics' polemic against, x, 20–21, 126; in
Detroit, 87, 94, 113; housing abandonment compared with, 95–96; in Lower
North Philadelphia, 153; scattered areas
of, 80–81, 96–97, 114; urban planning
linked with, 17–18; for Yorktown, 140. *See
also* abandoned housing and sites; demolition; housing condemnation; postrenewal
redevelopment
U.S. Department of Housing and Urban Development (HUD): Cecil B. Moore Homeownership Zone of, 161; current market-
driven approach of, 179; EDI grants of,
161; Nehemiah Housing Opportunity
Grant of, 149–50, 153, 161; Nehemiah
program of, 149–50, 161, 208; "New
Towns In-Town" initiative of, 1–2, 3–4;
redefined under Nixon's decentralization,
6–7; Section 8 new construction of, 83;
Section 108 funds of, 161; Section 223E
policy of, 92; Section 235 disaster and, 93–
94, 114; Section 236 low-income rental
program of, 83. *See also* Community Development Block Grants (CDBGs)
U.S. Department of Justice, 93
"used house" program, 81. *See* public housing, scattered-site type
utopianism, 2, 8

vacant lots and land. *See* abandoned housing
and sites
vernacular and historical traditions: preferences for, 172; reemergence of interest in,
19–20. *See also* row houses; suburban-style
design
Victoria Park (Detroit): current home values
in, 108; de-densification fostered by, 125;
design of, 99, *100*, 101, *102*, *103*, 106, 107;
design precedents established by, 108,
109–13, 160; entrance of, 102, *103*; Home-
A-Rama in (1992), 106, 107, 109; home
ownership focus of, 208; homes of, *102*;
later developments near, 114; low public
visibility of, 212; market and funding issues for, 103, 105–7, 160; New Urbanist
standards for third phase of, 125; origins
of, 98, 99, 101; pragmatic, market-oriented
approach of, 195; scale and cost of, 111–
13, 115–16, 207; site plan of, *100*; as suburbia in the city, 99, 101–3, 178; success of,
xiii, 107–9, 177

Victoria Woods. *See* Adams, Anthony; Carley, Garry

Ville Radieuse (Radiant City) design (Le Corbusier), 144

Vogel, Stephen, 101, 109

walkways: in Cedar-Riverside design, 4, 5; rail-to-trail paths, 124, 191; in *zeilenbau* developments, 136, *137*, 138–40. *See also* culs-de-sac; High Line; streets and highways

Warren and Wetmore (firm), ix

Washington, D.C.: housing types in, 50, *51*; moderate population losses of, 41, *42*, *43*, 44; population density of, *44*, 45

Washington Square neighborhood (Philadelphia), 82

West End neighborhood (Boston), 20, 114

West Philadelphia, 52, 57, 76, 82

white flight: in Detroit, 98; in New Haven (Conn.), 39; in Philadelphia, 128; in South Bronx, 22, 28

Williamsburg Houses (New York City), 17, 136

Windham Realty, 114–15. *See also* Clairpointe of Victoria Park development

Wissahickon Valley (Philadelphia), 75

Woodward Avenue (Detroit), 37, 109

Woodward Place at Brush Park (Detroit): de-densification shown by, 125; New Urbanist homes of, 122–23, 198, *199*, 201

Yankee Stadium, *23*, 24

Yorktown (North Philadelphia): bold design of, 81, 160; college students moving into, 170; context of, 208; historic row houses and, 156; home values in, 146; location of, *133*, *141*; midcentury row house design of, 140, 142, *142*, *143*; Poplar Nehemiah compared with, 159; reinterpretation of Philadelphia street grid in, 143–44; as revolution in redevelopment ideas, 142–44, 147, 178; successful design of, xii, 82, 146–47, 171–72, 210, 211

Young, Coleman: election of, 85; industrial and downtown rebuilding under, 73–74, 75, 96–97, 207; "new town" vision of, 97–98, 103; privately led redevelopment strategy and politics of, 87, 88; role of subsidies for development under, 110, 112; Victoria Park plans of, 106, 107, 109

zeilenbau (rows of buildings) housing blocks: antiurban effect of, 160; design of, 136, *137*, 138, 143; Poplar Nehemiah housing compared with, 156, 157; problems of, 144; row houses compared with, 138–39, *139*

zoning: inclusionary, 171; lack of influence of, 194; modernist planning and, 18; patchwork urbanism contrasted with, 214; reductive suburban application of, 219

Acknowledgments

Many individuals, places, and institutions provided valuable assistance and insights without which the writing of this book would have been impossible. Lawrence Vale's unfailing intellectual generosity made the commencement and conclusion of my writing much easier. Zane Miller believed in this work during a difficult middle period, and his interest and energy sustained mine. Charles Hoch urged me to find my voice; I hope that this book is a step along that road. Editors Robert Lockhart and Eugenie L. Birch at the University of Pennsylvania Press helped refine my work into publishable form. Sam Bass Warner, Anne Spirn, Eran Ben-Joseph, Susan Fainstein, Jerold Kayden, David Stradling, Larry Bennett, Rachel Weber, and Roberta Feldman all gave valuable editing and publishing suggestions. Daniel Campo was and remains an important touchstone for ideas about Philadelphia and all cities. Karen Gage introduced me to Detroit and is still the primary lens through which I see the city. Abe Brewster generously offered design talents at a critical stage. My research assistants, including Ann-Ariel Vecchio, Sarah Spicer, Jonah Stern, Allison Hu, Christina Calabrese, Geoff Moen, Franny Ritchie, Drew Pompa, Ellie Brown, and Christine Wu, were invaluable. My mother, father, siblings, other family, friends, urban lunch and hk cohorts encouraged me throughout.

While it may be true that "wherever you go, there you are," I find travel to be a productive, even critical, stimulus for thought. I was fortunate to have the initial idea for this book in the midst of a Salzburg Seminar in Austria, and to complete key parts of my writing in Montserrat, West Indies; Prudence Island, Rhode Island; and Chappaquiddick, Martha's Vineyard. Last of all, I am grateful to two institutions that supported my writing and thinking. The Massachusetts Institute of Technology provided an essential semester's leave and funding for research through the Linde Career Development Professorship, as did a Harvard University Graduate School of Design Junior Faculty Grant.

I dedicate this book to my wife, Lorena, whose wonderful spirit of kindness and joy sustains me every day.

www.ingramcontent.com/pod-product-compliance
Lightning Source LLC
Chambersburg PA
CBHW020340270326
41926CB00007B/262